AND
THE LEADER
IS... Mandy Avis

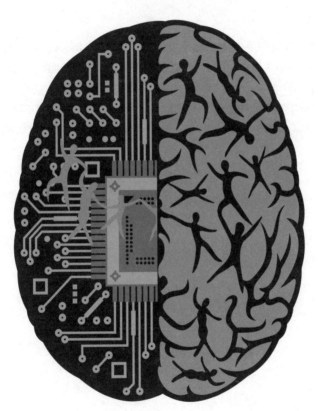

To Rachel

Thank you from the very bottom of my heart for your integrity, your passion, your unshakeable support, your inspiration and your love. You have taught me such profound lessons, and any success I've had at clarifying, synthesising, codifying and then narrating my beliefs and strategies, I absolutely owe to you. You are the golden thread of my life.

AND THE LEADER IS...

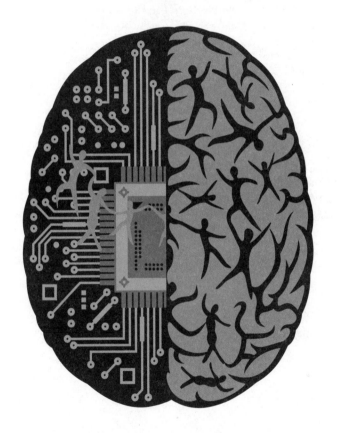

Transforming Cultures with CEQ

GARETH CHICK

First published in 2019 by Critical Publishing Ltd

British Library Cataloguing in Publication Data
A CIP record for this book is available from the British Library

ISBN: 978-1-912508-36-5

This book is also available in the following e-book formats:
MOBI ISBN: 978-1-912508-37-2
EPUB ISBN: 978-1-912508-38-9
Adobe e-book ISBN: 978-1-912508-39-6

Cover design by Out of House Limited
Text design by Out of House Limited
Project Management by Newgen Publishing UK
Printed and bound in Great Britain by Bell & Bain, Glasgow

Critical Publishing
3 Connaught Road
St Albans
AL3 5RX

www.criticalpublishing.com

Paper from responsible sources

PRAISE FOR *AND THE LEADER IS...*

And the Leader Is... is a bible of common sense; a book that cuts to the core of achieving great business results whilst caring for the people you lead, with expert techniques around management, team effectiveness and cultural change; but most of all a refreshing take on coaching as a skill for the real world leaders to inhabit to deliver real results. And it reads like a wonderful synopsis of the working sessions I and my team have had with Gareth over so many years. A tried and tested blueprint for those who are game enough to take the leap of faith into coaching. You will find a rich array of resources informed with practical guidance for leaders that will challenge and inspire you in equal measure.

**Fionnuala Meehan, VP Google Customer Solutions,
EMEA and Head of Google Ireland**

Gareth's book is supported by the wealth of his personal experience, illustrative anecdotes and insights. It is an incredibly useful resource for leaders who aspire to grow and learn along with their charges. His deep knowledge and passion for management skills, within and without the office, made for a rewarding and relatable read. He has developed a unique philosophy for interpreting the modern workplace, which has improved my own outlook when making major decisions.

Sofie Quidenus-Wahlforss, CEO, omni:us

I'm not quite sure how to say this. I started reading in what I imagined would be a somewhat detached, independent manner. The reality was quite different. I was not only engrossed, but it had a profound effect. I lived each point, putting myself in the place of the leader (and in some cases the led!) and recalling so many important moments and examples that brought the insights to life.

I loved the practical nature of the book. It doesn't speak to 'performance' in the traditional sense and it calls out (totally rightly) what the real role and purpose of leaders has to be in this day and age. And by the way, we are failing. It made me re-evaluate the role of self-managed teams and the specificity of things like how to run 1:1s, how to set up team meetings (and what they're for!) was just incredibly helpful. The notion of 'stewardship' is one of the most powerful in the book for me, cutting through the ego of the leader. This section should be prescribed reading for Chairs and Non-Execs. And finally I love the end.

It's like no other book I've ever experienced. It's intensely personal – the insights, the examples, the honesty. This is much more than a book. It's a deep journey, a ride you shouldn't get on unless you're really up for it – but then the same is true for leadership!

Alison Platt, Non-Executive Director, Tesco Plc

Truly insightful, providing a compelling balance of inspiration and practicality. This book will help you become a better version of yourself.

Jill Caseberry, FTSE250 Non-Executive Director

Gareth asks the tough questions and answers them instinctually. His candour strips away any tendencies of glossing over typical leadership books. He cuts right to the heart, so much so that rather than just reading the book, I found myself putting the book down, visualizing my own role, my flaws, but most importantly, my own opportunities.

Jennifer Kelly, VP Global Real Estate and Workplace Services, Google

During my time as an OD professional and as a leader I have had the fortune of reading many great books on coaching, leadership and teams. However, And the Leader Is... is even greater, with all of these areas more expertly placed in one book, giving you the tools to support you in being a great leader. It reminded me of two things, firstly it's what you do that defines you and secondly that you learn everyday. As a takeaway I am going to think about my 'Documents of Status' as I embark on the next phase of my leadership journey.

Becky Ivers, People Director – Expansion, Heathrow Airport

As a management book junkie, I read with a mind open to being engaged, enraged, entertained, challenged or inspired. Gareth Chick's first book Corporate Emotional Intelligence: Being Human in a Corporate World satisfied my every requirement, so I read it again. And again. So many questions were answered (even 'Which came first, the Chick or the Ego? Answer: the Ego, and Gareth has a great way to bring it into line'). The only thing that beats a great answer is a great question.

Gareth's writing demands that we continue to ask questions and And the Leader Is..., his second book, is a timely contribution to addressing those that seem unfathomable. Gareth is no slouch: he puts his wisdom to the test and we can all be beneficiaries of his experience. This is a great book... a yellow brick road to authentic cultural change.

Julia Hobbs, CEO, St John's Cymru Wales

From the moment I started to read And the Leader Is... I was transported into 'The Leader is Tina', I was visualising the 'leader' I aspire to be. This book is easy to read 'brain food', providing simple strategies to unlock human potential. This book is becoming my own personal coach. Genuine, obvious reminders, simple and fun and if you are a sceptic, jump right in with me to take some action and try it: I am.

Tina Jennings, HR Director, Global Consumer Brands, Walgreens Boots Alliance

I have never been asked to review a book before and it felt like a privilege. I thought it was brilliant. It's the one book every leader should have on their desk and be USING. I have marked so much in the book that I would like to refer back to which will help myself, my peers and my team. Maybe us leaders should read it every year to remind ourselves of some of the great leadership skills we should use and don't due to old habits! Let me know when it is out as I would love for my team to have this as part of their leadership toolkit.

Helen Verwoert, Global HR Director, Dr Martens AirWair International

This is one of the most practical, useful and well written business books I have read in a long time. I have already used some of Gareth's coaching advice and am seeing positive results. Gareth truly understands the positive and negative impact behaviours have on a business and is very clear on how, as leaders, it is our responsibility to act humanely as well as doing what's right for the business. Gareth shows us how to be more self-aware and to self-adjust in order not to negatively impact our team members and to facilitate them to step out of their comfort zones so they can reach their full potential. Whether you run a small or big organisation this is a must read and is one of those rare books I will read again and again.

Lulu O'Sullivan, CEO Gifts Direct and The Irish Store, and Member of Accenture Advisory Board

Thoughtful and pragmatic advice for managers who want to really make a difference in the workplace and be successful by their teams being successful. Practical tips that are absolutely achievable which will make a difference.

Deborah Parker, HR Director Corporate Functions Europe, XPO Logistics

CONTENTS

Meet the author	xii
Foreword	xiii
Acknowledgements	xiv
Introduction	**1**
And the leader is... *you*!	1
Transforming cultures with CEQ	1
CEQ v EQ	1
The four pillars of CEQ	2
Two books, but two parts of a whole	4
Section 1 – Coaching	**7**
Chapter 1 – Clumsy coaching	**9**
Why 'clumsy'?	9
The five myths of coaching	10
Human potential	11
Chapter 2 – Coaching recalibration	**15**
Recalibration	15
Trigger 1: Calm the fish	16
Trigger 2: Truly great feedback hurts	17
Trigger 3: Come from curiosity, not judgement	21
Trigger 4: Hold the person, not the problem	23
Trigger 5: Take people out of their comfort zones	27
Chapter 3 – Embedding recalibrated coaching habits	**33**
Our habits and their habits	33

Definition of coaching 38

The crux 40

Behaviour change 41

Chapter 4 – Coaching crafting **44**

Question crafting 44

Practical process 45

Coaching for ownership 47

Trigger 6: Create right-brain thinking 49

Trigger 7: Get their finest version to solve their problem 53

Chapter 5 – Coaching mastery **60**

From the sublime to the ridiculous 60

SuperListening 60

BreakThrough Coaching 66

Role play 68

Teaching and knowledge transfer 69

Our rewards 70

The coachee's plea 71

Exploding the myths 72

Section 2 – Leadership 73

Chapter 6 – Authentic leadership **75**

Authentic leadership – it's not big and it's not clever 75

Authenticity demands leadership 76

What is authenticity? 78

Our Golden Core 80

Our Shield of Pretence 81

Directive v consensual leadership 83

Chapter 7 – Establishing the leader version of ourselves **88**

Understanding ourselves 88

Personal core values process 90

Purpose and values 93

Establishing the 'leader' version of ourselves 101

Chapter 8 – Matching ourselves to our roles **115**

Stewardship 115

Now, what is the purpose of the role? 116

Strategies and behaviours 117

ACRC 119

Fernando – nobleman or fool? 123

Section 3 – Teams 125

Chapter 9 – Teams **127**

When is a team a team and not merely a group? 127

Coaching teams (aka facilitation) 127

The purpose of teams within a business 131

The place for targets 132

Account management 133

The three-dimensional matrix 134

Tuckman and Lencioni 136

Adapting theoretical models 138

Chapter 10 – The characteristics of high-performance teams **139**

1. Common purpose, inspiring vision, shared values, ambitious goals, great strategy 139

2. Clear structure of roles and responsibilities 140

3. Utter respect for each other as expert specialist professionals 141

4. Acceptance of individual idiosyncrasies and personal circumstances 146

5. Conflict embraced and used as a creative force 147

6. Honesty valued as the most precious commodity 149

7. Space honoured for rehearsal and celebration 151

8. Team is individuals' place of sanctuary and solace 153

9. A leader who is an honest coach and facilitator 155

10. 100 per cent commitment and personal subordination to the plan 156

Chapter 11 – Self-managed teams (SMTs) **158**

Principles of self-managed teams 158

Why don't fish bump into each other? 161

Summary 163

Section 4 – Change 165

Chapter 12 – Cultural change **167**

Cultural change – just another form of control? 167

The three pillars of cultural change 167

What is culture? More importantly, what is a 'winning culture'? 170

Why do we need to change? 170

The four dilemmas 173

The three classic mistakes and the two philosophical foundation stones 175

Chapter 13 – The cycle of ownership **176**

Five-stage 'cycle of ownership' 176

The job of the leader 181

Chapter 14 – The eight steps of cultural change **183**

Step 1: Be honest about what happens if we *don't* change 184

Step 2: Listen to customers and employees 185

Step 3: Set clear intentions and symbolic goals 185

Step 4: Slaughter some sacred cows 191

Step 5: Police non-negotiable structures and processes 191

Step 6: Turn the managers into coaches 194

Step 7: Create champions and CI teams 195

Step 8: Educate employees in the business model 200

Cultural change project planning – full steps example 203

Section 5 – Organisational strategies 211

Chapter 15 – The business management bit 213

A plan that everyone owns 213

Forecasting 214

The operating model 216

The philosophy of rigid disciplines 217

Key performance indicators 219

One-to-ones 219

Team meetings and communications 222

Management by objectives or OKRs 223

Strategy one-pagers 225

Know your balance sheet 228

Documents with status (I carry these next to my heart) 229

The results 229

Chapter 16 – Establishing a collaborative equity organisation 232

What is 'collaborative equity'? 232

But what about the alternatives? 233

Why haven't we listened to the voices before now? 239

The modern-day crusaders 241

Why a collaborative equity approach might just catch on *now* 242

Future leaders 245

Why collaborative equity is the 'acceptable' solution 246

The word of the moment is 'toxic' 247

A beacon of hope 248

Chapter 17 – This is all very well, but does it make more money? 250

Example 1: Pendragon Plc (1998–2000) 250

Example 2: Longwood Park (2003–2009) 257

Example 3: B&Q (2013–2014) 260

Example 4: SOFEA (2016 to date) 261

Example 5: Produce World (2016) 264

Example 6: Banbury Therapy Group (2009 to date) 267

Cynics, sceptics and evangelists 271

Further Notes 272

Index 275

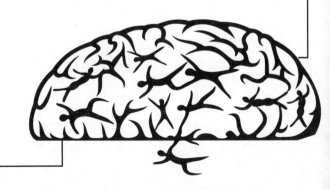

MEET THE AUTHOR

Gareth Chick is a 40-year corporate veteran with a global profile. His career has included hugely successful spells as CFO, CEO and Chairman in both public and private sectors, including private equity. What makes Gareth's experience unique is that he combined those executive roles with a part time career as a leadership trainer, researching psychology, neuroscience and psychotherapy to create leadership development programmes used now by many major global corporations. In the last 15 years Gareth has trained over 5000 managers and served as Executive Coach to over 200 senior execs including FTSE100 CEOs and Fortune 500 VPs. As Founder of Collaborative Equity LLP, 'promoting corporate cultures and sustainable business models of shared ownership, shared responsibility and shared rewards', Gareth acts as consultant to many global leaders, specialising in first time CEOs and start-up founders.

Gareth lives with his wife Rachel in a small Warwickshire village close to Stratford-upon-Avon in the UK – their four children are following their own paths in journalism, addiction therapy, teaching and acting. Though you would not know it to look at him, Gareth is a proud holder of a marathon-running world record – he is the oldest person ever to complete a marathon wearing a full 28lb rhino suit!

FOREWORD

I have known Gareth for nearly 30 years and to be asked to set down a Foreword to his new book is a great honour. I am now in my eighties and from my early years I have had the good fortune to meet men and women holding positions of leadership in business and government, representing many nations around the world. However, I have never before heard or read the practice and insight in respect of real leadership that Gareth has set down. The result is fantastic.

When Gareth asked me to write this Foreword, my mind went back to my time in Japan as a very young man, when I witnessed an amazing business and cultural transformation with the arrival of Dr Edwards Deming. Deming began the 'Japanese miracle', achieved through an insistence on the highest standards of quality and customer service, a totally involved and committed workforce, and the practice of kaizen (continuous and never-ending improvement). This led me to believe passionately in enabling organisations to combine the best of Eastern and Western practices to develop a totally new approach to human resource development and training. I then had an opportunity to put these ideas to work throughout businesses and with individuals worldwide.

Many organisations have introduced Dr Deming's principles, and tailored them to suit their types of business, and as we move into the digital age, we have an even greater opportunity to widen the qualities of improvement, but most importantly to always include and emphasise the human dimension. Gareth has outlined this so clearly, detailing the practical steps needed to become leaders in a new and exciting way. He clearly details the mindset needed in today's world for delivering results from the journey of hope, imagination and enlightenment that is required for the future.

I strongly recommend that Gareth's book should be referred to and made available to all centres of management and training. I only wish I'd had such information, guidance and understanding when I was younger. I commend all who read Gareth's book to fully realise that the role of leaders at all levels is essential to success, and to work tirelessly to realise the critical importance of the human dimension.

Never forget this – there is no greater calling in life than to develop the potential of another human being – as leaders we must take the wider and deeper responsibility for doing that for a whole community. If you are considering stepping into leadership in whatever situation, this book is essential in understanding the importance and effect it can have on the people you attract to the cause, and that true leadership is a calling and not just a job.

Tony Barnes

Member of Dr Deming's team, Japan

Former Director of the Europe Japan Centre

Former Board Advisor, Sony

Creator of the Dynamic Leadership Course, Institute of Directors

Founder of The New Beginning

ACKNOWLEDGEMENTS

I must start with thanking my mentor and friend Tony Barnes for doing me the immense honour of writing the Foreword. I could never have imagined nearly 30 years ago when I first heard Tony speak, that such a legend of business would be honouring me in this way.

I had 11 endorsements for my first book, but only after we'd gone to print did Matt Brittin ask me whether I'd noticed that they were all from men. So much for my diversity radar. I'd asked a select group of clients to review the manuscript with a view to giving me an endorsement, in hindsight in pretty much the two-thirds men/one-third women balance of my entire client network, but for one reason or another I had ended up with an all-male list. So I determined that with this second book I would balance things up. I have been humbled by the endorsements of 11 amazing women, every one a high profile and hugely successful leader. Thank you to Fionnuala Meehan, Jen Kelly, Sofie Quidenus-Wahlforss, Helen Verwoert, Becky Ivers, Lulu O'Sullivan, Tina Jennings, Deborah Parker, Julia Hobbs, Alison Platt and Jill Caseberry. Each one of you invested many hours of your busy lives to read the draft manuscript, and more than that, to engage deeply with the content. I can honestly say that your reactions to my book have already provided me with a greater reward than I could ever expect from 'mere' sales volume.

Throughout the unfolding narrative, I have wanted to tell my real-life stories with as much detail as possible while protecting the confidences that have been shared with me. Many stories are therefore anonymised; however, there are a few exceptions, where I've been given specific permission by the individuals concerned to tell their story. Thank you to Richard Kennell, Rachel Young, William Burgess and Kevin O'Byrne. I also want also to acknowledge the individuals named in the text who I have had the great pleasure of working with: Sir Ian Cheshire, Marian Green, Beverley Charman, Father Dermot Tredgett, David Grayson, Mike Morrison, Alan Sneddon and Geoff Webb.

In the opening pages of my first book *Corporate Emotional Intelligence: Being Human in a Corporate World* I took the opportunity of expressing my gratitude to a number of people who have been deeply influential in my career and my personal development; to some inspiring leaders that I have had the immense privilege of working with and learning from; and to a hugely supportive group of clients that actively encouraged and supported me in the creation of that first book. You know who you are and your names are there in lights.

So here in this place, while I want to give public acknowledgement to some additional very special leaders, I must give a second call out to David Frost, Peter Eglinton, Carole Stewart, Philip Lymbery, Ronan Harris, Fionnuala Meehan, Seb James, Kevin O'Byrne, Dave Geraghty, Mick Hodgins, Bob Bradley, Matt Brittin, Ross Baker, Alastair Brass, Jon Shaw, Eileen Naughton, Simon Charles and Gareth Morgan. Thank you all for your encouragement, your most generous support, your referrals and increasingly for your friendship.

The 'new' names are leaders who have impacted my life more recently plus some whom I've known for over 20 years, who have gone out of their way to provide specific support for my published work. Thank you to Nikos Kotalakidis, Darren Campbell, Eric Wahlforss, James Stevenson, Bob Bradley, Lindsay Tilley, Mark Stokes, Andrew Harland, Paul Coombes, Alex Belenky, Paul Tracey, Sandrine Lestringuez, Jose Pulpon, Fraser Brown, Lucero Tagle, Val King, Richard Kennell, Paddy Flynn, Derek Diviney, Roi Sagi, Mike Pilbeam, Martyn Fisher, Baur Sauranbekov, Jonathan Tole, Shane Holland, James Arrow, Jeremy Garlick, David Murdin, Caoimhe Keogan, Matt Starbuck, Paul Brazier and Peter Collyer.

My thanks once again to Di Page and the team at Critical Publishing, who made the process of production very smooth, and who were always on hand to give guidance. Once again the quality of Di's editing was magnificent.

Heartfelt thanks to my colleague Martyn Haworth who is quite simply the best leadership and management trainer I've ever come across. Since Martyn has the temerity to consistently outscore me in delivering the training programme material I created, that judgement is not hyperbole – not even just based on my instinct and experience – but a scientific fact.

My elder brother David has been a constant, reassuring, supportive and inspirational force in my life. As an experienced and hugely talented HR and employment law professional, Dave and I have shared many interesting debates, and his quiet, calm and unselfish encouragement has been one of the rocks of my life.

My children (I'm not sure if that's still the correct term as three of them are in their thirties, and even our youngest is now in her twenties) remain my most profound source of joy and inspiration. If my generation doesn't take our planet past a tipping point, the next generation will do things very differently, and Duncan and Leonie are the absolute embodiment of the integrity, courage, selflessness, community and creativity that will ultimately be our salvation. Stephanie and Tom have had a more involved journey with my work over the years, and I owe them the deepest gratitude for their love and constant encouragement. But I also owe them thanks for their practical advice and support – in Stephanie's case through our many long discussions on the subject of trauma and of transformational change (you try running a social care business under private equity ownership!) and in Tom's case through his supreme marketing and digital media expertise. Thank you the four of you. You know that all you need to do to make me happy is occasionally come and play Boggle with me, and in the future bring your own children to sit and watch *Noggin the Nog* with me.

Finally, and at the risk of duplicating my words in dedicating this book to her, I want to express my gratitude, appreciation and love to my wife Rachel. One of the loveliest aspects of writing this book was in telling the story of the amazing, groundbreaking organisation that Rachel founded, and of the incredible success she has had as a leader.

Introduction

And the leader is... *you*!

In my first book *Corporate Emotional Intelligence: Being Human in a Corporate World*, I introduced corporate emotional intelligence (CEQ) as a new and deeper level of thinking about our strategies and behaviours in our corporate working environments. I analysed the peculiar conditions of corporatism, with its foundations of power, control and fear creating the characters of the Corporapath and the Corporate Hostage, and causing the unique anxiety disorder CTSD – Corporate Traumatic Stress Disorder. Following the diagnosis, I introduced CEQ as the solution for us to individually and then collectively 'cure' corporatism from the inside out. I outlined the four pillars of CEQ, and I'll give a reprise of these in this Introduction.

In this, my second book, I complete my thesis by describing practical strategies, frameworks, tools, techniques and tips to effect transformational change with our newly heightened awareness and knowledge of CEQ. I chose the title *And the Leader Is...* as a way of connecting corporate citizens to the possibility of achieving a more authentic, fulfilling and enriching state of leadership themselves, for the unspoken end to the unfinished sentence is *your name*. The pause between the start of the sentence and the end is designed to conjure up the tense moment of unveiling at the end of whichever reality show is your personal guilty pleasure. There is a nervousness and apprehension in that momentary pause, until the name is announced, and the wild incredulous celebrations can begin. So I want you to engage with the exciting prospect that the leader is *you* – that *you* can be the inspiring leader, the one to change the world, or at least the part of the world that you work in right now. But if you want the exquisite and liberating moment of validation, I also want you then to engage with the responsibility that goes with the fact that the leader is *you*, in a way that impels you to hide no longer, and to gloriously if nervously step into a space of personal exposure and vulnerability. How delicious.

Transforming cultures with CEQ

And the Leader Is... is my main title, but to offer some support and assistance at that glorious but potentially terrifying moment of realisation that you are 'it', I've then completed the unfinished sentence for titular purposes with the subtitle 'swerve' of *Transforming Cultures with CEQ*. Make no mistake, I am calling you to arms – the leader is most definitely *you*. But I'm not abandoning you and I'm not leaving you bereft of protection. Lead with CEQ and you'll be an amazing leader and things will transform around you. Your presence will be sufficient, in fact it will be everything.

CEQ v EQ

Emotional intelligence (EQ) depends upon on calm, conscious reflection and a considered and intentional moderation of our actions and responses. When we have the luxury of time and space, this is profoundly effective. But our corporate working environments rarely if ever give us that luxury, thus denying us the real opportunity to reflect and then respond intentionally. We are operating in a constant heightened state of pressure, thus our brains are running high levels of cortisol and our bodies high levels of adrenaline. In critical highly charged moments of interaction with other human beings, our 'fight or flight' physiological imperatives will be so strong that any ability to act calmly is simply unavailable to us. EQ is of no use to us since we cannot access the EQ databank at that moment.

Even if we've trained ourselves to be able to access a more mindful state when we're feeling stressed and pressurised, the responses sourced from a calm space are so counterintuitive to the fight-or-flight messages bombarding our physicality that taking an action sourced from calm reflection will feel way too risky to execute.

And so EQ inadvertently plays into the old and seemingly unfathomable dilemma of short term versus long term, the dilemma of acting ethically versus doing whatever it takes, and the dilemma of people growth versus business results. Our intellects might well believe that focusing on long-term strategies, acting more ethically and focusing on people growth really will produce better all-round results. But our bodies haven't caught up. When it matters, our physiology dominates every single critical moment. The reality is that our intellect can believe whatever it likes – if our gut doesn't believe, then we're stuffed. And so we are seemingly destined to continuously reinforce the deeply grooved conditioned learning that allows us to act against our intellect in the moment – it's that inner voice that says, '*I know this is not the right approach; I know this is punishing for the other person and it's not how I want to be, but right now it will get the job done, and tomorrow when things have calmed down, I'll be how I want to be.*' Good intentions become deferred.

So we've come to believe that we *cannot* change, much as we'd love to. We're actually desperate to believe that a more ethical, human, calm and considered way of working and interacting with each other is possible, but it feels impossible to try it out. The moments of pressure are simply too critical and frankly too intensely packed together, one after another with no gaps. Therefore, in order for us not to experience the utter futility of this state of affairs, we've come to collectively adopt quasi authentic strategies and behaviours to stay sane. These 'authentic' behaviours are certainly rational and intentional, but they have at their root a desire to fool others around us and to compensate for and even to salve the shame and guilt we inevitably feel. The inevitability of the way the corporate world is and our sense of being trapped within it cause us to have learned the wrong lesson, and hence we're solving the wrong problem. Since we're all colluding in this, we constantly reinforce our learning and our consequent behaviours. We stay gloriously in our denial and in our fear.

If we are to stand any chance of extricating ourselves from the worst aspects of corporatism, we have to develop our CEQ – a deeper emotional intelligence that is truly and readily accessible in our most intense moments of pressure.

The four pillars of CEQ

1. OUCH! Our unconscious controlling habits

2. Promoting positive learning

3. Transparency and vulnerability

4. A grip on reality

OUCH! *Our unconscious controlling habits*

The first pillar concerns the crucial physiological confrontation of how we actually behave when under pressure – the habits that have been developed through constant conditioning, and that have become unconscious and automatic. These behaviours in some perverse way feel ethical since we have no choice but to do what's needed to serve the cause in that moment. But they are neither inevitable nor acceptable. They only 'work' (seemingly in the moment), because everyone around us is trapped in the same insanity.

We have to break these habits, and that only comes about by practising new ones until they're in our muscle memory.

Promoting positive learning

In my experience, the vast majority of behavioural learning that goes on in corporate environments is conditioned. We learn mostly how *not* to behave because of perceived sanctions and threatened consequences, and how *to* behave because of rewards.

Of course, there is phenomenal positive learning going on in technical skills such as engineering, coding, design, research, accounting, manufacturing, packaging, etc. Experimentation and failures are the lifeblood of growth and development in these areas of our businesses, and so we have developed ways of protecting these areas from the ruthless consequences of the outside world in 'laboratories', whether physical or virtual. But when it comes to learning how to behave, how to make the right decisions for the good of the cause, how to collaborate, how to communicate, how to organise ourselves and how to allocate scarce resources, we've collectively failed to learn positively. We have to start bringing the methodology from our labs into our meeting rooms.

Transparency and vulnerability

Much is written on the subject of vulnerability nowadays, and that's fantastic. It can only be a good thing that vulnerability is more widely feted as a positive attribute for leaders and managers, and is therefore more openly embraced within the corporate world. However, corporatism is brilliant at surviving; at learning how to look like it's embracing modern, more enlightened leadership concepts and then at manipulating corporate citizens into a corporately acceptable version. So I am not interested in a manufactured vulnerability as part of an overt strategy to appear more human. I'm interested in the true human vulnerabilities of flaws, mistakes, uncertainty, tiredness – of struggle.

Our corporate cultures have come to eschew struggle – it simply doesn't feel safe for people to get things wrong or to show weakness or hesitancy or indecisiveness, yet these are naturally occurring states in any path of learning and any path to arriving at the best possible strategy, particularly when we are setting people very stretching objectives, and when external events can derail us at any moment. We have to celebrate struggle; we have to seek it out, welcome it and reward it. We simply have to stop punishing people for struggling, and as leaders even if we are not overtly creating threat conditions around struggle, we have to acknowledge people's fears of appearing weak.

This also means we simply have to make it OK for people to express emotions at work. I've witnessed an almost systemic denial of human emotions in the corporate workplace, to the extent where we've become scared of doing things that will predictably evoke strong emotions. Human emotions are both beautiful and profoundly effective. Bring them on.

Finally, the greatest way of forcing vulnerability into the open is to make everything possible transparent. A lack of transparency fostered through a fear of breaching confidentiality or of somehow skewing behaviours under observation actually means that we promote secrecy, and this is fundamentally what allows unnatural, inhuman and at times abusive behaviours to go unwitnessed. As a leader I promote the maximum transparency in terms of the sharing of facts, since I have a profound belief that it is the community as a whole that can best solve the problems at hand, and thus move us collectively more efficiently towards our goals in service of our mission.

A grip on reality

So much of what constitutes our 'real world' inside our corporate environments are artificial and intangible structures. We treat the org chart as if it were a solid and linear physical structure, we treat targets as if they were immutable states of being once achieved, and we treat milestones and key performance indicators (KPIs) and metrics as objects in their own right as opposed to indicators that are there to guide us. And in all of this we lose our grip on what is truly real – the people we have relationships with who are affected by our actions: our families, our friends and our work colleagues. How often have we damaged or even sacrificed an important relationship with someone we care about, simply to ensure that someone we've never met doesn't get a bit miffed? So, as leaders, we have to be stewards of cultures that keep everything in perspective, personally focusing on compassion over competition, genuinely fostering ethics and values and principles to run the show and encouraging people to be truly human at work. And we should do these things first because it's the right thing to do, as an act of faith in humanity over corporate subservience. But with CEQ what we then find is that doing these things quickly and progressively releases profound human potential in service of our common causes. And that is both surprising and transformational.

Two books, but two parts of a whole

While this is my second book, my original plan was always to write one single work – my motivation was to synthesise my learnings and practices. Having written a 40,000-word manual to accompany the Coaching Excellence programme I designed 15 years ago, and having written and designed unique training products around leadership, teams and change, in 2013 I decided to put everything I knew into a book. What I wrote then, five years ago, has actually ended up forming the guts of this book.

But the process of synthesising, as it so often does when we codify what we know, revealed to me precisely what was unique about my approach. My 'discovery' of unconscious controlling habits and my development of solutions that we can practically access and utilise under pressure, showed me that underpinning everything was my deep understanding and appreciation of corporatism and corporate behaviours.

So I founded a new business, which I called Collaborative Equity, and I created a brand around what I realised was actually a new form of emotional intelligence, CEQ, which I was able also to use as a form of acronym for Collaborative Equity. I purchased the domains ceq.com and ceq.co.uk, and then I put this near-completed manuscript to one side, and embarked on the research and investigation into neuroscience, psychotherapy and psychology that turned into the analysis that is my first book *Corporate Emotional Intelligence: Being Human in a Corporate World*.

When I wrote down the solutions you'll find in the following 17 chapters, I knew they worked, because I'd utilised them myself as a CEO and chairman, and then I'd progressively seen them utilised by others. But I didn't fully appreciate why they worked until I'd done the research. And this is why *Corporate Emotional Intelligence* is book one, and *And the Leader Is…* is book two.

While each of my books stands on its own merits, I believe the combination of the two books forms arguably the most important work on corporate leadership since Dr Edwards Deming's writings of the late twentieth century. Deming's *14 Points for Management*, devised and refined through his experiences in leading the team that rebuilt Japanese industry after the Second World War, combined with his seminal work *Out of the Crisis*, published in 1982, revolutionised business strategies and practices around the world, resetting the accepted frameworks for generations to come. Without Deming there would have been no Toyota, and arguably therefore no Intel, no Microsoft, no Apple, no Google, no Alibaba and no Amazon.

If Deming were still alive, I think he would be sounding another clarion call for us to revolutionise our business practices. I think he'd have discovered CEQ long before I did and he'd be lecturing, practising and leading the cause. It's why I'm profoundly grateful to Tony Barnes, then the youngest and now the last surviving member of Deming's team, for his personal support and his advocacy for this book.

Section 1
Coaching

Chapter 1
Clumsy coaching

Why 'clumsy'?

With an awareness of OUCH! – our unconscious controlling habits – we've realised that we have become so skilled with these that they have come to feel 'natural'. Breaking these habits means putting something else in their place. We cannot simply stop doing one thing, we need to *start* doing another. Since controlling feels so natural, coaching will feel decidedly unnatural and so we have to be prepared to be clumsy as we start coaching. The good news is that clumsy reinforces vulnerability and our humanity and trustworthiness.

Leadership theory tells us that there are many leadership styles and methods; however, I like to talk about just two opposite styles – directing and coaching. I consider teaching to be a separate process; one that is hugely necessary and beneficial, but separate to, and in support of, either of the two prime styles.

Directing people means telling them precisely what to do (and probably how to do it), how to report to you, and maybe what they will get when they are successful. This style is all about control. Things will be done my way, and then all will be well and everything will go to plan.

I am not saying that this style is wrong – it's not. In certain circumstances this style is not only correct, but essential. Giving clear direction and telling people precisely what to do can make people feel very safe and feel highly motivated to carry out instructions. I recall an incident that really brought this home to me. I went out on a day's sailing with a client, having never sailed before. I was nervous because I simply did not know how to do things. The ropes were a mystery to me and the sail positioning to the wind was counterintuitive. So my client had to be very precise in his instructions to me – and the more precise he was, the more confident I felt. He was reluctant to give me orders and wanted to give me an opportunity to discover things for myself – until a crisis point when the wind suddenly changed when we were slicing through the water at eight knots. I missed my cue and in an instant I experienced all the emotions of failure – I was letting my colleagues down and I did not know what to do and started to panic. Luckily my client went into extreme direction mode and screamed a very precise instruction in my ear. He was not polite. His voice contained urgency, and frustration with me. He swore. And it was exactly what I needed. In that instant I felt relieved and safe. I pulled the correct rope through and tied it off, and the crisis was averted. He gave me the leadership that I needed right at that moment.

> *He was not polite. His voice contained urgency, and frustration with me. He swore. And it was exactly what I needed. In that instant I felt relieved and safe.*

If directing is all about control, coaching is all about growth. Directing is giving people our solutions. Coaching is the opposite – not giving solutions but getting the other person to perform to their best; finding methods and processes and structures that enable others to come to their own solutions and choose their own actions. And just where are they supposed to get this coaching from if not from us as their line manager – their 'performance' manager?

So knowing it's OK for us to be directive at times, and knowing we're going to be a bit clumsy as we start to coach, we can at least make the change. What people want more than anything else is clarity. They just need to know what's expected of them. Our problem is that, knowing that there are just the two styles of leadership, instead of being clear about which style we are using, we try and mix the two and find a continual middle ground of a style. This is not helpful to people; in fact it is highly confusing. People want to be coached most of the time, and then are prepared to be directed as an exception. Trust and respect grow when people know that we are genuinely attempting to coach them, even if we are clumsy sometimes, and this buys us the right to direct them clearly and strongly when it is necessary and appropriate.

We need to consciously choose the style we are going to employ, moment by moment. We cannot delegate by abdication, even when it sounds incredibly supportive, even possibly enlightened. For when people are left alone, they will come to decide for themselves that their objective is not achievable and they will start constructing their perfect reasons for when they are held to account for 'failing'.

Poor forecasting is endemic in organisations and it has this moment of decision at its root, for people don't choose to tell us when they have decided that the target is not possible. Their exhortations that the target is still possible may sound highly committed, but in reality they have started the positioning of the excuses.

If only all the energy that was put into selling our excuses was put into achieving the stated objectives, business performance would be revolutionised. And this is where the adoption of a cultural change to having coaching as the predominant leadership style is utterly transformational in organisational success, since suddenly the truth is exposed and ruthless honesty comes to the fore in a collegiate spirit of simply wishing to achieve more and grow, and for everyone to be fulfilled in the process.

The five myths of coaching

The biggest problem any of us have in achieving excellence in coaching is that we tend to believe the myths that surround the term itself. 'Coaching' is a term much used in the world of 'modern' leadership; however, when asked to define it we struggle. What would your definition be?

So what are the myths that we are guilty of being seduced by?

First of all we believe that coaching is 'soft and fluffy' – that coaching is not being tough on people or driving better performance out of them, but that it is being more gentle and understanding, and needs an immense amount of patience to allow people to come to their own decisions and processes. This then leads us to the second myth – that it takes longer to coach people than to simply direct them, and it is this belief that stops us from investing in the skill development needed. It is the same barrier that stops us from delegating to people, since it is often quicker to do it ourselves than to explain to someone else.

Myth 3 is that teaching people is coaching them. In other words when we are explaining a process or a guideline or a company rule to people, we tell ourselves that we are coaching them and we often confuse the two.

But the most restricting beliefs are Myths 4 and 5 – Myth 4 is that we genuinely tell ourselves that we know how to coach, and Myth 5 is that we are already coaching our people. I often hear in my workshops '*I already coach my people*', when in fact we need to realise that when we believe we are coaching, we are usually being more inclusive and consensual, and perhaps even more polite, but we are not coaching, we are simply directing people more subtly. We may even be guilty of manipulation.

And notice that when we say that we 'need' to be better at something, that sentence usually ends in an unspoken 'but': '*Of course I need to be better at coaching and I need to coach my people more than I do, but... I just don't get the time to spend with each of them/ I do my best/I am better than I was ten years ago.*' Silent 'buts' basically mean than we have no intention of changing – listen out for them. The phrase 'I need to...' rarely leads to urgent action or embedded change.

> **The phrase 'I need to...' rarely leads to urgent action or embedded change.**

Human potential

What percentage of your personal potential are you currently delivering in your work?

Made you think, didn't it? It's a question that raises so many different issues for us:

What *is* our potential? Do I really want to give 100 per cent at work, or do I want to save some for home? Can anyone ever get to 100 per cent of their potential? My brain hurts just thinking about it, so can't I just be happy as I am?

After we've all thrashed around a bit, I guess what we can all agree on is however much of our potential we are delivering, there is more to come. We all have a sense that we could be achieving more, giving more of ourselves and all the passion, enthusiasm and sheer depth of capability that we possess. We might be working as hard as we can, but we could probably all be working smarter. So what is stopping us?

Listing the external factors that are holding us back is the easy answer to the question of what is stopping us delivering more of ourselves into our work, especially when we are under pressure. And these factors are of course very real on a day-to-day basis. However, when we get ourselves into a fixed belief that only when certain things happen outside of us will we be able to fulfil our potential, we have entered a dangerous zone.

When we step back and breathe and analyse things, we realise of course that the key to delivering more of our potential lies squarely within ourselves. We must change ourselves, and that takes two things: courage and having a great coach!

When someone asks their boss what they should do about a problem, how often does the person asking actually know the answer?

When someone asks their boss what they should do about a problem, how often does the person asking actually know the answer?

At the very least, how often could they work it out or find the answer for themselves? Although we might struggle to put a number on the first question, when we think about it we do know that it is a pretty high proportion of the time. With the second part of the question, the answer might even be pretty close to 100 per cent. We know this, and yet it is a constant source of frustration to us. How much more efficient our businesses would be if only people did the job we paid them to do, and if they only 'got' the fact that part of what we pay them to do is think for themselves and solve problems, or do we have to end up doing everything ourselves; thinking of everything; worrying about *everything*?

The critical question of course is not how often people come and ask, but *why* they come and ask if they really know the answer or could easily work it out for themselves? Yes, you've guessed it – maybe it's more to do with us than it is to do with them. Blaming them is easy and often quite enjoyable, but the answer is to look at the way we manage them. If we genuinely want our people using their initiative, thinking for themselves and solving their own problems then we need to change the way we manage them – we need to become genuine coaches.

The reality is that people come and ask because we reward that behaviour. It's a habit they've learned. Maybe they are seeking reassurance, or maybe they're fearful of getting it wrong, but why would that be the case? Unless, of course, their experience of us is that we can be predatory at times. Us? Surely not...

The reality is that our habits have created their habits. If we want them to develop new habits, we *have* to start with ourselves.

And remember the key word in the question above is 'problem' – we are not talking about technical facts or processes that people need to be taught. If it's their first day in the business and they come and ask where the bathroom is, there is very little point in saying '*Where do* you *think the bathroom is?*' Teach them what they don't know. Now if they come and ask on day two, they're just being lazy and using us as a crutch... so coach away!

If coaching is about growth, and if taking the risks is going to be worth it, just what could this 'untapped potential' in people look like? And if we are going to release it, how do we know that it will come out in an orderly and appropriate (controllable) fashion?

The question regarding the percentage of personal potential people are currently delivering in their work is one I have asked hundreds of times to individuals and groups of managers. And in any group the average answer invariably comes out to about 65 per cent. The range of course is often huge – from 20 per cent to 100 per cent – and we all interpret the question slightly differently, yet it's as if we all instinctively know that there is 'more to come'.

Now if I asked the question in terms of effort or work rate or hours worked, I know I would get answers of 100 per cent and maybe more! Because we all know that we can't work much harder or put many more hours in. Recent advances in technology have pushed management 'productivity' to new levels. We can all now work more hours per day on more things, and the latest daily 'holy grail' for managers is an empty inbox. What insanity!

The other thing we instinctively sense about our potential, is that we don't need to tap into much more to give a step change – the sense that another 5 per cent could transform our confidence, our skills, our performance, our achievements.

When we are fearful of judgement, we stop ourselves from trying something different. It's as if we have to be guaranteed of success before we'll even try something. Thank God that business success is not dependent upon managers learning to ride bikes. Remember what it took for you to learn to ride a bike – basically you had to make a fool of yourself by falling off hundreds of times and by having to have a parent or carer run along behind you grabbing at your saddle and shouting inane encouragements at you. But, of course, you were not conscious of this, or if you were, the desire to ride was greater than your desire to look 'cool'.

I remember going surfing with my son Tom when he was 15, when neither of us could surf. He learned much quicker than me, due simply to the fact that he had more goes than I did in the same amount of time we were out together. My strategy was to wait for a really good wave that would give me a chance of a decent attempt – he just tried every wave that came along. I spent most of my time standing up in the water waiting for a 'great' wave. He spent most of his time falling off. I had about ten attempts. He probably had 100. He wanted to learn to surf. I wanted not to look stupid.

I spent most of my time standing up in the water waiting for a 'great' wave. He spent most of his time falling off. I had about ten attempts. He probably had 100. He wanted to learn to surf. I wanted not to look stupid.

We say that people are our biggest asset, and then we don't invest the highest standards of leadership in them. So how do we bring out that extra 5 per cent of people's potential? Great question, and having the awareness to ask it of ourselves means that we are halfway there! As a coach, my job is to help people perform at their peak, as much of the time as possible, and certainly more often than they would if I was not around. In doing so, I help them extend their peak beyond what they believed it to be and beyond any level they've yet achieved.

Nine times out of ten, when people come and ask us as their manager what they should do, they know the answer. They certainly know where to look for the answer, even if the solution is not obvious. How inefficient is that? Now I hear you saying that *your* people don't just come and ask you. No they probably don't – they are far too subtle for that; nevertheless, they do know how to put you in a position where you will give them the answer.

So the real question is, why do they come and ask? We need to realise just how important it is for any employee to please their boss – yes, even you. So when they are about to hit the edge of their comfort zone, instead of risking a unilateral decision to go outside, they come and see you.

They have learned that this is the safest thing to do, and not only that, but that they will be rewarded for coming. Yes, rewarded. They have learned that if they venture outside their comfort zone and it goes wrong, you will give them that funny little judgemental look that says 'you did *what*?!' and you will be all hurt and cross that they went ahead without clearing it with you first, because if they had you could have saved them.

Actually the saddest thing here is that maybe our people have learned that if they venture outside their comfort zone and take a risk (showing the initiative that you are always asking of them) and it goes right, you might still sanction them! It sounds like this: '*You took a real risk and actually you were lucky it worked this time, but in future you need to run that sort of thing past me, or at the very least inform me in advance so I am prepared in case I get challenged by my boss.*' We say that we trust people and that we want them to use their initiative, but do we actually reward that behaviour when they do?

But do we 'reward' mistakes? Maybe the reality is that the reward for coming to ask what they already know is, of course, that you treat them well. You are in fact flattered that they have come to you in such circumstances because it reinforces your position in the hierarchy. You do after all possess greater wisdom and experience, and what's the point if they don't come and ask you sometimes?

There is something a bit Machiavellian going on here. If they come to you and you engage and give them the answer, then you are on the hook when it goes wrong. They manipulate you into being co-responsible for their objectives.

So if we want to stop this behaviour we have to change the risk–reward paradigm. Instead of rewarding them for coming when they know the answer we have to make *this* the situation they do not want to experience, and conversely reward them for coming to us when stepping outside their comfort zone. If someone comes to me as their coach when they are still inside their comfort zone, they are going to get short shrift. If they come when they need me to hold them outside their comfort zone, they will get rewarded. They will quickly come to understand the behaviour that gets rewarded. And for me that means I have to work hard to be ruthlessly consistent in ensuring my words and my actions match.

Chapter 2
Coaching recalibration

Recalibration

When running my Coaching Excellence programmes, I often refer to this part as 'rebooting to factory settings' to communicate two critical aspects of this initial engagement process. First, hard-pressed managers will almost inevitably be sceptical of training, and rapidly engaging them with the metaphor of themselves and their brains being computers that can be rebooted and that there is a science to these things can really help their logical side to be open to engaging. Second, it hints at the idea that all we need to do is to restore ourselves, our strategies and our relationships to the most natural state we were all born in.

This process starts with an honest assessment and inventory of our unconscious controlling habits, and so let's remind ourselves what these are:

⊛ We ask closed questions *(like machine gun fire!)*

⊛ We fill silences *(anything over a few nanoseconds with so much cortisol banging around)*

⊛ We answer our own questions *(if we waited for them for God's sake...)*

⊛ We let people answer a different question *(we can't be rude, and besides we probably didn't notice anyway)*

⊛ We make statements *(since they are clearly lacking motivation, our words will inspire them)*

⊛ We give multiple inputs *(it's quicker to dump out a stream of consciousness, it being so valuable)*

⊛ We use 'we' instead of 'you' *(we want to be inclusive and we are scared of being direct)*

⊛ We issue instructions *(tell me, explain to me, take me through your thinking...)*

⊛ We interrupt and talk over people *(only if what they're saying is nonsense, of course...)*

⊛ We finish people's sentences for them *(well we knew what they were saying, but they were taking forever...)*

We unwittingly train people to be dependent upon us. We create co-dependent people out of bright, young, talented, independent thinkers. Our habits create the very culture that we find so irritating and frustrating and with which we so quickly lose patience. And so we enter the vicious downward spiral as our habits get worse not better, and as we find ourselves reliant

We unwittingly train people to be dependent upon us. We create co-dependent people out of bright, young, talented, independent thinkers. Our habits create the very culture that we find so irritating and frustrating and with which we so quickly lose patience.

on management strategies and techniques that we know in our hearts to be wrong. We simply have to break our habits and we know this, but the issue is that we are actually unaware of the real habits that we need to change and so we end up beating ourselves up for not being able to better control our frustration. And as we get angry with ourselves, we project that frustration onto our people, making them worse!

Armed with self-knowledge, and confronted with OUCH!, we can now truly recalibrate ourselves. This is where our seven triggers come in. The first five will be outlined here, with triggers 6 and 7 being discussed in Chapter 4.

Trigger 1: Calm the fish

Years ago I met a professor of fish biology at Bournemouth University; a world-leading expert on predicting fish behaviour in reaction to changes to the oceans and their environment. She told me that the greatest skill she had to develop was not reading charts or looking down microscopes or understanding complex algorithms. No, none of these. The greatest skill she'd had to master was the ability to calm herself down into an almost Zen-like state before she entered an ocean or a tank of fish, otherwise the fish will 'think' she's a predator and bugger off. And if they think she's a predator and act accordingly, she cannot then take their behaviour as an accurate predictor of how they will actually react in natural conditions in the wild.

What the hell has a fish biologist got to do with me, I hear you ask? I manage people, not fish… well, our working cultures are highly pressured. It's all about deadlines and targets and timescales and comparisons and metrics and KPIs, so we and our people are under constant pressure. And under pressure, our physiology tells us that we have to stay safe. So culturally its almost inevitable that our employees will default to safety, rather than habitually being expansive, creative and energetic. We then find this quite frustrating, and since we are our people's physical environ-ment, it's no wonder that they often feel a predatory energy from us. If we walk into a meeting, a one-to-one or even an ad hoc conversation by the water cooler, and we are carrying the slightest anxious energy, our people will pick up on it instantly and their 'fight or flight' reflex will be triggered. It won't matter if that anxious energy we are carrying is nothing to do with them, if it was caused by something else that happened to us earlier or by something that we are worried or preoccupied by. They'll think it's them. The 'fish' will bugger off – of course they will not do physically do this, since walking out of a meeting with the boss is the epitome of 'career limiting', not to say discourteous. So the 'fish' stay and act like they are listening, even like they are agreeing, and our egos don't allow us to notice, although the evidence is clear.

So the first 'trigger' we need, as an instant and unconscious signpost for us to coach, is simply 'calm the fish'. This alone will help us to better regulate our own energetic state. But this trigger also helps us communicate openly and honestly. Sometimes it's asking too much of ourselves to completely manage our frustration, impatience and irritation, but if we can go into a meeting owning our own state, and then communicate to the people assembled how we are and that it's not because of them, we can stay authentic but with calmed fish around us to move forward positively.

Trigger 2: Truly great feedback hurts

We simply have to give our feedback honestly and with as much care (in the proper sense of that word of 'caring' for the other person) as possible; not sanitising it or sugar-coating it as this leaves people unclear. They have to *feel* it, otherwise it won't register and is therefore not available for them as valuable data for them to really consider. How many people

They have to feel it, otherwise it won't register and is therefore not available for them as valuable data for them to really consider.

do you know who've had the same feedback for years and yet do nothing about it, or worse seem to wear it as some sort of badge of honour?

The biggest problem we have with giving feedback is that we believe it involves passing judgement on people. In other words that we have to tell them they are not doing well enough, or not doing it right. These are judgements, and I don't know about you, but if someone judges me I tend to defend myself. After all I am my own worst critic and I spend a lot of time judging myself, so I don't need others to judge me. What I *do* need is feedback – information. And that is all feedback is – information. It should be factual and evidence-based. The best example I can give is the video replay that any athlete would watch with their coach after a game or match. Video replay contains no judgement – it is simply a factual rerun of what happened, of what the athlete actually did and what happened as a result. The great thing about feedback is that when it's given well, it's often all we need. When we get high-quality feedback as to what we did and what the result was, we know what to do to correct things next time.

I believe it should always be owned personally. If I have heard something about you from someone else, my best course of action is to relay it to you from my own observation – to own it myself. Now I don't subscribe to blatant dishonesty, and would always encourage others to pass their feedback themselves, and after passing my own observations I will often find a way of encouraging a conversation between the two parties. The problem is that passing on someone else's feedback is fraught with danger if the other person decides to deny the information. And there is something of an abdication in my view if I am passing on feedback that I don't own.

Another pitfall of feedback is to wait for 'the right time' to give it, especially to wait for an appraisal that may be weeks or months after the incident. It is also difficult to 'call someone in' to receive feedback – you know the sort of meeting that we all dread, lose sleep over, put off if we can and then end up 'getting through' rather than giving real value to the other person. Have the courage to stop the world and give feedback in the moment – when replaying the tape for someone is going to be undeniable.

Telling someone how you experience them is useful as it can give an indication of how they might be impacting others as well. But be wary of being definitive. The 'fact' that the other person's particular behaviour makes you feel uncomfortable, nervous, intimidated, excited or inspired may say more about you than it does about them.

The great gift of the coach giving feedback is more than just a piece of information about that moment or that incident, however. The real added value is to help the person identify their patterns (their habits), whether sabotage or success. We all have sabotage patterns – things that we do to ourselves to snatch defeat from the jaws of victory – and we all have success patterns – things that we habitually do that work for us and always put us in positions of influence and power. When as coaches we help others to see these, they can control the bad ones and play up the good, thereby instantly raising their performance.

Having said that we need to be wary of our judgements and be very non-judgemental in order to coach people, we do need to make judgements about what the other person *needs* from us along the way. Maybe they need confidence and courage? We can give that through our feedback. Maybe they need some humility? Again, we can give that. If we are sincere in our approbations, we can tell people that they have what it takes. We can tell them they are good, great, wonderful, beautiful, talented, courageous, creative, etc. We can tell them we believe in them and that they will find a way through. After all at times, if we don't believe in them – who will?

Receiving feedback

But what about receiving, soliciting feedback? As a leader, we have a duty to be a role model – to be an exemplar of the behaviours we want to see in others. If you want to be successful in giving feedback, a great place to start is by asking people to give it to you – and to encourage them to be both direct and honest. The rules of receiving feedback are to smile and say thank you. Never defend yourself, never explain why they are wrong. Others may lack skill at giving feedback and therefore it may contain judgements, but be big enough to rise above this and hear the informational content. It is the act of a big man to hear feedback, accept it and not defend himself.

It *is* OK to seek more details or information if you genuinely don't understand what you are hearing, but never cross the line into interrogation because you will simply send the message that you don't really want feedback, you just say that you do.

Honesty in feedback is one of the great fundamentals of team-working and team-building. Most team-building devices are simply trying to give an environment whereby communication takes place between team members in a supportive and collegiate manner.

You set the example. As with everything in coaching, however, you have to ask the right questions. Here are some good examples:

❀ *What do I do that inspires you/adds value?*

❀ *What am I doing when I am at my best?*

❀ *What do I do that irritates you/gets in your way?*

❀ *What do I need to start/stop doing?*

Remember you will need to ask each question more than once to get to the truth.

Feedback using values

Just as we can really get our values into the organisation through using the language in our questions, the other opportunity is with our feedback. This is slightly harder to do without sounding or being judgemental since we are almost deliberately comparing behaviour to the inherent code in the values; however, it again does the two jobs in one.

Often a good technique for feedback is to make your observation and then immediately follow up with a question that gets them to reflect on what you have said. This ensures that they cannot avoid the feedback – either they have to acknowledge it and accept it, or they have to enter a debate with you.

The following four values are those of a major national retailer in the UK:

⊛ Proud – I am proud to work for the company

⊛ Valued – I feel valued and appreciated

⊛ Trusted – I trust the company and they trust me

⊛ Successful – I am able to succeed

We can craft great questions using these, as we shall see in an upcoming section, but we can also use them to give feedback. It took me just a few minutes to design the statements below, but the trick will be to simply use these as examples.

One more thing, notice how I have deliberately given alternate examples starting with the words 'I', 'You' and 'Your' – don't be afraid to be direct in giving your feedback, after all we should only be afraid of such directness if we are passing judgement on people. If we are stating facts, or making observations, then we are not judging, and our intervention will be treated as helpful not damaging.

Proud – I am proud to work for the company

⊛ *I don't get any sense of pride from you in this*

⊛ *You don't seem proud of your team*

⊛ *Your team are obviously proud of what they have achieved*

Valued – I feel valued and appreciated

⊛ *I would not feel valued by you in this instance*

⊛ *You showed appreciation and look at the result*

⊛ *Your team are feeling unappreciated*

Trusted – I trust the company and they trust me

⊛ *I trust you and you could push further and faster because of this*

⊛ *You have a high degree of trust from your team*

⊛ *Your colleagues don't seem to trust what you are proposing*

Successful – I am able to succeed

- 🌐 *I don't see how your planned outcomes really equal success*
- 🌐 *You achieved that success because you...*
- 🌐 *Your team simply don't feel successful*

We have created many moments of magic along the way in our journey of becoming at first clumsy and then skilled coaches, and feedback gives us access to the second of our seven triggers.

But the most excruciating lesson for us as coaches is to acknowledge that truly great feedback – the type of feedback that really makes people stop and think and take action – hurts! And the last thing we ever want to do to another human being is to hurt them. But if they are blocked and battling against the wrong obstacle, then *someone* needs to tell them, and as their manager, their coach, that responsibility falls to us.

When working some years ago with the then chief medical officer, Liam Donaldson, I met his 'maverick' deputy, Professor Aidan Halligan. Aidan was to become one of my dearest friends before the world sadly lost him in 2015. Aidan was brilliant, but could be 'difficult'. His ideas and methods were right, but he often lost people along the way. It bothered me that this situation was known, but no one seemed to have told Aidan! But it wasn't my job...

One morning as I walked down the wide corridor towards Liam's office, I saw Aidan walking towards me. The annoyingly inconvenient voice on my shoulder said: *'Now's your chance – tell him.'* In the few seconds that passed before we would have to acknowledge each other, I talked myself into and then out of giving him feedback several times. But ultimately I cannot leave these things alone. We passed each other with a courteous acknowledgement but without stopping – I'd only met Aidan twice so we were not on social speaking terms. I turned as he walked past me and jumped: *'Aidan, do you have a moment?'* No way back now. Aidan was immensely perceptive, so I suspect he knew from my demeanour that this was a request to be accommodated. We walked to his office and I sat with him for probably no more than ten minutes and I let him have it. I told him he was brilliant but that he was getting in his own way and that his style was getting him rejected. I told him he was about to fail, and that he needed to decide if he could adapt his style to make the change he was advocating more palatable for his audience to hear and engage with. Aidan sat back and simply said *'thank you'*. He then asked me for some advice on how he could do what I had advocated. It was the start of a very special relationship for the two of us. Some years later we were at an event, and someone asked us how we had met. Aidan told the story, but to my amazement he added a small postscript. He said that in the two years that he had spent in the Department of Health, my giving him that feedback was the greatest 'act of kindness' anyone had shown him.

> *He said that in the two years that he had spent in the Department of Health, my giving him that feedback was the greatest 'act of kindness' anyone had shown him.*

How does the saying go? *'If you set out to be liked, you'll end up being disrespected. If you set out to be respected, you'll end up being liked.'* So take courage and give your people the most profound gift you can. Treat them like adults and they will respond in an adult way. Give them professional respect, and they will respond as professionals. And even though they may not like you in the moment, they will end up appreciating you for it.

Advice

> *Advice is something we ask for when we know the answer, but wish we didn't.*
> Erica Jong, *How to Save Your Own Life*

Giving advice is tough for any line manager because of the hierarchy dynamic. How can I ignore a piece of advice from my boss? In most organisations this would be 'career limiting'. But in coaching we are developing a relationship where we are there to help the other person get the best out of themselves. They are learning that, as their boss, we are more concerned with them than with the business result at hand. In this spirit we can develop a relationship where they can ignore our advice and we will be perfectly OK with this. After all, as we learned very early on and as they have found with us in this new relationship, if we wanted them to just do what we ask of them, we would be open and direct and honest about it and issue a directive.

Advice is best given as a question that they need to ask themselves. This way we can give our advice, not as a beautifully gift-wrapped solution that they would be mad to ignore, but as a haunting question that nags at them until they engage with it and take it into their decision-making thought process.

A powerful way of expressing your concerns is to preface your sentence with '*My worry for you is...*' or '*The risk I think you run if you... is...*' This allows you to put a legitimate concern on the table without causing offence or directing the person to do or not do something specific. It leaves them with the dignity of their own choice. This is also a way of being able to express a judgement you have reached, without making your feedback judgemental.

But ultimately we may need to be very direct, with a '*you need to...*' message, and again this will be absolutely taken on board if we are trusted as their coach, They will look back at us and say, '*You're absolutely right.*'

Trigger 3: Come from curiosity, not judgement

We have to use curiosity when asking people why they did things or what is stopping them from acting, since we humans make our decisions subconsciously and emotionally, although we convince ourselves that we make decisions rationally. Actually what we do is, having made our decision subconsciously or emotionally, we pile in the rational justification. So if we put people under pressure in our 'interrogation' of their motives for action or inaction, they will surely give us their left-brain answer, ie, their logical justification, which will therefore be defensive and ultimately not the real reason. When we use curiosity, we allow the other person to feel accepted and not judged or threatened, and thus we can allow them to explore their real reasons, which will ultimately have been driven by emotions – maybe of fear, excitement, anger or elation.

I was confronted as a young general manager with having to prove my belief in these fine words – one of our delivery drivers had returned from a drop having severely damaged the front of their vehicle. I mustered all my curiosity as I asked him what had happened. When he hesitated I knew he was about to lie to me, so I calmly reminded him that he was safe, and that I genuinely wanted to understand what had happened and that I would not be angry. So he went for it, and explained that he had run into the back of another car because he was looking at a pretty girl on the side of the road. Every fibre of my being wanted to scream at him that he had been a bloody idiot. But I had to be trustworthy in that moment, to reward his honesty – after all he knew he'd been an idiot, but now he had exposed himself to my judgement, and he could have lied. Sam Goldwyn once said '*I expect people to tell me the truth, even if it costs them their job*.' There was, of course, a consequence for the driver – fessing up cannot in itself absolve people from taking responsibility, but he did not lose his job and I made sure that he knew how much I respected him for telling the truth.

The first key to wisdom is constant and frequent questioning, for by doubting or through being curious we are led to question, and by questioning we arrive at the truth.
Peter Abelard, 1079–1142

I like this quote is because it tells us that curiosity is a core principle for us to base our coaching on. People who are naturally curious often make great coaches, because they ask the questions that others avoid.

Questions are powerful – infinitely more so than we give credit for before we start asking them in bucket-loads. They work so well because they multitask for us – they work on several levels, but basically they do two jobs at once. They make the other person think, and start the process of them accepting responsibility, and they communicate so much of the position that *we* are taking as the coach – acceptance, confidence, belief, the fact that there *is* a solution, the fact that there are other options, support, the fact they are not alone, etc.

I'm often asked by people how they can make this coaching skill more natural. I simply invite them to notice that coaching is actually the most natural human relationship communication skill and we've known it all our lives. I invite them to notice that it is our corporate behaviour that is unnatural. Let me ask you this. At what age were you at your finest as an asker of open questions? Yes, that's right. About four years old. Four year-olds ask stunning open questions, but more than that, they are then ruthless with us if we fob them off with a bullshit answer. So if we could ask open questions (without any training) when we were four, how is it we find it so tough 30, 40 or 50 years later?

At what age were you at your finest as an asker of open questions? Yes, that's right. About four years old.

So here is the third of our seven triggers. Be aware when you want to ask a question that is really motivated because you have judged the other person or the situation, and instead go for what you are curious about. This is another area where our physiology helps us out. People know when they are being judged, and they defend themselves. Ask someone a question that comes from judgement, and you will get a defensive or evasive response; maybe even a lie. It won't matter if your question is legitimate. But ask them from a place of genuine curiosity, and it's completely irresistible, and you will get both a truthful and a revealing answer. Curiosity is an incredibly attractive human quality and people will be motivated to respond with the truth, even though they know that revealing the truth could create a consequence for them.

Trigger 4: Hold the person, not the problem

Although we need to study the facets of how we create and maintain rapport with people, the good news is that we human animals instinctively know when we are in rapport – when we are 'connected' with another human being. In fact it's what we crave, and for many (me included) it defines our spirituality and gives meaning to life. It's what I live for, and is its own reward, just as much if not more than the 'punch the air' euphoria of achieving a goal.

Curiosity is an incredibly attractive human quality and people will be motivated to respond with the truth, even though they know that revealing the truth could create a consequence for them.

But at work this connection often scares us, as we are wary of getting 'in deep' with people. We just work with them and the last thing we want is to get *close* to them. They might abuse the closeness, or even worse we might have to reprimand them or discipline them or even fire them in the future, so we tell ourselves that we must retain a separation from our people, just in case. The problem with this is that instead of interpreting this as drawing and maintaining healthy boundaries with people, we tend to interpret it as having to stay 'aloof' from people – in other words our own lack of self-esteem or self-confidence and our poor assertiveness skills push us to rely on the dreaded hierarchical authority over others.

I understand those who say that it is dangerous to make your work colleagues your friends, but all I know is that it is friendships that often see companies through tough times. If you are going to do the whole 'know/challenge/believe' bit, then you are going to get close to people whether you like it or not. So why not like it? You are going to end up caring about people, so why not embrace this? They will certainly end up caring about you, since very few people, if any, in their lives before will have shown them the type of leadership that you will.

The great thing about human emotional connection is that it is a constant – it can, of course, become damaged by betrayal of trust, and it might well follow cycles dependent upon people's personal circumstances, but the quality of the relationships you build with your people will stay strong, and will constantly communicate your support for them. Thus every action you take including, when it's necessary, actions that might seem overly autocratic or dictatorial, will be accepted within the supportive frame-work you have created. Thus the athlete who needs to be screamed at by their coach to get them across the line first, when their whole body wants to give up, will not feel the abuse, but will take energy from the encouragement, knowing that the coach is only acting inhumanely because they believe so deeply in their athlete's ability. This is why as leader you have to invest in the relationship unconditionally, because your only concern is for their success. You are there for them and them alone.

It is your acceptance of them, your non-judgementalism, your unconditionality that is the foundation for trust and mutual respect. Of course, the reason we struggle with the whole respect piece is because we have told ourselves that our self-worth only comes from our ability to solve problems. We do not value coaching in itself, so how could we be respected by others simply for our coaching? The reality, however, is that once the trust is there, our people do not want us to solve their problems

> *Once the trust is there, our people do not want us to solve their problems for them – for all we do is deny them their sense of achievement and success.*

for them – for all we do is deny them their sense of achievement and success. Once trust is there, what people are desperate for is coaching, and the better we are at it, the more respect we will earn from them.

Now for a revolutionary statement. I believe that the prime purpose of human resources (HR) within any organisation is to help create better relationships between ever-more highly skilled people – between peers and colleagues and between bosses and their people. Of course there is the functional specialism of making sure the company operates within legislation, but that's just the technical stuff. The real stuff is about recruitment and selection, induction, appraisals, career planning, training and development and cultural change,

Why do we use psychometrics if not to help people understand each other and thus form stronger teams? Why carry out 360-degree feedback if not to facilitate the shared journey of discovery we are embarking on as a community of people? Why bother with attitude surveys if not to assess what the managers and leaders need to do differently to gain greater employee commitment and creativity? Why exercise so much time and professional resource on recruitment, induction, appraisals and training if not to facilitate higher performance through better team-working, attitudes, culture and skills?

I am constantly amazed at the levels of disconnect between operational managers and their HR departments and processes. What is that all about? Why is HR often seen as some sort of enemy or as people who simply don't understand what it's like at the sharp end, and who therefore come up with lovely theories that won't work practically? If operational managers accepted that HR's role is to help them have better rapport, then they might just use some of the tools so carefully created for them and use them well. And if the HR tools are substandard, they might just work with their HR colleagues to generate tools that are high-standard.

Coming back to our own coaching, we often believe that to coach someone we have to set up some sort of formal coaching session. Personally I believe in one-to-ones, but I don't subscribe to overly structured coaching sessions in a normal working relationship between a person and their line manager. Rather, I believe that coaching, being the now predominant leadership style we are employing with our people, is just the way we are with people, so actually what I am looking for is to be more opportunistic, and to use moments or spaces when I am in greatest rapport with people, most connected to them, to coach them.

When my daughter Steph and my son Tom were in their middle teens, and I had just separated from their mother, I knew that asking them about 'stuff' at a time that suited *me* was doomed to failure, bringing forth the ubiquitous single-syllable grunts so typical of the humans that arrive in our lives at around the age of 13. I used to say that my kids were the only people I knew who could consistently answer my most carefully crafted open questions with 'yes' or 'no' answers. So I learned (and it sounds so obvious, I know) that I had to be opportunistic with them – to only 'coach' them (ask questions and offer advice) when we were really connected – and that my job was to work to create the strongest and most frequent connections, and to be aware of them so that I could make use of them. My greatest conversations with Steph and Tom – when I found out what was *really* happening with them and how they were really feeling about things, and when they would listen to and value my words of fatherly wisdom – were odd moments driving them home late at night, or eating a burger at half-time when we were at the football – situations when I was not threatening to them, when I was simply accepting them for who they were and loving them for it.

A good technique to use when you have rapport with people is to attach them to past events so that they can experience the sort of state that they need to move forward. Of course, they have already told themselves and you the solution that they need to enact, but there is still something stopping them. For example, if they need courage to move forward, get them to relive a past success when they had to be truly courageous. Their courage will visibly rise in front of you, and you can then get them to use this to gird them for their current challenge. If they need to demonstrate more humility in their current situation, get them to relive a situation when they did so successfully in the past – again they will become humble in front of you, and you can then steer them towards the solution they have already expounded.

One of the greatest skills for building rapport is learning to hear bad news without displaying frustration. It's tough to hear bad news, but it's so much tougher to give it. Don't ever shoot the messenger or you won't get the truth again, or if you do you will hear it sometime after others have known. This means that we have to be in a constant state whereby people are more important than problems, whereby our compassion for another person in pain overrides our impatience at whatever has gone wrong with the plan. Being in rapport or being deeply connected to someone is the only way to guarantee that you will hear the truth, so we have to ask ourselves how much we value the truth – or are we still guilty of entertaining hope as a strategy? Just check out the accuracy of your forecasting system.

Being 'in the moment' with people requires constant self-regulation. Managers tend to live in the past (the other person has failed to do what we've asked, or they've been exhibiting pre-judged behaviour) or the future (the other person needs to do something or achieve a certain objective) rather than being in the present moment with that person. We judge them (we carry their past into the meeting) and we doubt they can do what's really needed (we carry their future into the meeting). Understandably, the other person picks up on this and reacts accordingly (defending themselves, getting their excuses in early, and generally taking demotivation and lack of confidence away from the meeting).

Leaders need to stay 'in the moment' with people and deal with them as they are today. Only then can we judge, as their coach, what they really need from us to achieve their objectives. We have to leave them more energised and confident, even if we've had to deliver some tough feedback and advice, and achieving that starts with acceptance and compassion.

And so we get to the heart of how we actually change our behaviour to have a chance of being successful in coaching others.

in our interactions with people, we always focus on the problem at hand, and as such the other person almost gets in the way.

We must learn to 'hold the person, not the problem'. This sums up our issue – that in our interactions with people, we always focus on the problem at hand, and as such the other person almost gets in the way. So there we are (as their coach), using all our resources to solve the problem, and in the process communicating to them that they are actually part of the problem. We inevitably leave them feeling like bit-part players in some grand performance where we are the star, feeling judged by us as being inferior – we are 100 per cent guilty of being the brake on their energy and the barrier to them taking a radical or creative approach to solving their issue. And all of this without realising what we are doing, without realising that we as managers are perpetuating an environment whereby everything revolves around us yet blaming others for not stepping up, not showing initiative. We create the classic paradigm of the chasm between manager and subordinate – where we blame them for not showing enough initiative, and they blame us for not allowing them to take risks or be themselves.

So how do we 'hold the person'? Well the trick is to focus (physically through eyes and ears, and so eventually through the heart) on them – concentrating on what serves them as an individual. We need to trust that everything we need to know as a coach is there before us, if only we pay attention. We need to listen – and boy is that hard.

And slowly, the more we practise this, the more we will enter a profoundly connected world, where we will see things in others that we had never even glimpsed before. The deeper we look, the more we will see, including the magical prize for any coach – stuff that the other person does not yet realise about themselves!

Now we can coach them, because the issue at hand is merely today's issue. Tomorrow there will be another. Issues will come and go, but the path for the other person to grow and develop all that they have and all that they are – well, that is ongoing and never-ending. And it is a beautiful experience that is the true privilege of responsibility for others.

As we practise this essential change, we will find it tough. We must constantly keep this mantra in our minds – 'hold the person, hold the person' – and we will need to constantly repress the solutions that come up for us and seek to define our navigation of the conversation. It really is like a physical act: first noticing the solution that has come to us, or the path that our left brain wants to take the other person down to get them where we want them to go, and then suppressing it – physically pushing it down or forcing it out of our minds, so that we can get back to noticing and listening to the other person. I have been coaching for many years, and yet I constantly have to be aware of this pattern within me, of how easy it is for me to slip back into problem-solving mode, of how hard it is for me to exorcise an idea from my brain once it's popped in there. So take heart. Awareness is everything – don't try and be perfect at it.

When we listen we hear so much more than when we don't. Sounds obvious doesn't it? But we need to realise that when we are not listening, we are relying on our pre-judgements. When we are under pressure, we are meeting a person we have already put in a box, and so they stand no chance. Just how are people supposed to get us to change those judgements we are holding? They have to either do something completely extraordinary, or rely on some external event to give us 'no choice' but to trust them with greater responsibility.

When we 'hold the person, not the problem' it's amazing how skilful we are at interpreting body language and non-verbal communication. Only then can we 'sense' what people are really communicating. Carl Jung said that if the conscious mind was like the skin of an orange, the outermost 1 per cent of the fruit, the subconscious was everything else. We think we are highly developed animals, yet we pretty much ignore and devalue the power of what is going on *sub*consciously. The coach, how-ever, sees it all; sees the denial and self-delusion that is actually guiding the motiv-ation of the other person.

And as we start to appreciate this skill, this fundamental change of our approach as a leader of people, we enter the truly magical world of the virtuous circle – where we can enjoy the most fantastic results and the most rewarding relationships. And we can absorb into our leadership DNA the *most* fundamental change we need to make if we are to become genuine coaches – that we should exercise all our creative energy on the subject of what we need to do to assist the other person to improve their own performance.

Trigger 5: Take people out of their comfort zones

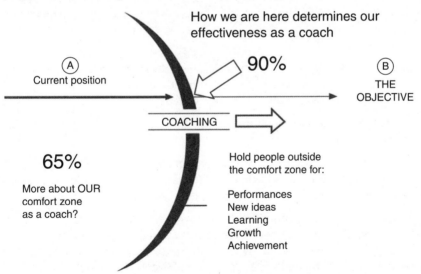

How do we *know* when someone has hit the edge of their comfort zone? Here's another way of looking at the comfort zone. We are at position A, aiming for our target at position B. Have you noticed that your company only ever sets you object-ives that can only be achieved by you performing to extraordinary standards and methods? So somewhere along the path we hit the edge of our comfort zone and then we have a choice. What typically happens is that we decide not to go outside, and therefore we have to give up on achieving the target B. But if we give up on the target, we need have a story that excuses us. So we come up with reasons why we cannot achieve B, and since we are now turning all our energy and creativity into these reasons, they are always 'perfect' and thus cannot be denied or countered.

If B is a sales target, our 'perfect' reason may be that B was *always* unrealistic, but we all knew that and where we will actually end up will still be a good result. If B is a customer order, our 'perfect' reason may be that our competition has done some-thing underhand or uncommercial to win the business that we, of course, on our high ground, would not stoop to. If B is the development of a person under our leader-ship, our 'perfect' reason may be that something that they did along the way caused us to determine that they clearly need another 12 months' experience before we can promote them. If B is a market share position, our 'perfect' reason could include any one of a multitude of external events that were both completely unpredictable and outside our control.

The most powerful 'perfect' reason to brandish is one where the boss is actually included. So maybe the reason I did not meet my commitment to get that piece of work to you, is because you asked me to go to see that customer last week. In other words *you* changed my schedule, thus clearly making me miss the deadline. Of course I did not tell you when you diverted me last week that asking me to do something extra would cause me to break my commitment.

How often have we gone to hold someone to account for not completing on a commitment they have made, thinking to ourselves *'This had better be good...'*, only to reluctantly let the other person off the hook because their excuse is *so* plausible, and only because it would *so* unreasonable of us to insist that they should still have met their commitment.

We are experts at perfect reasons (excuses). They always mask a fear – fear of failure, fear of taking the necessary risks, and the most powerful fear of all, fear of the judgements people will make about us should we fail.

A good coach will listen for these and then move the person outside their comfort zone again by challenging.

But how do we hold people outside their comfort zones? It's up to us to determine what tool to use to get them outside their comfort zone – from gentle persuasion and encouragement at one extreme, to a kick up the backside at the other.

But then we need to hold them outside so that they experience what it's like. For only outside the comfort zone will people perform at a higher level, learn from new experiences, grow and, most importantly, achieve things they had begun to believe were not possible, or perhaps had never dared to believe were possible.

People gain enormous confidence from achieving things. It's infectious and it gives a huge positive momentum. This is the starting point for bringing out the true untapped potential of our people.

If I were to ask you to tell me a story of something you achieved in the past, of which you were incredibly proud, you would tell me a story of how you had come out of your comfort zone. After all, why on earth would we be proud of something that had been easy for us? And the pride that comes gives us a taste of achievement. And achievement builds tremendous confidence. So the time to really challenge people is often immediately after they have achieved something extraordinary.

And going back to our conscious focus, the reality is that if as leaders, we make the experience of being outside their comfort zone one of fear, then the things people will consciously focus on will be defensive and safety-based. They will do everything in their power to get back inside their comfort zone, including lying and blaming others. If, however, we make that experience exciting, then the things they will consciously focus on will be expansive, creative and energetic, and the transformation in that moment will be palpable and beautiful. More than that, they will want that experience again for it is a more deeply rewarding experience than following orders.

A coach takes a person outside their comfort zone, and holds them there while they learn and grow, however uncomfortable this might be for the coach. The trick is to make the person feel safe and uncomfortable at the same time.

> *A coach takes a person outside their comfort zone, and holds them there while they learn and grow*

A leader takes an entire community outside its collective comfort zone, and makes the journey exciting, not frightening.

Make people feel valued and supported when they are outside their comfort zone, not judged and fearful.

> *A leader takes an entire community outside its collective comfort zone, and makes the journey exciting, not frightening.*

There are two comfort zones – our own personal comfort zones, which are set by our natural, innate personalities and past experiences, and the cultural comfort zone, which is the collective comfort zone we find ourselves in and strongly influenced by – and this is 100 per cent set by our leaders and the people who we feel have power and authority over us at work

Targets

> *When the Archer misses the mark, he turns and looks at the fault within himself. Failure to hit the bullseye is never the fault of the target. To improve your aim, improve yourself.*
>
> Gilbert Arland

I want to describe a really stupid situation. You are watching the Olympics on the TV and the archery comes on.

The archer steadies himself, pulls back on the drawstring, his hand almost imperceptibly shaking as he regulates the tension between the frame of the bow and the strings, and then sets about taking aim. This process seems to take minutes rather than seconds, his movements are so deliberate and measured and controlled, becoming ever-more imperceptible. The archer takes aim, reducing the already minuscule movements of his hand to a state of almost unnatural stillness, so that in fact the only movement of the arrowhead in the channel he has created with his fingers, is due to the impact of his heartbeat on the bow.

In this state he completes the final act of preparation – a hair's-breadth trajectory adjustment for the prevailing breeze that will surely work on the arrow as it speeds towards the target.

And then the arrow is gone – unleashed in a fluid movement that ends with the archer 'following through' with his whole being. A few microseconds later the arrow 'thuds' into the target. It's good, but it's not a bull. The arrow lands in the target some four centimetres to the left of the bull's-eye. The archer thinks for a moment, then walks the 50 metres to the target, picks it up, moves it bodily four centimetres to the right, removes their arrow and walks back to take his next shot.

Now there is some logic to this. The archer cannot readily think of what he did wrong, and yet his arrow missed the bull's-eye by four centimetres. Clearly the obvious reason is that the target was in the wrong place. And yet not only would this be a totally stupid response on his part, he would immediately be disqualified.

Yes, I know it's a stupid story, but the reality is that we allow people to do this every day – we go through the fatuous process of designing and agreeing targets, and then enduring weeks or months of progressive renegotiation as the results start to unfold. Of course there are exceptional circumstances when we should adjust objectives and targets, but we're far too lenient. The target is the target. If people say they cannot achieve it, the very worst thing we can do is let them off the hook by moving the target. *Now* is the time for our coaching skills to come into their own.

- 🏵 *I understand that the cat died and that I diverted you last week, but how will you now get back on track?*

- 🏵 *I understand that our competitor has dropped their price by 50 per cent, so what will you now need to do differently in order to win the business from the customer?*

- 🏵 *I agree it is unfortunate that Charlie is going to be off sick for a month, so what is your plan now to meet your original commitment?*

And other such questions. Now we're coaching!

Ambition

And now to the bit where we really start to bring out people's latent or hidden potential. It's easy to do, once we have the basics in place. We simply challenge the other person to stretch themselves towards goals and objectives that are further ahead than they had been thinking. Maybe than they would ever dare think.

Ambition. It's one of my favourite places. I am at my best when I am helping someone to stretch towards an ambitious goal – when I see that look on their face, when I sense the energy and excitement rising – of what might just be possible if only they believe. And my belief in them is often all it takes to unlock their own ambition.

Think back to a wonderful time in your own life – a moment when you achieved something very special. Often what makes it so special is that sense of humility that accompanies the pride – the feeling that we still cannot believe that we did it, that this is really happening to us. I believe passionately and wholeheartedly that people are capable of truly extraordinary achievements, and of experiencing the joy that goes along with it. I have witnessed it time and time again. When business leaders give me the all-too-common lament that they cannot get enough good people, I have a simple response – look around, you've got them already, but if you are unable to lead them to greatness, maybe they need a new leader.

> *When business leaders give me the all-too-common lament that they cannot get enough good people, I have a simple response – look around, you've got them already, but if you are unable to lead them to greatness, maybe they need a new leader.*

Of course the bonus is that achievement is self-perpetuating and highly infectious. Once we have tasted it we want more.

I believe that a good coach can help someone live their life like this, constantly looking for the possibilities to expand and grow and achieve miraculous things. They don't have to be big things, in fact they can be tiny, but they are different and they add value, just as the greatest customer service comes down to the tiny details or the smallest gesture. The big things are easy, because they are one-offs and can be planned and executed. In fact it is the small stuff that is hard because it can go unnoticed, because we have to do them all day every day and because it can feel like there's no respite and no hiding place.

But this profound belief is matched and balanced with my belief that people need respite, nourishment, compassion, understanding, acceptance. No one can be innovating and striving for growth every day. Sometimes the most superhuman act is to get up and feed the children – and that simply *has* to be enough. On that particular day, it's everything.

In an organisation that is going places, there should be no hiding places. I like the environment of honesty – that if you want to hide for a day or to get back under the duvet, you can go and do some comfort work, openly and honestly so that we all know where you are and what you are doing. So much better than the culture of conning and skiving and whatever else we do to get a break.

It is achievement that develops self-confidence. What are you doing to help your people achieve great things for themselves? What are you doing to construct a culture around you of excellence and extraordinary performance? We worry about being seen as unreasonable, so we let people off the hook sometimes. Don't. They can take a rest when they have climbed the mountain, climbed back down again and packed all their gear away.

Resources

We are starting to see that organisations are operating on a superficial autopilot mechanism, and that we need to expose the realities and help everyone to a new level of awareness. Here's another typical paradigm within businesses.

We are struggling to achieve our objectives, so we put more pressure on people, who respond by asking for more resources – more time, more people, more advertising, more budget, etc. And how do we respond to their requests? First we accept them, since we sort of know that we would feel the same in their position, and we do not want to be accused of being unreasonable. Wrong – but we'll come back to this.

Having accepted the legitimacy of the request, we have to respond, or we have to accept that the target is not possible anymore. But what if we have no more money or budget? Well I guess we could give more time by extending the deadline or I could exert more pressure on you, since it is clear that you (or possibly your team) are not working flat out. If I kick you harder, just maybe you'll kick all your people harder and maybe everyone will raise their game and we'll win by everyone working longer hours under more pressure. It's easier than having to think hard about alternatives that will take us all outside our comfort zones, after all!

Try this the next time someone wants more time to write a report – ask them how long they need; then when they say 'a week' or whatever they respond with, ask them precisely how long it would take them if they physically sat down and wrote it right this second. The truthful answer will be something like 30 minutes. So it's about priorities, not time. It's about the mental space people legitimately need, not the physical amount of time the activity will take. It's about people feeling fearful of starting a task they know will be really tough.

And if we give in and add people, even when we know it's going to be counterproductive, we are often not surprised that things get worse and not better. This is where your experience as a manager might need to set the structure – you may have to be very directive on stuff like this, and then coach people to work within the structures you have set.

The trick is not to accept that no more can be done to achieve the objectives with precisely the current resources. The trick is to risk appearing unreasonable. The trick is to coach people to get back outside their comfort zones and find new creative ways to keep moving forward. Don't move the target, or at least don't move it unless external circumstances have significantly changed, or until you are convinced that every strategy has been exhausted.

> *this coaching lark is more about our comfort zones than those of others. Are we prepared to risk being judged as unreasonable?*

And so it dawns on us – this coaching lark is more about *our* comfort zones than those of others. Are we prepared to risk being judged as unreasonable? Are we prepared to go outside *our* comfort zone and meet our own fear of the judgement of others head on?

Chapter 3
Embedding recalibrated coaching habits

Our habits and their habits

Once we become aware of the real habits we need to break, we achieve a new self-awareness, and then it's simply practice. And our clumsiness as we practise, our vulnerability as we transparently seek to develop new habits, is the very medium through which we inspire change in our people, who respond in a heartbeat. Every single time. This is the fundamental vehicle on which we build cultural change, away from command and control, to a truly empowered workforce. Coaching is the way. But not coaching as we think we understood it; coaching through breaking OUCH!

With our new awareness we will quickly realise the extent to which people avoid taking personal responsibility. Since *our* habits have bred *their* habits, we can notice some of their habits listed below.

- *There isn't enough time (you overloaded me from the start)*
- *I don't have the resources (you didn't let me have what I need)*
- *I've helped you out on other things (you distracted me)*
- *The target was always just a hope (you knew that when you set it)*
- *I didn't know that was the target (you were unclear)*
- *External events have changed things (you should lower the target)*
- *Other departments have let me down (you don't hold them to account)*

Employees pressurised to hit unrealistic targets work on excuses rather than objectives. They are highly skilled at this and collude with each other, becoming practised and highly skilled at the following attributes:

> *Employees pressurised to hit unrealistic targets work on excuses rather than objectives. They are highly skilled at this and collude with each other*

- Noticing when the boss is unclear (for future reference)
- Appearing to agree without ever giving express commitments
- Never answering a straight question, yet sounding like they have
- Always looking stressed and overloaded
- Being seen to work long hours
- Sending emails in the evenings, on weekends and on holiday
- Helping the boss out on other things whenever possible
- Noticing when the boss fails to meet one of their own commitments (for future reference)

❀ Exaggerating or even exacerbating mistakes made by other departments

❀ Playing up the impact of external events

❀ Blaming others for everything that goes wrong

❀ Always using the pronouns 'we' and 'you' rather than 'I'

❀ Never ever committing to a specific timed action or decision

❀ Letting other people off their commitments

I don't want to overplay the negatives here, since I know you will tell me that your people do not behave in the way(s) I'm outlining. That may well be true, but in my experience many employees do find themselves in the unenviable position of having to pay attention to protecting themselves, and the real risk is that their creativity in developing self-preservation strategies has become so good that we've stopped recognising it for what it really is. If you look at the list above, it's pretty damning, and you'll see that I've linked the power and effect of our controlling habits with the other major controlling factor in our corporations – unreasonable timescales and growth targets.

If you *really* listen to people as you coach them, you'll realise just how conditioned people are to these behaviours. Our habits have created their habits. Once noticed, we simply need to be accepting of their situation, compassionate even for the position we've put them in, and then earnestly and consistently go about winning back their trust. And we can do this very fast, since it is profoundly how people want to be at work. They simply need some licence, some consistent permission and facilitation to gain confidence in the 'new' way. And I promise they will break their habits in response, in celebration even, of you striving to break yours. This is the gateway to the joy and the transformation of working in a coaching culture.

The next thing we will notice as soon as we start taking care in our choice and crafting of our questions, is that people do not answer the question we've asked them; they answer the question that's safest for them. And again they have become skilled at this. In the chart below you'll see some prime examples.

The question we ask	The question they actually answer
What do you think?	What do I want you to think?
What are you trying to achieve?	What are you doing?
How do you feel?	What do you think?
What could you do?	What have you done?
What could you do?	What can't you do?
What are you struggling with?	What have you been doing?
What's the problem?	What's happened?
How did the problem arise?	Who's to blame?

The question we ask	The question they actually answer
How will you solve the problem?	What is the problem?
What will you do next?	What are you already doing?
What could you do differently?	What have you done so far?

Ask short questions so you can repeat them word for word; make your questions unavoidable. The key is to make our open questions non-threatening (ie, genuinely open) and then calmly repeat them if they're not answered. Many people have an almost visceral fear of repeating a question, but if the repeating of the question is done with care, if it's done calmly, gently but firmly, then what actually gets communicated is certainly a correction, but a correction that's taken as a mark of professional respect. In other words what they receive unconsciously from us is a belief that they *can* answer the question, rather than any form of punishment for *not* answering it in the first place. This is one of the most simple and effective ways we have of breaking old, outmoded and irrelevant habits in others, and instilling a new-found enthusiasm for getting to the heart of an issue really fast. This becomes exhilarating and, lo and behold, transformations abound.

Closed questions

Perhaps the biggest habit change we need to make is to stop asking so many closed questions. We ask them because we have a flowchart in our mind, a decision tree created by the left-hand side of our brain, and we are attempting to get the other person to agree to our solution. We ask closed questions either to control people – by asking a closed question

Perhaps the biggest habit change we need to make is to stop asking so many closed questions.

to which the answer we desire is obvious – or when we genuinely don't know the answer but we need to determine which way to go next in our flowchart.

If we *are* aware, then we excuse ourselves by saying that closed questions are quicker, but they are *hugely* judgemental. I cannot stress enough how powerful they are in controlling people. We get the answer we want, giving us a greater feeling of control. But this control is an illusion – a total illusion. Getting a yes gives no guarantee at all that the other person will do what they have said yes to, or if they do they will probably not carry it out with passion and enthusiasm and energy and total commitment, because it's *our* solution and not theirs. Or if they do and it goes wrong they will end up blaming us, or making excuses for themselves.

Using closed questions has a further downside – it means no one explores the 'shades of grey' that tend to be closer to reality. Why is it that we go into such extremes at work, assuming that everything is either black or white, zero or 100 per cent?

We can ask people *'Are you committed?'* and get a *'Yes'*. Or we can ask them *'How committed are you?'* and get an entirely different answer. We might hear them answer *'I'm completely committed'* or *'Well, pretty committed'* or *'Actually, I'm not feeling very* committed' – if we ask the closed question and get a 'Yes', we move on. If we ask an open question, we will get a richer answer that probably demands a follow-up.

So here is our flowchart. We get presented with the problem, and instantly our solution comes into our mind closely followed by the flowchart template we will use to get 'them' to the solution. The left brain bombards the other person with closed questions that determine the flow, and gets the other person where we want them to go.

The real issue, of course, is that we are the ones that are now guilty of restricting the creativity used in the whole process, ignoring the potential solutions that lie outside the flowchart template we have created – we have become the limiters.

We talk too much

We talk too much, but we find it hard to shut up because we believe it's the way to get the best out of people, first of all to motivate them and second to tell them what to do. When it seems not to work we become like the stereotypical Englishman abroad when the 'foreigner' does not speak our language – we just talk louder and slower. Strangely enough they still don't understand, but all parties get more frustrated. And they simply think we're very stupid.

The trouble is that fundamental brain chemistry gets in our way – because the other person's brain works seven times faster than we can speak. So while we are speaking, their brain is thinking all sorts of stuff. We would like to think that they are thinking *'Wow, this is fantastic stuff! I feel so motivated to do what the boss is asking me – more than that, I feel so lucky to work for such a great boss and I am going to so grateful in the future and change my attitude to become exactly how he wants me to be.'* Yeah, right. Unfortunately they are more likely to be thinking *'What exactly is he trying to say? What does this mean for me? How will this affect me? What do I have to do now? When is this going to end? Why can't I work for someone else?'*

Even after delivering the most inspirational speech, will our people have made the decision to follow us unconditionally, or will they be waiting to see what happens next? It depends what their experience of us has been in the past. If we tend to have a short attention span, blowing a bit hot and cold on the latest problem or opportunity, they might well have learned to wait and see whether our energy level stays high or whether our attention moves on. If we are a bit of a control freak, they may have learned not to take the initiative but to wait for our precise instruction. If our pattern is to be too trusting of others and not at all concerned with the detail of how things proceed, they may have learned that the right thing to do is to start, but not take any risks.

You see, the problem is that we are so clear in our own minds of what we mean, we assume that others have received a crystal-clear communication from us. We rely on telepathy. We convince ourselves that we have told people everything they need to know. After all we sent them an email about it three weeks ago. We make huge and appalling assumptions, and having made them our view of the world is set, and it's up to others to play their part. We then fail to understand why they get confused or seem unclear. What's wrong with them?

Of course, by force of personality, authority and passion, we are able to get our people to say 'Yes' to us; to agree that the course we have set or the solution we have devised is the right path. And this is our biggest danger – that we can get people to say 'Yes' to us, when in their hearts they are saying 'Maybe' at best, and 'Over my dead body' at worst.

we can get people to say 'Yes' to us, when in their hearts they are saying 'Maybe' at best, and 'Over my dead body' at worst.

Us doing all the talking feels like we are in control and that we have gained commitment from people. Actually it guarantees nothing and is a highly risky strategy. We simply have to get them talking to us – and to do that we have to ask them questions.

We tend to make statements when we don't want to change; when we are in fact defending a fixed position. We make statements to justify our position, to convince others that we are right and they are wrong, to bring people round to our way of thinking. As managers we have to be highly aware of the power of our statements, not only because they tend to bulldoze people into compliance to 'our way' rather than commitment to their coming to their own solutions, but also because they will be used against us in perfect reasons (excuses). Conversely we tend only to ask questions when we genuinely want to learn, when we truly don't know the answer or when we are genuinely curious.

So one of my rules is don't ask a question to which you have a non-negotiable answer!

The legitimate use of statements

So when should we make statements? Simple:

- to lay out the problem or set context

- to set the challenge

- to give facts (or feedback!)

- to give clarity of expectation

If we follow these guidelines we will communicate so much more clearly. It will be uncomfortable at times for us and for others, since the truth of situations is often uncomfortable, and since the required course of action may involve us navigating unchartered waters, but then raising the bar is not going to involve doing what we've always done.

Questions v statements

How do you create a climate where the truth is heard? The first thing is to increase your questions-to-statements ratio. Have someone track it and see if you can double it in the next year. The leaders in our studies asked lots of questions. They were Socratic. By asking questions, they got the brutal facts, as well as lots of insights and ideas.

Jim Collins, *Good to Great*

Leaders talk too much and make statements, rather than listening and asking questions.

Robert Sutton, *The No Asshole Rule*

Prepare clear statements of your non-negotiables; have these ready to repeat, mantra-like. Then prepare great open questions you will ask, to learn and to prompt thinking and debate. Jim Collins' book *Good to Great* is one of the defining works on management. And if Jim Collins can sum up in one simple dynamic the best and most frequent advice he gives CEOs as '*increase your questions-to-statements ratio*', then this gives us a clear indication of the simplicity of the change we must make in ourselves.

The most beautiful thing about asking open questions is the very fact that we have to think about what we are doing. This act of conscious care calms us down, the feeling of threat passes, our adrenaline and cortisol levels reduce, blood flows back into our frontal cortex, and we regain control of our rational and emotional faculties. The bonus in all of this is the unconscious energetic communication that takes place between us and the other party – as our adrenaline levels reduce, so do theirs. As we calm down so do they. As we take care, they receive care from us. As they feel cared for, they trust us and are therefore much more likely to consider our question carefully and give us a truthful response. Wow, now we're actually getting somewhere.

Our millstones

1. *Let me tell you what you need to do*

2. *Leave it with me*

3. *Have you thought of... (or even worse, Don't you think that...)*

4. *I trust you; You know what to do; My door is always open*

And so to our millstones – those classic phrases that habitually and perpetually come out of our mouths. Numbers 1 and 3 above are variations on the theme of 'here is the solution'. Number 2, 'leave it with me', basically means that I cannot think of a solution in the time I can allocate to debating this with you, so I will devote time to it later when, of course, I will come up with the solution. Many people know the story of the manager who takes monkeys (problems) off the backs of his people, only to end the day with 50 monkeys on his own back, while his people swan off for the evening completely monkey-free. How often have you complained that you wished your people would care about the job as much as you do, like some sort of indispensable martyr? But how can they care, when you do all their thinking for them, when you have trained them not to care, but to leave it all to you?

Definition of coaching

So now we can agree our definition of coaching.

❀ Releasing people's full potential, while making them accountable for results

❀ Helping them to total clarity and commitment for what they need to do

❀ Transferring your knowledge and experience with your questions

Coaching is *not* a normal, everyday, superficial, 'matey' conversation... it is a structured dialogue, controlled by the coach, with a direction and an intent. It is an adult, professional, authentic discourse on the crucial business issues. The purpose of coaching is to realise people's full potential while holding them accountable for results. The process of coaching is to help people to come to a position of total clarity and maximum commitment for what they need to do. The byproduct of coaching is the transfer of your knowledge and experience in the process.

> *Coaching is not a normal, everyday, superficial, 'matey' conversation... it is a structured dialogue, controlled by the coach, with a direction and an intent. It is an adult, professional, authentic discourse on the crucial business issues.*

Furthermore, it is an adult, professional, authentic discourse on the crucial business issues. Transactional analysis (TA) teaches us that in relationships with others, people play one of three roles – parent, adult or child. Too many times at work we are trying to be the parent – the caring leader with greater wisdom and experience than those for whom we have responsibility. However, when we play the parent, the other person is almost bound to play a child. The child may, of course, be compliant and well-behaved, which will get them a reward from us, or the child may be disruptive and... well, childish. So we should be aiming for a real adult-to-adult dialogue. Much more efficient, and much more rewarding.

We must liberate ourselves from the belief that we know what is best for others, that we help people best by taking decisions for them, and that we care for them best by exercising responsibility on their behalf – paternalism may have noble motivations, but it creates dependent children not empowered adults.

Once we understand all this, we are freed from having to rely on our old habits, and we gain permission to behave as a coach, however unskilled or clumsy we may be at it.

Coaching is a leadership intervention that creates raised performance and a different outcome. Done well, coaching can:

1. Facilitate different thinking

2. Motivate committed action

3. Embed new long-term habits

It may be daunting to think about starting to coach people. However, if we think of coaching as simply a leadership intervention – a one-off act that can make a real difference – we may just give it a try.

As a one-off intervention, what we are doing when we coach someone is to be their structure to allow them to think differently. If they are stuck and genuinely don't know what to do next, then their thinking is blocked and they need help to think differently. When we have facilitated this different thinking, we then need to have them reach a new level or place of commitment to action.

And in doing this not once but many times, we achieve the added bonus of embedding in them new long-term habits, so that they manage themselves and coach themselves into greater self-awareness, with more choices of thought process or actions.

We should not be hesitant about challenging a person with a potential meaning for them to fulfil. It is only by doing this that we evoke their purpose from its state of latency. A coach moves someone from latent to active.

A coach is an eye specialist, not a painter. A painter tries to convey to us a picture of the world as they see it, or more often as they want us to see it. An ophthalmologist helps us see the world as it really is through our own eyes.

As a coach, my prime role is to help you perform at your peak, more often than you do without me, and in doing so to help you extend your peak beyond what you believe it to be and beyond any level that you have yet achieved.

As a coach, I must both lay down and adhere to strict boundaries between us in our relationship of coach and client. Leaders need to create clear boundaries (as well as clear roles and responsibilities). There needs to be a clear and almost physical distance between leaders and followers, without the leaders becoming aloof, detached or unapproachable. The dynamic needs to be clear that a target is unchangeable, that a task or responsibility will not be bought back by the leader once accepted by the person.

Those boundaries are as much about our behaviour as they are about the behaviour of our people. Our boundaries are as follows:

- Share the problem not the ideas
- Share the facts not the solution
- Share guidelines not decisions

If we discipline ourselves to live by these boundaries, we will educate people very quickly that they are accountable, and that we are here to coach them, not to solve their problems for them.

The crux

All this works because of a simple physical truth about human beings – that when we are forced to think about something, we have to take some responsibility for it. And the longer we are made to think about it without being able to pass it to someone else to think about, the more responsibility we have to take.

Try this simple exercise. Take a burning political issue of the day, one where opinions are easily polarised and expressed with passion and total conviction. Listen to someone give their view. Now ask them some questions that make them think about it a bit more deeply. And now ask them what they would do if they had ultimate responsibility. The truth is that we all find it easy and comfortable to give views on something we are not responsible for. We find it harder and way more uncomfortable to give views when it's down to us to make a decision.

So let's make the game simple. Our people have clear responsibilities and object-ives. These responsibilities and objectives are theirs. All we need to do is to keep it that way. That means not accepting that an objective is unachievable, and not solving their problem for them. It means helping them to think differently about their problem and encouraging them to find an alternative action that will take them forward. Simple.

And the reality is that we learn more about someone's true ability and potential by coaching them than we ever do by giving them solutions. And when we learn about them, something truly magical happens to them. They emerge butterfly-like from the fixed judgement chrysalis we had put them in, and we see something in them that surprises and delights us.

> *we learn more about someone's true ability and potential by coaching them than we ever do by giving them solutions. And when we learn about them, something truly magical happens to them. They emerge butterfly-like from the fixed judgement chrysalis we had put them in, and we see something in them that surprises and delights us.*

Behaviour change

But maybe this coaching lark is becoming too difficult. Why can't we just tell people what to do and have done with it? Why can't people just follow instructions or, even better, just get on and do what they get paid to do without us having to fret about what they are doing?

Well of course they can, and in many, many cases they do just that. However, we are completely blind to the ways in which *we* get in their way or throw them off course. And we underestimate the vital importance of coaching to support people in having the courage and confidence to perform to their very best. So I'm afraid we have to keep going on this coaching lark.

This behaviour change is the hardest part for us, because it involves the almost unthinkable risk of changing the very thing that has made us successful. And why on earth would we want to take that risk? Let's understand how we got to be a manager in the first place – because we demonstrated to others in authority that we possessed the ability to solve problems and marshal resources to implement our solutions. It's a skill that is highly (*most* highly) prized in organisations. If we demonstrated this skill at a very early age then we got to manage people very early. And once we got on the management treadmill, the way to make progress was to get noticed higher up the tree, and to solve bigger and bigger problems.

The more problems we solved and the better we got at motivating others to implement solutions, the more successful we became and the better we got at it. It was a virtuous circle for us – it was like everything else in life: the more we practised the better we got. And now here we are, solving problems all day long – it's what we do and it's who we are. If we only knew it, we even create problems for ourselves to solve. A life without problems for us would not be worth living! It is so much of an ingrained habit that we now do not know when we are doing it. It is a truly unconscious competence. And we are fabulous at it. In fact it has become an addiction.

We sometimes lose good people who move onto bigger and better things in a different company – but we tell ourselves that they are not really ready for the job they have found and it will all end in tears. We often complain that our people do not show enough initiative, but explain this to ourselves by reasoning that we cannot expect them to be like us. And so the insanity starts and grows until we have become the monster – the block on growth, the barrier to people developing their potential, the problem. We think it's them but now we know it's us. We have to get out of the way, we have to change. So let's make a start.

Practice

Imagine you are the coach of a Grand Slam tennis champion. You have watched all the video replays with her of her recent matches, and you have seen that her success rate on hitting a running forehand down the line over the high part of the net is only 33 per cent. You work out that if she could improve that to 66 per cent, she would win two more break points per match – enough to win critical matches and move her closer to the World No. 1 ranking and, more critically, winning more Grand Slam tournaments.

So you take your pro out onto the tennis court and make her hit 1,000 running forehands down the line, occasionally suggesting adjustments, but mainly adding value through being your pro's discipline. Eventually and progressively, the ball goes over the high part of the net and lands inside the line more frequently than it does not. The muscle memory of your protégée develops to the point where she can hit the shot in her sleep.

In his seminal book *Outliers*, Malcolm Gladwell postulates that in order to become truly excellent at anything, we have to practise for 10,000 hours. Let's think about this for managers in business. To achieve 10,000 hours in business equates to four years of working a 50-hour week. So if we have been managers for four years, we have done the requisite number of hours to… I would love to say, become excellent, but the reality is that we have spent our 10,000 hours becoming the manager we are today – doing enough to succeed, but probably nowhere near excellent, and nowhere near being the best in the world. So what went wrong? Well the simple truth is that we have been practising the wrong things. Someone once said that 'practice makes perfect'. This is a lie. The truth is that 'practice makes permanent'.

So we have to learn how to practise, then what to practise.

Open questions

> *I keep six honest serving men*
>
> *They taught me all I knew*
>
> *Their names are **What** and **Why** and **When***
>
> *And **How** and **Where** and **Who***

Rudyard Kipling

So let's start by practising the most fundamental technique we will need – open questions.

But just why are open questions so powerful? Well they force people to think, because they do not communicate what you believe to be the 'right' answer, thereby genuinely putting the responsibility onto the responder, and we have already seen the power of this. And if we underestimate the degree to which people will avoid 'thinking' then listen to Bertrand Russell who stated that '*most people would rather die than think*'. He was observing the situation whereby some people seem able to tolerate failure if only they can blame someone else. In fact, when people feel disempowered (perhaps by a boss who uses a lot of closed questions?), they gravitate towards blaming others because they are simply not in a position to take full responsibility.

This zone is one that may be familiar to us as managers – where it seems as though others are more concerned about watching their own backs than doing what's right for the company. They seem to exert their energy on making excuses, rather than getting the job done. And we blame them… Open questions work like magic. They make people think.

How do we know they are thinking? Well, first of all they go quiet and then their eye contact, which up to that point has been adoringly on you as their leader, goes off somewhere else. And if you can hold yourself calmly and stay emotionally connected to them while they stare out of the window, they will feel safe to explore their thoughts. What the neuroscientists will tell us is that the unconscious eye contact movement is the neurological signal that the other person is searching for the answer to the question in some other part of their brain, since the answer is not to be found in their frontal cortex. If it were there already, they would hold your gaze and give you an immediate response.

How do we know they are thinking? Well, first of all they go quiet and then their eye contact, which up to that point has been adoringly on you as their leader, goes off somewhere else.

The other beautiful thing about this flicking away of the eye contact (and it is a beautiful thing) is that it is an unconscious communication of trust. If you don't trust me, there is no way you're going to take your eyes off me. This is a sublime space, one in which I am being a true coach – and notice it has the bonus of creating a beautiful human moment of connection and intimacy. It's impossible to create such moments all the time, but the good news is that we don't need that many. Humans can operate on a very scant diet of such moments, because the nourishment infused in those precious seconds is so rich. Truly it is ambrosia. Achieve these moments opportunistically but regularly, and you can afford for them to be on autopilot most of the time.

Chapter 4

Coaching crafting

Question crafting

- Use **who, when** and **where** for facts – it's not important that *you* know the answers (in fact it's dangerous!) but it will help them realise what they know and what they do not know about the problem, but *do not* get seduced into the drama that is their problem
- Use **what** for goals and objectives
- Use **how** for process and options
- Use **why** for motivation and confidence (be careful!)
- **Would, could** and **might** give choice and therefore safety to create

So if asking open questions is so fundamental, we better get good at them. We better realise that question crafting is one of our core processes. I work really hard to craft the best possible questions I can. And then it's simple – I make them answer! Of our six open questions, each has its own unique purpose. 'Who', 'when' and 'where' are often looking for facts so we can stretch the other person to consider other factual data. However, we should be wary of asking these three questions as the risk is that we will get seduced into the drama that is their problem and end up inevitably offering solutions.

Most of the questions I ask are 'what' questions. 'What' is looking for the objective or the purpose and often a simple 'what' question is all it takes to unlock someone's thinking since they become clear on the goal. 'How' is looking for process or options and 'why' is for motivation or to give confidence. We do need to be a bit careful of asking 'why' questions, as if there is the slightest threat, anxiety or adrenaline flying about, a 'why' question can be received as accusatory and will produce a defensive answer. Unless the trust levels are very high, I often try and convert a 'why' question into a 'what' question. For example instead of asking *'Why didn't you delegate the meeting to your junior?'* I might rephrase it as *'What made you decide that you needed to take the meeting personally rather than delegate it?'* In doing so I respectfully endow the other person with having made a conscious decision. If they did then they'll calmly explain their thinking. If they didn't then they will have no issue in telling me this and then very likely moving straight to self-correction.

Getting even more subtle, using 'would', 'could' and 'might' give choice to the other person. Asking someone *'What are you going to do?'* is asking a left-brain question forcing them to give you a decision. We tend to ask this type of question far too early in our exchanges, because we want to get on with things. Asking them *'What could you do?'* or *'What might you do?'* are right-brain questions that communicate to them that it's OK for them not to give us *'the'* answer, but to spend a few minutes exploring options. Again as a coach we are doing everything in our power to be non-threatening, and yet we can be asking the most challenging questions. This is how we start to become more skilled as coaches, and when the joy of being a crafter of great questions starts to overcome the more ingrained desire to be the problem-solver.

Practical process

⚛ First 10 per cent – connect, acceptance, calm the fish!

⚛ Next 70 per cent – questions and listening *(new thinking, creativity, growing confidence)*

⚛ Next 10 per cent – feedback and advice *(reflection and learning)*

⚛ Final 10 per cent – decisions and solutions *(ownership and commitment)*

So the steps follow a logical process, although the skills of giving feedback, offering advice and transferring knowledge can be added in at any time, like sprinkling salt as a condiment.

We can even simplify it further by following this really rough guide to a coaching session – and a 'session' might only take a few minutes. If we have a finite time available, we should always start by building rapport – calming the fish! Hopefully because we've invested in a strong relationship of trust, we already have a strong rapport in place. But we need to check in and demonstrate again that we support the other person – that we care about them and believe in them. Something as simple as a smile, a genuine expression of warmth and kindness, might suffice.

Then we can start crafting our questions that are going to form the structure for them to think differently about the problem or challenge they are facing. And most of the 'session' should be taken up with questions, since then the other person will be doing most of the talking (and thus thinking) and will gain the most from the time. These questions are for new thinking and creativity. So we should have a large 'stock' of questions at our disposal – and this is where we need most work and practice. We'll go into this in much greater depth later. Remember, however, that nine times out of ten they know the answer and that what they really lack is the courage to go and do what they know they should, so often our questions are aimed at what is stopping them from acting.

With the bulk of the time used to explore new thinking and creativity, we come towards the end of the 'session' and so we might well need to add in some add-itional ingredients – namely some feedback and maybe even some advice. This allows us to reflect back what they have said and how they have been, to give them the awareness that raises the important stuff right into their conscious mind so that it is harder for them to keep it buried or run away from it once we have finished. It allows the other person a chance to see that they have learned some-thing during the 'session', making it easier for their confidence to rise and stay high for what is needed ahead. This is a part that we sometime shy away from because it can sound to us as if we are trying to get them to acknowledge how good we are as a coach, but remember that's our stuff not theirs – our comfort zone not theirs – so just do what's needed to help them; take the risk that they will think we are showing off or want to be praised. Teachers deal with this all the time, and since as someone's coach we adopt the role of teaching and educating and guiding, it goes with our new territory. Funnily enough, people are so often consumed with their own thoughts as a result of our coaching that they are oblivious to the techniques we are using anyway.

Finally, however, it is our job to get the other person to make a commitment. And this is where so many of us fail the other person at the final hurdle. We do the hard part in helping them to their solution, but then we leave them the luxury of slinking back into their comfort zone before they have irrevocably committed to action.

Finally, however, it is our job to get the other person to make a commitment. And this is where so many of us fail the other person at the final hurdle. We do the hard part in helping them to their solution, but then we leave them the luxury of slinking back into their comfort zone before they have irrevocably committed to action. And we know that once back inside their comfort zone, the perfect reasons will take over again. So we have to 'close' them to ensure that they truly own their solution and that they have the courage and the confidence they need to act. If they were 'merely' friends we could let them off the hook, but we are their coaches – their performance managers – so we must close them.

Turning closed questions into open ones

Once we become more conscious of our closed-question habit, we can consciously control the habit. But stopping something is hard. We need to start something in that moment and one technique is simply to hear the closed question in our head all the way to the end and then play a game with ourselves to turn it into an open question.

So here's an example. We are listening to the other person recount their story and we hear a thought in our head – '*I wonder if his client really supports him in this (and I bet he doesn't!). If he doesn't have his client's support, it could be chaos.*'

The reflex question we hear forming in our head is: '*Are you sure your client supports you in this?*' But the risk with this question is that the other person will give us the convenient answer, not necessarily the truth.

Here are some alternative ways of asking pretty much the same question. Notice how much more powerful these are:

⊛ *To what extent do you have your client's support in this?*

⊛ *Where does your client sit with this?*

⊛ *What does your client want from you right now?*

⊛ *What has been the tone of the conversations you've had with your client on this?*

⊛ *If your client were listening to this conversation right now, what advice would they be giving you?*

🌐 *How important is it to you that you have your client's 100 per cent support on this?*

🌐 *What would you do if you knew your client was dead against this course of action?*

So again we are endowing the other person with the intense respect of them either having thought about all these things, or being able to consciously reflect upon them in front of us if they have not.

While we can have a concern for them, and we might even share that concern as a piece of feedback or even advice, we cannot live their life for them and we cannot tell them what to do. As experienced as we are, we cannot know for sure what's best for them. We can only serve them by helping them ensure that they've thought through every angle and dealt with every concern.

Coaching for ownership

🌐 *What are you waiting for?*

🌐 *What are you doing to help make it happen?*

🌐 *What if you knew it was never going to happen?*

🌐 *What are you doing to support them?*

🌐 *What will you do if it does not happen?*

🌐 *How long are you going to wait?*

🌐 *What if you had to act today?*

🌐 *What's stopping you?*

🌐 *What do you suspect you'll end up doing?*

Then there are the questions that you can use if people are excusing themselves by blaming someone or something else – externalising. We all do it. It's natural to blame something else if we are blocked and feel that we have tried everything or when we simply do not know what to do next or, more often, when we get fixated on something we have been promised or have been expecting.

A typical example in business is where the IT system does not (yet) give us a report we 'need' in order to be able to act, or where we are waiting for information from another source. So these questions go to the heart of ownership. My experience is that when asked these questions, and when forced to answer, people tend to come up with what proves to be the final answer – the best solution. Everything they are saying is actually a series of very powerful reasons for them not to act, not to risk.

And if the habit of asking open questions is critical, then another habit we need to develop is being insistent in asking the same question until we get an answer. A typical answer to some of the above questions will be '*It's not as simple as that*'. Just keep going… because the other person has just admitted one of their biggest blocks – the fact that they overcomplicate things. Overcomplicating things is extremely convenient. It gives us more time to procrastinate and a great excuse if we fail. But as a coach, our role is to help the other person simplify things, to reduce their issues to basics so that they can see clearly what is blocking them.

Some great coaching questions

I ask a lot of 'what' questions. I'm not that bothered about the 'how', since my experience is that people are not normally stuck on the how, although if they are then this will come out and can be addressed by some teaching and advice. I'm even not that bothered about the 'why', since how we got here can wait for the post-mortem!

So these are my favourite 'what' questions. Carry them round as a 'stock' to be called on at any time. Sometimes just one of these is all you need to unlock someone's thinking. However, having said they are my favourites, they are by no means the only questions you will hear me ask. These are true 'open' questions in that they contain no hint of potential answers, which is powerful, but neither do they contain any helpful context or potential avenues of exploration. And so the real trick is for you to add that context to your questions and to truly personalise them.

Adding context means you can give some strategic structure to the other person's thinking, and you can add your experience in your questions.

- *What do you think?*

- *What are you trying to achieve?*

- *What would you do if you had to decide right now?*

- *What's stopping you?*

- *What bothers you most about this?*

- *What are you struggling with?*

- *What's the real problem?*

- *What options are there?*

- *What else could you do?*

- *What's the right thing to do?*

- *What do you suspect you'll end up doing?*

And if you can only remember three?

- **So what?** sounds so blunt doesn't it? Yes it is, but it's a very effective question, and if your relationship is strong, the other person can take the bluntness. Ask this one until you have genuinely got to the real issue.

- **What else?** communicates that there might well be more to the problem, or that there may be other potential solutions. Ask this one until they are spent or about to do you violence.

⊛ **What's next?** communicates that it's now up to them to determine their next step, which might not be a full solution, but will certainly be a forward movement.

Trigger 6: Create right-brain thinking

We need at this point to come back to brain science. The brain is physically made in two hemispheres – the left side of the brain controls all the rational, logical, digital processes and structures, and is the side that makes the decisions. It is hugely judgemental. My contention is that there is very little scope in the modern business world for creating more productivity here. We have already talked about the technology that has raised management 'productivity'. It is the left side of the brain that judges people on first impressions (and they tend to stay judged since we make no time for reassessment), and that lands in seconds on the right course of action when faced with a problem. So when one of our people brings us a problem, what comes up first is the judgement we hold of that person, followed quickly by the solution to the problem they haven't even finished explaining yet!

And then there's the right-hand side – the side that is creative, playful, sensitive, emotional and haphazard. All this is fine, of course, and we sort of recognise that we need these things in our businesses, but the right-hand side of the brain has one big drawback – it has no sense of time deadlines. And everything has a deadline (even when one has not been communicated or even created). So the simple truth is that the right-hand side of the brain, while we recognise that a more creative solution may be forthcoming if we bring it into play, can only be evoked in a most inconvenient package.

Questions to access right brain

We ask *'What are you going to do?'* far too early. This is the rather Tigger-like energy that makes us follow the 'fire, ready, aim' methodology. We need to hold off on the action-oriented question until the end.

In our mission to craft the very highest-quality questions, we just need to keep in mind the structures that can guide us – one of them being to ask questions that access the right brain. There are literally hundreds and the key is to find your own favourites – ones that are very much personal to you and your own style. There are five categories, and so the left brain can have something to do (task it with asking one from each category, for example) while our right brains come out to play. Right-brain questions contain the energy of hope, possibility – and most importantly human connection. We don't need to understand the other person's problem – we simply need to understand them.

One of my favourites is *'What ideas are you playing with at the moment?'*, because it deliberately uses the word 'play'. The question conveys an acceptance that having a bit of fun or not taking things too seriously is OK, thus taking some of the pressure off

One of my favourites is 'What ideas are you playing with at the moment?'

the other person, and it also gives the steer that maybe the answer lies in thinking more creatively – maybe even inviting others in to play too. And notice the power of the simplest of right-brain questions, 'What else?' This communicates that there could well be other solutions, it's simply we've not uncovered them yet – and then watch their eye contact flicker as they go deep into their neocortex, mining for possible answers. The harder you make them work here, the more likely they are to find a little jewel of an idea within their own brains.

The right-hand side of the brain is where we feel our human emotions – not the mammalian, primeval, limbic emotions such as anger, disgust and fear, but the more 'human' emotions such as jealousy, joy, sadness, shame, guilt, disappointment, pride. Whether we like it or not, it's our emotions that are so often in control. Neural research has demonstrated that our decisions are not made by our conscious minds – we just think we are making conscious decisions. The fact is we make all our decisions emotionally and then use logic and reason to justify them. Under pressure, we tend not to ask people how they are feeling, since we are looking for logical and rational solutions, and frankly because we are afraid of the 'messiness' of human emotions or even being rejected for asking a question that has so clearly come from some fluffy training course! But that is to block a profound and arguably the richest source of data and fuel for the other person. If we coach them without giving them permission to access and honour their emotions, we are severely limiting their performance.

But this is also where we will need to be on our mettle as coaches, because particularly with emotional questions, you may need to repeat the question until they answer. Here's a game you can play with left/right-brain dynamics. Ask someone a 'feelings' question – how do they feel about the current issues they face, etc. Then listen, inevitably and predictably, to their answers, '*I think...*' (left brain). Politely say you understand that's what they *think*, your question was how they *feel*. Play the game until they get the point, or until they hit you.

Politely say you understand that's what they think, your question was how they feel. Play the game until they get the point, or until they hit you.

Right-brain questions are so hard because we land on the first glimpse of an idea that we think is novel like a eureka moment and then the Left-Brain Tyrant immediately swoops in to process it into action, slamming it into the bank and shutting off any further innovation. To continue at this point seems random, pointless and frankly a waste of time. It's been proven that gut feel is actually the adaptive unconscious having learned from prior experience – but we are simply unaware that we have learned, thus it's just a feeling, a sense (that we potentially end up not trusting).

Notice their gestures when they are engaging as you want them to (eg, excited hand gestures) and mirror them.

'*What else?*' – the most powerful right-brain question; the left brain banks the first acceptable idea that comes along! But we need to ask '*What else?*' until the person has dug into the furthest crevices of their mind and has truly exhausted their thinking and their ideas.

I also really enjoy giving people some challenge on achieving their objective in half the time, or with ten times the cash – in other words, examples that are *so* far outside the current thinking that only *new* thinking can encompass them. One of the things that people are guilty of when they are stuck in a bit of a fear rut, or when they cannot escape the restrictions of thinking in a risk-free way, is that they tend only to think incrementally – a sort of kaizen way of improving things in small if inexorable iterations. Trying to improve something by 5 per cent is severely limiting of itself in the type of thinking people apply to the problem, whereas being forced to think about doubling something or halving the time taken forces a completely different approach.

And notice the classic questions to power the imagination – blank sheet of paper, magic wand, start again... these questions work like magic because everyone wants to access the power of their imagination and be liberated from their anxiety.

The embodiment questions again really facilitate the incredible power of the right brain to think like someone else and even to instantaneously fill ourselves with the qualities of another. When we bring an admired character or even their hero into the room, in a heartbeat the person feels all of the qualities of that person that they so admire. It's impossible for me to bring my dad to mind without me immediately having his qualities inside me and to immediately predict what he would think and do in my place. Amazingly useful data for me to consider, and 30 seconds ago that data was denied to me. And then you asked me a question. This is also the place where we can appeal to the nobler motives of the other person, bringing in guiding principles or values, or getting them to consider a higher purpose, thus lifting them out of the anxiety of the current drama.

And finally, trusting our instincts, our senses, our gut. Since we make most of our decisions emotionally, gut feel is an incredibly important part of this. And so are our senses. Notice the classic '*What does a great solution look like?*', which I promise will immediately invoke the eye contact flicker as they search for a visualisation. We are incredibly visual creatures, with 70 per cent of the processing in our brain being in pictures. Now if we were dogs, that 70 per cent would be all about smell. And while I would not necessarily urge you to go and ask the question '*What does a great solution smell like?*', never underestimate the power of smell. Walking into a department store at Christmas to the odour of sage and onion stuffing makes us feel good (they pump it through the air conditioning, the manipulative bastards). And when we show prospective buyers around our flat or house to sell or let it, and we've done the 'brew coffee and bake bread' thing, even though the buyers spot it and comment on it, seconds later they're falling in love with our home.

Thanks to Edward de Bono's work in the 1970s and 1980s we have the benefit of the 'brainstorming' session. And we have all been there. The boss takes us all away for half a day and stands at the end of the table explaining that we are all going to be creative for four hours, and then there's an awkward silence, followed thankfully by someone suggesting something ridiculous that makes everyone laugh and breaks the tension. Then we have a really enjoyable session with loads of good ideas, including a few fantastic ideas, all up on flipcharts tacked up round the wall. Some poor sod is delegated to type them all up, and we all go away saying that it was a great session and how everyone had really enjoyed it and we *must* do it again soon, and then the notes come out on 15 pages of unintelligible bullet points and none are followed up and everything goes back to the way it was except we are more frustrated now – all because we don't know how to have creativity as an integral part of our culture, as opposed to something that we have to manufacture specially. And this is the key – we need to make creativity a normal part of the way we do things, and to celebrate the respective strengths and roles of *both* sides of the brain.

> *The intuitive mind is a sacred gift, and the rational mind a faithful servant. We have created a society that honours the servant and has forgotten the gift.*
>
> Albert Einstein

A century ago, Einstein knew that we were already creating a world that was far too dominated by left-brain thinking. I wonder what he would make of our modern-day corporations? I am sure he would marvel at our achievements, but I suspect he would weep at our stupidity. We all work in massively left brain dominated corporate cultures, where hitting deadlines and targets has become the almost sole measure of our performance and of our worth. This denies us our humanity, and it denies our organisations any sustainable quality.

If we are going to gain access to even the smallest part of that 35 per cent untapped potential in people, the key is the right-hand side of the brain – that is where the untapped potential lies, in more creative ways of thinking, problem-solving and working. So our job as a coach is to create space for people to use the right-hand side of their brains, by creating structures for them to think differently – and of course we do *that* by asking great open questions.

I often refer to the left hemisphere as the Left-Brain Tyrant – its behaviour and its constant nagging are truly tyrannical. It cannot tolerate subordination of any kind.

And I refer to the right hemisphere as the Right-Brain Saviour – it truly is our salvation, not simply because it unlocks that inexhaustible human potential and creativity, but because it restores our common humanity at the same time, giving us back the precious nourishment of human emotional connection.

So here are some examples of right-brain questions:

Possibilities

- 'What ideas are you playing with at the moment?'
- 'What are some of the crazier things you've considered?'
- 'What other possible options might there be?'
- 'And what else…?'

Emotions

- 'How do you feel? How are your team feeling?'
- 'What reaction might you get to this?'

- ⊛ 'What bothers you most about this?'
- ⊛ 'What concerns does this bring up for you?'

Imagine

- ⊛ 'What if you had a blank sheet of paper? A magic wand?'
- ⊛ 'In an ideal world, where would you start?'
- ⊛ 'What if I gave you another ten people/£1 million/six months?'

Embodiment

- ⊛ 'What would [admired character] do?'
- ⊛ 'What values or principles could you use to guide you?'
- ⊛ 'What would best serve our purpose/vision/mission/goal?'

Senses

- ⊛ 'What's your instinct telling you?'
- ⊛ 'What's your gut feel?'
- ⊛ 'What does the ideal solution look/sound/feel/taste/smell like?'

Trigger 7: Get their finest version to solve their problem

Maslow's hierarchy of needs

Abraham Maslow came up with his seminal 'hierarchy of needs' in the 1960s. It is a simple model of human motivation, moving up in a hierarchy until we become motivated by the ultimate desire to 'make a difference in the world' and be remembered for achieving something special.

Maslow said that the most basic of human needs was survival, and that only when this desire is satisfied do we 'move up' the hierarchy to the desire to be secure, in other words to survive tomorrow as well. Only once we feel secure can we be motivated by the desire to be loved and to belong, followed by the desire to be important and finally to the ultimate that he called 'self-actualization' (he was American!).

The trick for us as line managers looking to coach our people, is to convert this into a model that works within organisations and working cultures. Survival cannot mean, therefore, that we must seek food and shelter today, but that we can do enough to maintain the confidence of those who hold power over us. And we all know and understand the concept of security at work. Part of the reason that Maslow used the concept of a hierarchy for his model is because he noticed the parallel to the organisational hierarchy, and the fact that the higher up the organisation people went, the more they were motivated by the higher levels of his hierarchy of needs.

One lesson I have had to learn and relearn over the years is how close 'shop floor' employees are to the bottom of the pyramid. One whiff of the word 'change' and they are in immediate fear of losing their jobs. Never, ever underestimate the power of this fear in organisational change.

However, for me Tom Peters really summed this up for us as managers in organisations – that 'everyone wants to be part of a winning team, but everyone yearns to be a star in their own right'. In other words, we should be able to largely ignore the bottom two levels, since most employees are now salaried and thus have at least four weeks' potential notice of losing their jobs, and very few are at the highest levels where they can make decisions on matters of organisational destiny. Most are concerned with levels three and four. So we as coaches need to work on these two levels, without ever underestimating the degree to which people can drop down on the slightest uncertainties.

We often make the fundamental mistake of assuming that what would motivate us will naturally motivate others. This is almost automatic when we are under pressure and not thinking consciously of our coaching strategies. Therefore our mission when coaching people is again to listen to them and hear where they are blocked – at what level *they* are telling themselves they need to find motivation. Then you can get them talking at a different level. If they need courage to do what's right, we need to appeal to the higher levels. If they are complacent or need a shove, then we need to remind them of the precariousness of their situation if left inactive or unattended.

Robert Dilts' logical levels

In 2001 I had the great pleasure of meeting Robert Dilts, one of the 'gurus' of neurolinguistic programming, in California. I had come across Dilts' work through a Sue Knight coaching programme I had taken. I like this model precisely because it is 'logical' – it had appealed to my left hemisphere.

Dilts' model, heavily influenced by the work of anthropologist Gregory Bateson, simply says that when we communicate about a problem at work, we will do so on one of six levels, and that the key to coaching is to understand which level the other person is communicating at, and then to give them a structure through our question selection that allows them to communicate on another level. Dilts said that 'a problem cannot be solved at the level at which it presents itself'. In other words, as a coach, all we have to do is to listen hard, work out which level they are on, and then ask a question that they have to answer at a different level.

Level 1 is 'environment' – the way we dress, the environment that we put ourselves in, the people we associate with, the type of car we drive, the symbols we choose, the designer (or not) labels. We judge people on first impressions, often before they have spoken, so we must be accessing some communication from them. If someone is presenting their problem at this level, they may not even be speaking about it! If they are then it will sound very much like their surroundings are to blame – the workplace itself, maybe the company, maybe their colleagues. It's not that they are consciously avoiding taking personal responsibility, it's just that they are stuck in denial.

Level 2 is 'behaviour' – this is how they are behaving or acting, or what they are actually doing. Problems expressed at this level will have a lot of action words in; they will be describing what they have tried and how it has not worked. They may say that they do not know what to do, or how to behave, or that the problem is the activities of third parties.

Level 3 is 'skills' – this is about their competence or their feelings about their ability. So they may communicate that they know *what* to do, but not *how* to do it.

Level 4 is 'values and beliefs' – this is about what they believe and may contain lots about their values or sense of right and wrong. So they may communicate that they do not know what 'the right thing to do' is.

Level 5 is 'identity' – this is about who they are or maybe a doubt about their role in the problem or as the leader or person responsible. They may communicate here that they feel inadequate, or convey a sense that they want to run away or avoid the role or identity they have been given or adopted. They may communicate that they feel unable to act because it is 'below' them or maybe above them.

Level 6, the pinnacle, is 'purpose'. This is perhaps the ultimate spiritual ground for people. This is about their purpose in life, or their 'mission' in the business, not just their given objectives, but the sense of the vision that they are seeking to achieve or lead their people to. While people may spend a great deal of time actively involved in, and thinking about, Levels 1 to 3, Dilts said that it is Levels 4 to 6 that drive our motivations and our sense of satisfaction in our work.

Dilts said that when all levels are in alignment then we have achieved a true spiritual place, and we will be at our greatest power and also our greatest sense of peace, since we are being who we truly feel we are, we are doing what we were born to do. This is what some people describe as 'effortless' – when our achievements seem to flow naturally. Now I don't know what your spiritual beliefs are, all I can tell you is that this is very much *my* bag in terms of spirituality.

if people reside predominantly in the bottom three levels, then boredom, habit and fear can rule the day. However, when people live (and communicate) more in the top three levels, then they are accessing more of their true potential and power

Dilts said that if people reside predominantly in the bottom three levels, then boredom, habit and fear can rule the day. However, when people live (and communicate) more in the top three levels, then they are accessing more of their true potential and power, and they are more likely to be able to find their own courage, their own passion and their own energy – and thus their own solutions and accountability (and successes and failures). The top three levels expand the comfort zone.

When we listen to people, do we really hear what they are saying, or are we simply interpreting? The moment we start to interpret, our left brain has begun the process of cutting us off from more data and of coming up with *the* solution. And we do this all the time unconsciously. From this point on, we are guilty of driving the other person towards *our* solution, even though we think we are coaching them with some great questions.

If we truly listen, and then coach on the basis of what people actually *say*, rather than what we think they mean, then we really help them to be clear, and we create an honest and unequivocal communication between us. This is why the logical levels are such a useful tool, because they discipline us to listen and react only to what the other person has actually said. The real bonus from this technique is that we educate people to be completely clear in their communications with us (and thus with themselves) and we create a culture of truth, fact, honesty and clarity.

We can use the logical levels to 'bring the best person into the room' to address the issue at hand – the person we interviewed; the person operating at their peak – *that's* the person we need addressing the issue, not the hesitant, unconfident person who may be presenting themselves to us at the moment. When I get you talking at the top three levels, by asking you the right questions, then I bring the courageous, passionate, enthusiastic, energetic and totally committed person into the room – and *that's* the person I will then take back down to the bottom levels into the detail of the issue and I will ask *that* person what they are going to do about it.

When coaching, if we purely concentrate on behaviour then we can fix problems in the short term, but get little learning of patterns and real causes. When we recognise patterns we have a choice of repeating or not repeating. We need to become more generic in coaching rather than striving for the single solution to the particular issue that is at hand.

So listen, work out where people are and then ask a question that shifts them to another level. If they are 'stuck' at a lower level, you might get them talking about what they are good at (skills) or what they think is important (values). If they seem stuck on principles or identity, you might get them to consider what action they need to take (behaviour) or how their inaction is affecting others (environment).

Here are some guideline questions you can use at each level:

Environment

- *Where are you with this issue at the moment?*
- *What are you bogged down with?*
- *Why can't you seem to move forward?*
- *What's stopping you from making progress?*

Behaviour

- *What are you doing about the problem?*
- *What plan are you executing?*
- *What's the very next action you are going to take?*
- *What strategy are you using for solving the problem?*
- *How are you behaving at the moment?*

Skills/capabilities

- 🌐 *What do you need to learn to move forward?*
- 🌐 *What is it that you feel you need to be more competent at?*
- 🌐 *What is the quality that you have that should be helping you most here?*

Beliefs/values

- 🌐 *What is important to you about this issue/situation?*
- 🌐 *What's the right thing to do?*
- 🌐 *If you were to use the company values to guide you, what would you do?*
- 🌐 *What principles are you using to guide you through this?*
- 🌐 *What do you feel strongly about with this issue?*

Identity

- 🌐 *What type of manager are you trying to be?*
- 🌐 *What is your reputation and what do you want it to be?*
- 🌐 *What are you doing when you are adding most value as a manager?*
- 🌐 *Why were you the best candidate when you were selected to be the manager?*
- 🌐 *What qualities would a world-class manager be using more of right now?*

Purpose

- 🌐 *Why did you take the job?*
- 🌐 *How does this role fulfil you at this stage of your career?*
- 🌐 *What are you striving to achieve in your role?*
- 🌐 *What does the company expect from you as the best possible incumbent for your role at this time?*
- 🌐 *How long have you been in your role and how far through your mission are you?*

Genuinely listening and not interpreting what people are saying is tough, but this is why the logical levels are such a useful tool, because they discipline us to listen and react *only* to what the other person has actually communicated. When we have assessed the level at which they are presenting the problem, which will usually be at one of the bottom two levels, all we need to do is to bring the best version of that person into the room, and then ask *that* person to solve the problem.

How do we do that? Well, we do what we did at their interview – the thing that gave them the structure with which to impress us with their attitude. We ask them questions at the top three levels. We get them accessing their passion, their strength of feeling about the issue, their energy and enthusiasm, their courage. We reconnect them with their core – their internal source of (almost unlimited) power. And once we have *that* version of the person in front of us, we can then deliberately drop our questions right down to the bottom levels and get *that* version of the person, the finest version, to solve the problem.

Both versions of the person – the one who is bogged down and struggling, and the one who is passionate and courageous – know what the answer is, but the one who is bogged down and struggling is never going to get there. And the more we mix it with them down in *environment*, the more we conspire with them to keep them struggling and fearful.

When we are coaching someone, and when we really listen to the content of what they are saying, we will notice that they are invariably stuck down in the weeds; they may be thrashing around down there, engaging in action or indeed they may have gone into some form of 'freeze' whereby they've become so scared to act that all their creative energy is targeted at coming up with those great excuses we looked at earlier.

And the reality is while they may find *an* answer down there, it will be at best a 'sticking plaster' solution and at worst it will solve the wrong problem, allowing the embers to smoulder and reignite more destructively somewhere down the road.

We cannot collude with them and join them down in their drama. It's theirs, not ours. If we join them down there we may feel like we're 'getting in the trenches with them' thus showing solidarity and truly inspiring them as we basically tell/show them what to do. So tempting, but do not be seduced.

> *Instead, we need to metaphorically lift them out of the drama, attach them to the real power and fuel they possess in their sense of purpose, and in their values*

Instead, we need to metaphorically lift them out of the drama, attach them to the real power and fuel they possess in their sense of purpose, and in their values, and in appealing to the finest identity they aspire to.

But people can also get stuck on principle, and the more senior the manager, the greater the scope to 'hide' in fine words and obfuscation. If an employee on the shop floor hides, today's production quota will be missed. If a marketing director hides (no offence) it can go unnoticed for months... so as well as having the ability to lift someone out of the weeds and reattach them to their principles, we also need to know when to push someone out of their humbug into action!

And remember there's no change without action, so the key in all of this is to leave the person back on the right road – back at floor level, stuck neither in the basement nor in the penthouse, but with a clear and practical strategy and perhaps, for good measure, a clear next step that gives them confidence to break an old pattern, to truly learn from the experience and to consciously develop new skills. And thus personal growth genuinely leads to extraordinary results.

Hidden depths

We are judged by others on the data we present to them – what we choose to show and what we have no awareness we are showing. So quite naturally they judge us on that. They judge us on our appearance and our mannerisms, then on our behaviours and, crucially, on what we say. And in a pressured world, once they've judged us, we stay judged. We stay in the pigeonhole they've put us in. Because we expect people to behave according to their pigeonhole, we react to them accordingly, and so the vicious circle starts.

And in a pressured world, even if our company has a terrific talent planning process, it takes something truly extraordinary for others to see us differently and change their minds about us. So we're on a loser really. We are nervous of taking risks because we don't want the beast to be let loose on us, and yet only something extra-ordinary on our part will change our leaders' minds and cause them to re-rate us.

But below the surface we have hidden depths – all of the good stuff: our passion, our principles and beliefs, our courage and the remaining 35 per cent of that all-elusive potential.

No wonder it is so hard for organisations to truly unleash the extraordinary potential of their people.

Chapter 5
Coaching mastery

From the sublime to the ridiculous

When we're savouring the crafting we're doing with our questions, and we're really feeling and seeing the difference, then we can start flexing our coaching muscles towards the extremes of our range – we can push at the sublime and we can push at the ridiculous, and we can move seamlessly and very rapidly between the two. The sublime is the deepest human connection we can achieve – the ridiculous is the most directive and challenging we can be when we are completely trusted. We achieve the sublime through SuperListening, and, having established the trust and emotional connection, we achieve the ridiculous through BreakThrough Coaching.

SuperListening

Everyone longs to tell their story and have it understood and accepted.

Carl Jung

When we give someone the space to tell their story, the whole issue unfolds before us. If the person is really blocked, they will meander around and frequently apologise that they are making no sense. If we can be patient and learn to enjoy the stories, the golden thread that will take the person towards their solution *will* emerge. Once people feel understood by us, they're ready to change, ready to follow us.

And so to the hardest skill of all – listening. How many times has someone (maybe your partner?) told you that they don't want you to solve their problems for them, they just want you to listen. Or maybe you have had feedback in the past that you need to be better at it. The problem we have of course is that a) we don't believe it adds any value because it has no action associated with it, b) we believe it allows people to 'wallow' in their problem and their inactivity, and c) that it's inconvenient – it wastes time when everyone knows what needs to be done. Listening to someone else is perhaps the single aspect of coaching that leads us to believe the myth that coaching is 'soft and fluffy' and that therefore coaching gets in the way of our drive for performance and results.

And yet we crave to be listened to ourselves; invariably it will be the thing we criticise *our* leaders for the most. What strange animals we are – we value things for ourselves, but do not value them for others. The reality is that listening to someone is a hugely valuable act and a really good use of time. Often it is all people need – they simply need to hear themselves talk the problem through with a 'sounding board' and perhaps also to feel the silent input of another human being honouring their position, accepting their fears and flaws, and not judging them for being foolish or stupid or frightened or incompetent.

As children we are brought up on stories; we learn through the power of storytelling. One of the most comforting phrases of my childhood was *'Are you sitting comfortably? Then I'll begin.'* We live our lives in stories. We make sense of situations and events by constructing stories around them – our own version of what happened and why. We see events through a filter that is unique to us – our physical position with reference to the event itself, but also down to our values and beliefs – our pre-judgements of the people involved. That is why two people can have such differing memories of the very same event. They have told themselves different stories. Two sides in a conflict need to understand that their account is not the factual view, merely *their* view. If two sides in a conflict are to be reconciled and brought back to some sort of harmony, then they need to honour the view of their adversary. They do not need to agree, they merely need to accept that their opponent believes something different and respect that. This was the incredible wisdom of Nelson Mandela and Desmond Tutu's insistence on the Truth and Reconciliation Commission after the fall of the apartheid regime in South Africa.

So listening to someone tell their story is hugely important. Yes it can be time-consuming, but it's not the time we begrudge, it's the fact that we get bored easily and our conditioned sense that we could, nay should, be doing other more productive things. Our attention deficit disorder kicks in. Learn to listen. Learn to really listen; actively listen by empathising with the speaker, feeling their emotions and sensing their state of mind, for this is our path to a deeper and more meaningful and fulfilling connection with others – our path to trust.

But we know this, so clearly what we need are some practical tools to use – to know what to listen out for to assist us in knowing what to do as their coach when they have finished talking. Fundamentally we humans have three methods of receiving information: judgemental, sensing and curiosity.

1. Judgemental

In this mode we are not listening, we are filtering incoming data through our own internal conversation. We are in fact listening to the voice in our own head, rather than objectively taking in new information from the outside. Instead of hearing the other person saying they are struggling, we hear the voice in our head which says 'What on earth am I going to do with this person?' We are in this mode a *lot*. The crazy thing is that the other person knows full well that we are not listening to them, but keeps going. Not only do they know that we're not listening, they can sense the judgemental energy we are emitting, and

Instead of hearing the other person saying they are struggling, we hear the voice in our head which says 'What on earth am I going to do with this person?'

they put their own characterisation onto the voice in our head. It is not a benign voice that they hear. It is a voice of threat and condemnation. In this mode, we cut across people, interrupt them and finish their sentences. We allow our frustration, irritation and impatience to show. Our responses are not conversational or curious, since we have no motivation to join in what feels to us like a useless conversation. Energetically we convey judgement and we let the other person know what they should do next – which either will be some unhelpful variation on '*just get it done*', or it will be to tell them to give it back to us so we can do it properly. This mode is abusive and damaging, and with overuse it creates the negative conditioned learning that severely limits human potential and organisational growth. It creates CTSD (Corporate Traumatic Stress Disorder). Be aware, and then don't do it!

2. Sensing

This is our wonderfully underused and seriously mistrusted ability to correctly inter-pret non-verbal communications. As a species we've been around for close to 200,000 years. We've had complex language for maybe the last 5 per cent of that evolution – so we did OK for 190,000 years with little more than nuanced grunts. And now we think words are everything. But we are seriously skilled at reading non-verbal communication – we pick up the slightest physical cues and even micro-expressions and we know exactly what they mean. We have that skill, but we've stopped acknowledging it and we've certainly stopped trusting it. We know when someone is not saying something, and we know pretty well what they're not saying. We know when someone says they're fine, and actually they're struggling. We know when someone says yes they can, and what they really mean is no they probably can't. It's so easy to choose to take their words as the truth, especially if it is exactly what we wanted to hear. If our inner control freak has forced a *Yes* out of them, then even if we know they'll probably fail, at least everyone will know where the blame lies… and frankly if I was to stop for a moment and challenge them, then all that will happen is they'll learn that it is OK to fail, and I can't be having that! Better that they feel the pressure to achieve, and who knows, they might even surprise everyone. We simply do not allow people to be human. We know how they are feeling, and we choose to pretend that we don't. They know that we know, and they know that we know they've not been honest. But if we have the power, then the dynamic is too stacked against them. Survival says '*Tell them what they want to hear, since nothing else will be acceptable anyway.*' This dynamic is at the heart of everything that is wrong in the corporate world.

3. Curiosity

A magical thing happens when we choose to listen intently to the content of the communication – to the words, phrases, descriptions, metaphors, similes, poetry of what someone else is saying to us. We get drawn into the narrative, we become intrigued, curious and desperate to know how the story ends. And so we naturally ask open questions to understand more and receive further and deeper informa-tion. And since the speaker picks up on our non-verbal signals of acceptance, validation, witnessing, approbation, excitement and curiosity, they are inspired to tell us more; not just of what they already know of the story, but of what they can uncover in their unconscious mind, what they haven't known or clarified up to this point. Curiosity is the most attractive human quality, and we have absolutely no problem with this mode of listening outside of work. I think it's really sad that we have become so scared of intimacy in our working relationships

As well as being more self-aware of our own state of mind, and being able to recon-nect with the speaker, it really helps if we have some things to watch out for. Let's not just listen, let's SuperListen. When we really start to listen to the words and become intrigued by the story, and when we really pay attention to the non-verbal communications and start to notice the smallest physical cues, we enter a whole new level of human connection – of trust.

In SuperListening mode we will hear the denial (fear) in people's communications. We will hear them distracting themselves and us from the real issue; we will hear them deflecting us; we will hear them softening the truth to make the situation seem less urgent. We may even hear them drop into the third person to describe the protagonist in the story (themselves!). We will hear them gloriously describe how things are *not*, instead of how they are; of how they are *not* feeling instead of how they *are* feeling.

When we are really listening and really noticing, we'll hear what appears to be just a 'throwaway' comment. An example might be '*Oh, he's a nightmare*' or '*If that client asks for one more piece of information, I'll swing for them.*' Even more interesting are the little things that people say under their breath – as if they don't want us to hear. And yet they've said it aloud. When challenged on these, the speaker will immediately refute it or issue a call-back, telling us they didn't mean it; that it was '*just an expression*'. Well there is no such thing as a throwaway comment. These are little but significant betrayals of truth, of strength of feeling or point of view.

There is an expression that comes from the world of psychotherapy that says '*when the mind moves, the body moves too*'. When we are listening and really noticing, we'll see the movement of the body that betrays an unexpressed thought – a smile, a tapping of the fingers on a desk, a grimace, a raising of an eyebrow. Noticing this, and then asking the other person what they thought was not only helps them be clear in their feelings, beliefs and strategies, it's a hugely powerful communicator of the care you are taking of them and for them. Listening at this level of intensity and attention is a real act of love, and the effect of being cared for in this way is profound.

> **Listening at this level of intensity and attention is a real act of love, and the effect of being cared for in this way is profound.**

When we're really paying attention, we'll notice the sentence they can't finish. These sentences will be prefaced with phrases such '*So what I need to do is...*', '*I'm going to speak to them and tell them...*', '*I believe the right decision is to...*' If only we were brave enough to finish the sentence! The problem is our inner protector hears us about to irrevocably commit, and it hijacks us just in time, by stopping us from completing the sentence. Since this protector has been so exercised in the past, it has got a lot of practice, and so it's become highly skilled at hiding what just happened from the audience. The skill is not to leave a silence at the point of halting the sentence, but to swerve away from the disastrous outcome, into a conclusion to the sentence that sounds plausible but offers no commitment whatsoever.

So if my brain has started the sentence '*I'm going to speak to them and tell them...*' and if my brain, left to its own devices, is on a collision course to finish that sentence with the words '*that what they are asking for is not possible, and that therefore they either find another supplier, or they agree to our proposal*', my inner protector will jump in, since there really is no way back from making such a statement, and since the consequences of such unilateral action are too scary to contemplate. My inner protector realises what is about to unfold, around about the words '*and tell them...*' (ie, just in time) and jumps in to save the day. The sentence ends up sounding like this: '*I'm going to speak to them and tell them... because the problem we have is that we're just not in a position to give them what they want for the budget they've made available.*'

Hang on a minute, that doesn't make sense. I did not complete the sentence. But I completed a sentence, and since the sentence I did complete is not contentious and contains no scary actions, my audience are unlikely to pick me up on it. Of course my coach would say '*You're going to speak to them and tell them... what?*'

I listen to many conversations where all these cues and signals are in evidence, and yet are just not noticed. So actually I listen to vast numbers of non-conversations. Two people end up agreeing that things are tough, agreeing that it's someone else's fault, and agreeing that there's nothing they can do. When this happens at the end of a meeting, we can simply agree to having another meeting, so we can get away with inertia.

Three answers to get to the truth

Finally, let's come back to the immense amounts of licence, permission and encouragement that people need to struggle, to be honest and to be vulnerable.

> *it takes three goes at answering a tough question for people to respond with total honesty.*

I've realised that it takes three goes at answering a tough question for people to respond with total honesty. The first answer is their 'scout', the second answer is the 'correct' answer, and then finally their third answer will be their 'truth'. The 'scout' answer will not be an answer to the question at all – it will be wholly designed as reconnaissance, the scout sent out to survey the lay of the land and the position and strength of the enemy, and to report back. Now armed with more intelligence about what the acceptable or desired answer is, we can give that 'correct' answer. Normally of course the 'scout' does the job and we're not asked a second time, but if we are then our second 'correct' response nearly always kills the transaction, since the other person has what they want. Why would they pursue things now? But of course our coach notices that we've yet to speak our truth, and asks again, with every ounce of acceptance and compassion they can muster to let us know we are safe. And so we answer for the third time with our 'truth'.

Here's an example. The other person asks me '*How long are you going to work with X to help them achieve their objectives?*' The scout says, '*I need to work with X for long enough to be fair to their talents but always bearing in mind that if X doesn't start meeting their objectives quite soon, I might need to make a change.*' Notice how beautifully the scout does its job. It sounds in control, like I'm well-aware of the issue and not avoiding it; it demonstrates my balance and my competence. It is in many ways a very plausible answer, one that I cannot really be criticised for. But notice it studiously avoids answering the question. And notice that the answer is quite long, containing all elements of what could be the 'correct' answer. This means that while I am talking, I can be gauging your reaction to each element, picking up the intelligence I need to work out what answer you are looking for. At the outset I may not know whether you believe I should have already sacked X, or whether you believe that he's brilliant and simply needs more time and attention. At the end of my 'scout' answer I will have collected all the intelligence I need. If you repeat the question, 'So, how long?', then I can give you what you want, for example, 'I need to act quickly since this has gone on for too long already' (right answer!). Although notice again it still avoids the specifics of timescales. But in fact I may not need you to repeat the question since once the scout returns to camp, I might simply volunteer the 'correct' answer. After all, I can't have you thinking I'm not on top of things.

But since you're my coach, and since you want only the best solution for me in my performance as a manager, you've not given anything away. The scout returns with nothing! Actually of course that's not true – the scout returns with intelligence that says this is a genuinely open question and my coach is just wanting me to get to my truth. It's just that I don't trust the scout. I mean what sort of scout comes back and says 'Don't worry they're not the enemy, they just want to be friends...' Poor foolish, naïve scout.

In that case my 'correct' answer might hint at my truth, since I cannot repeat the scout answer, as that would be too obvious. And the gentleness of the enquiry coming back – 'How long?' – will finally persuade me that you can be trusted, and so here comes my truth: 'I need to have a clear conversation with X and see significant signs of achievement within one month, or I will have to make a change.' So now as your coach I know how to help you, with questions like 'What would constitute acceptable progress inside one month? How will you persuade X's colleagues to support him/her to succeed in that timeframe? What's the most impactful thing you could do that would help X to believe in him/herself?'

If I were your coach/manager in this situation, this is where I have to be completely clear in my own agenda. If I believe that X is never going to make it and that you are procrastinating through fear, I may need to offer you that as feedback, and then my questions would be very different. If I believe that X is brilliant but needs a good six months, and if as your manager I am prepared to suffer a shortfall in achievements over that period, then again I may need to offer that as feedback or advice. Owning a strong belief or agenda upfront is a sensible strategy as part of our contract of trust.

The most valuable thing we can do is to recognise the language they employ and use it back to them. People have very definite ways of expressing themselves and will convey much with their choice of language. A great technique is to craft questions back to them using the very same language they have used already – sometimes without emphasising it, and sometimes deliberately placing emphasis on the word or words that you have heard from them. Sometimes it's valuable to simply repeat a word and ask them what they mean by that. Using this method allows the other person to uncover the more subconscious thoughts they have been having, and once the words are out of their mouths, our good friend physics takes over. Their words are like an energetic version of tomato sauce – once it's out of the bottle, it does not go back in. They just need to hear themselves.

SuperListening feedback

We then need some forms of words, some phrases that we can use to preface our feedback, with introductory phrases that telegraph what we are about to do and why. Phrases such as:

- ⊕ *'A judgement I might be guilty of making...'*
- ⊕ *'There was a voice in my head saying...'*
- ⊕ *'What I noticed (and how I interpreted that)...'*
- ⊕ *'I got a strong sense that you are feeling...'*
- ⊕ *'Where I felt you were being less than 100 per cent honest...'*
- ⊕ *'What I found intriguing (and therefore a question I have)...'*
- ⊕ *'What do you mean by...?'*

This is how we build trust. We need to make every question come from them, rather than from our own agenda or our own solutions. As coaches we are looking to uncover and assess their capacity: their competencies and gaps or blind spots they may have, their courage, since if they are confident they'll probably make *any* decision work, and their commitment to specific new actions. Even when we've heard a commitment, we should help further, since one way to fob a coach off if the coaching is getting too uncomfortable is to issue a *'So what I need to do is...'*-style response. Making verbal commitments is easy – carrying through actions that involve risk and discomfort are an entirely different thing, so as coaches we need to persist and ask them what might stop them from acting – let's make them do the work they fear in the session and show them they can do it.

BreakThrough Coaching

So now we move from our ability to create the most sublime human connections and trust to the other extreme in developing an ability to be really tough and even directive in our coaching when we need to be. This is where we consciously bring an appropriate use of our authority as their line manager to bear, with a more conscious directing of them to their resolution. We can only use BreakThrough Coaching techniques if we have built a very high degree of trust, so this comes after SuperListening.

We'll focus on what the other person is really struggling with, remembering that struggle is inevitable, struggle is good. And we're looking to find the breakthrough question – the question that if the other person hears themselves give an unequivocal answer, they have solved the problem.

One powerful technique is to use superlatives (most, fastest, worst, greatest) in our questions. This means that the person has to compare facts and opinions in their head and arrive at a single answer and this is an incredibly helpful cognitive process for them to undertake. Superlative questions are also 'unavoidable' – if we ask someone what is most scary, they cannot say they have no fear as that is avoiding the question. So with BreakThrough Coaching more than ever we have to repeat questions word for word when we hear an answer that seeks to avoid or distract or deflect.

With BreakThrough Coaching we're going to immediately challenge their use of certain phrases such as *'unacceptable'*, *'I need to'*, *'I don't know'*. They cannot describe a situation as unacceptable if they are in fact accepting it through their lack of action. I've had to confront clients many times with the 'lie' that is the phrase *'it's unacceptable'*, and the confrontation of the disconnect between words and actions is uncomfortable but incredibly helpful. I don't care if you end up accepting the situation, but please do so consciously and positively and supportively, and not sullenly and grudgingly. And it's easy for someone to tell us that they *need to* do something and then not follow through. Again they've said the right thing, but there is a complete disconnect between their words and actions. So if you have no actual intention of doing what you say you need to, please stop saying it. But if you really need to, then how and when…

And when someone says they don't know, that's rarely true. They may, of course, genuinely believe that they don't know, but once said as the truth, there's no further exploration. People often don't know that they know – so when pushed, people frequently come up with potential answers. What most people mean when they say *'I don't know'* is actually *'I cannot think of any alternatives that would work or be acceptable, and since it is not possible for me to take risks, I have to shut down and close off my part in this and give it back to you or someone else.'* As their coach, all we need to do is push further – *'What do you suspect could be the answer?'* is a good question to pose after an emphatic *'I don't know'*, since the question acknowledges that the answer might have some fear attached to it.

The proper use of closed questions

It's in BreakThrough Coaching mode that we will engage in the proper use of closed questions – insisting on a yes or no answer to force the other person out of their procrastination or their fear, forcing them off the fence one way or the other. This is especially useful when we have no attachment to which way they jump, but they need to get on. *'Do you believe that…?'* is a great way to prompt the jumping one way or the other.

> *the proper use of closed questions – insisting on a yes or no answer to force the other person out of their procrastination or their fear, forcing them off the fence one way or the other*

⊛ *Do you believe that you have sufficient time to develop X into the role?*

⊛ *Do you believe that the client will ever sign a contract?*

⊛ *Do you believe that X will make it?*

When the person hears themselves give the emphatic binary response, they can finally put all of their energy into a positive strategy. I've known people wrestle for months with tough issues, when what they needed at the start was to land on one clear and positive strategy and get on with it.

In BreakThrough Coaching mode we need to provoke, to be prepared to be the lightning rod for the other person's emotions, showing them how to use the emotional energy for its correct and positive intentional purpose. If they are frustrated but trying hard not to be, we may need to provoke that frustration and let them vent it on us. So while we would normally be very wary of 'abusing' someone by interrupting them, in BreakThrough Coaching mode we've built such trust that we can consciously interrupt them if they're not answering our question. We simply must take them outside their comfort zone, and to do anything less is simply not serving them. One way to provoke someone is to deliberately use language that they might react against, whereas in SuperListening mode we used *their* language back to them to build trust and demonstrate care. So if they say they're a bit apprehensive about an upcoming meeting, we might ask them what they're scared of.

> *One way to provoke someone is to deliberately use language that they might react against, whereas in SuperListening mode we used their language back to them to build trust and demonstrate care.*

Finally and in the spirit of making them do the work in front of us, we can ask them *'What's stopping you?'* And then *'If you had to decide right now...?'* This is another way of forcing them off the fence, and once they've landed on a decision, we can move into helping them plan the 'how' of the action entailed.

Role play

Staged role plays for pitches, presentations, etc, are enormously helpful, and really play into the culture of rehearsal as a positive and hugely enjoyable part of innovation and experimentation. But in coaching we need to be able to do spontaneous role plays where we will drop into a role for just a few short minutes, with the objective of testing the other person's resolve and giving them practice in their fear. Typically this will be when the other person has voiced that they need to have a meeting with a third party, and where they are fearful of how the meeting will go. When you decide to use role play you have to be directive and not allow the other person off the hook. They'll resist if they can, so be firm. While you might need a couple of details of the character you are about to play, you don't need too much, since your job in playing the role is not to do an impersonation or even try and predict how that person will react; your job is to give an honest reaction to the inputs you are given. Your job is to give the other person a stretching practice, so avoid answering questions or taking any personal responsibility if you can. Be defensive, resist, distract them, blame others, etc. Resist until you cannot, and then hold the moment because you'll both feel the difference. It will be when the other person has finally been honest, clear and direct. You will both feel this moment – it is inescapable. Stop the role play immediately and feedback what happened and how they did it. Show them they cannot just survive, but thrive. We know when someone is too scared to be direct and we also know exactly what it is that they want to say to us. We will respect them if they are honest; it could be the breakthrough we need, and it could lead to an amazing partnership going forward.

The feedback is then what they did really well, what they did that made it easy for you to resist, and what they clearly wanted to say but were too scared to be honest. Don't be afraid to stop the role play if they struggle for too long, and give them a strong direction to practise a different tack.

Teaching and knowledge transfer

This brings us to a potential Achilles heel for coaches, and something that has been levelled at me in the past – that it's all very well me asking all the questions and never offering solutions or advice, but people *do* want to know what I think, and denying them this makes them feel cheated in some way; maybe even leaves them feeling that I am guarding myself and not making myself vulnerable, thus giving me enormous power over them. Watch out for this. Trust will only perpetuate if the other person gets to know you as well as you getting to know them.

It's important to them from a personal self-esteem point of view, and it's important to them for efficiency – to ensure that they are not having to re-tread old ground if I can save them from making obvious mistakes.

Now we do have to be careful here, since the hierarchical dynamic can come into play if I add suggestions. Also, facilitating people's developing *without* learning directly from mistakes is not equipping them to get by without you, but nevertheless I now try and be more aware of this and give people more of a sense of my views and experience through adding my thoughts as additional data for them.

As a teacher, a role that I believe coaches must adopt at times, the job is not to tell people what to do or how to do it, but to give them the skills of research, analysis, communicating, working in teams and problem-solving. So I refer people to all those rules and guidelines and sources around them – the company vision and values, the budgets, the processes, the methods – maybe even the people within the organisation who are specialists.

The hardest part about being a coach is that we have to constantly be self-aware – and that way we consciously choose what devices or techniques or tools to use. And it is this self-awareness that can help us in those challenging cases when we simply know the answer and we sense that the other person is about to make a terrible mistake – and we have the power to save them. Dangerous territory.

Don't be afraid to go into teaching mode when you need to, and when you go, go gloriously! Tell them you are teaching them things. I've observed great leaders running internal 'masterclasses' for employees, and they are both vibrant and hugely appreciated sessions for all concerned. This is where we need to consider every employee as a performer,

> *Don't be afraid to go into teaching mode when you need to, and when you go, go gloriously!*

and allow them to demonstrate and teach their skills to others in an overt process of education. Another example is where an experienced sales manager goes on sales calls/visits with their team and literally shows them the job – people learn so fast from watching and then having a go. When an organisation embraces education and learning at its core, then growth accelerates like night follows day – of course not always the growth that was planned or even desired, so this can really piss off the control freaks who've made their minds up that the world needs to look a certain way in a certain timeframe. This is why the core mission and purpose is so vital, why the values are sacrosanct and why the value proposition has to have central status, for when education and learning rule the day, the business will organically go where it wants to, where it is *needed* to by the customers and the marketplace. So educate people in the vision, the values, the business model, the finances and the processes. And remember the biggest single factor in teaching is the example we set – so always strive to be a great role model.

When you have to move out of teaching into a more directive style, you can try a halfway house first and that is to position yourself as their 'expert counsel', not their teacher or even their director. An expert counsel will say, '*I understand you are the client and will make the final choice or decision on what you want to do, what's best to do – but I am an expert and I strongly advise/counsel you to do X. The reason I say that is that my concern if you do not, the risk that you are really running, is Y.*'

Adding your experience is, of course, trickier, but self-awareness helps and then there are three techniques to embrace – one is to add your experience as an additional piece of data. After all, your experience is factual (it actually happened) and therefore is available to learn from and build on. But it's only part of the mix, so add it into the ingredients rather than giving them the finished cake. Second, use your experience as an additional source of coaching questions, or craft questions around your experience, but the trick here is to come 'above' the solution or detailed action that your experience would lead *you* to and make your question more strategic. We have to avoid the *leading* question. And this is tough because we've become quite skilled at them! Finally one lovely way to give your experience is to tell them a story and leave them to conclude. People love stories, there's something therapeutic about the process, but again the trick is to give them the data and leave them to reach their own conclusions, and thus their own committed decisions and actions.

Point out sources of information and research as additional pieces of data for them, or simply ask them what research they've done. Ask them what the market research is telling them, what customers or other stakeholders are advising. If they haven't asked, they might just realise they're missing an important angle (without you telling them what that angle is!).

When you 'know' *the* answer, ask yourself if it is in fact just the way *you* would do it? Check your ego, check your inner control freak – and let go of your need for control.

Our rewards

Finally, let's tune into the world's favourite radio station – WIIFM: what's in it for me?

You see, when we allowed ourselves to exercise our egos and tell people what to do and enjoy ourselves by solving all the problems, it was so much fun. Our enjoyment not only came easily, it came instantly. That's what adrenaline does. It's addictive. It makes us feel great – strong, invulnerable, brilliant. And so we like instant gratification – that feeling that we can go home having slain the dragons and earned our money – even if it is only that we have cleared our inbox.

But now we have to coach, we are denied all this. So what's in its place?

Well, we have, of course, touched on this when we spoke of the deep connections we make, and that sense of knowing when we have helped someone grow – when they achieve something and WE know that we created the conditions for them to achieve it. All very well, but it's all too enlightened – we do at times need to hear that we are good. So listen out for it – all the feedback is there if we only listen. It simply sounds different.

If you ask great open questions you will get direct feedback quite often – people will never say '*thank you, you have been an outstanding coach*', but they will betray their admiration and the value they place on you in their responses. First of all their honesty means that they trust you, possibly to a degree that they have *never* trusted anyone before. They may even say, '*I've never told anyone this before*'. They will say, '*That's a great question...*', and you should allow yourself to feel proud and acknowledge the praise.

Coaching is the only management skill I know that can elicit immediate and spontaneous positive feedback. '*That's a great question*', they might mutter, as their eyes look to the distance, engineered by your coaching.

But the biggest compliment they will pay you will be their willingness to open themselves up in front of you and to be vulnerable. This is often silent, and their eye contact may well be somewhere else, but enjoy the moment because it is precious – and *you* created it. '*If I'm really honest...*', they'll mutter, and you know that your coaching, your presence has given them the safety and permission they need to be vulnerable.

> *the biggest compliment they will pay you will be their willingness to open themselves up in front of you and to be vulnerable. This is often silent, and their eye contact may well be somewhere else, but enjoy the moment because it is precious*

We have to learn to get excited about being creative in our coaching, rather than being seduced into solving their problem. So when they are silent and looking away – when you've achieved the 'eye contact flicker', they are thinking and you are being a great coach. For God's sake stay silent! Pat yourself on the back (momentarily), savour the connection, the humanity, the joy of the sheer intimacy of human interaction, and then complete the process in whatever way serves them best – sometimes by asking for a specific action plan, and sometimes leaving them with the respect and dignity of knowing that they've done the work they needed to do and *we* don't need to know what action they will take.

The coachee's plea

I am often asked what managers should do when they encounter someone who does not want to be coached. In my experience this often comes with a loaded belief in the person asking that not everyone wants to or is capable of being coached. In my experience every single human being wants to be coached, and if they are presenting as if they don't then it will be either because they are mistrusting of us as coaches or because they have never really been coached in the past and so do not believe in it. I've coached people in all parts of the world and had wonderful interactions and impact.

If someone presents to you as not wanting coaching, then you need to work on trust first of all. And part of that trust-building might have to be real clarity on the fact that coaching is not optional when they work for you. You *will* coach them – it's your job. If coaching is going to be our predominant management style or technique, we cannot have team members who opt out.

So when you approach a member of your team or a customer, or an internal or external stakeholder, then remember they are silently and unconsciously asking something of you. This is their plea:

I am bright, intelligent and capable. I am prepared to live or die by my own decisions and actions. I am my own harshest judge. I do not want to be denied the opportunity to exercise all that I am and all that I have, however much I may feel like running away or being rescued. I may be stuck, I may be anxious, but I am determined to get through this on my own – to have my own successes (and failures!) and my own achievements. So please don't solve my problem for me. Please don't judge me as being foolish for getting myself in this mess (!) or for struggling to know what to do next, even if the solution seems crystal clear to you. Please don't take this opportunity away from me, or deny me the privilege of finding my own path through this. Please just coach me. I am out of my comfort zone and I need you to hold me out there while I learn. Please just give me what I do not possess at this moment – a structure for my thinking and my own decision-making process, and help me find the courage to take the risks I need to take. And maybe give me something of your strengths – the stuff that comes naturally to you but that I struggle with. Challenge me; inspire me with your confidence in my ability to achieve the best possible result. Believe in me. And then leave me to get on and do it for myself.

Coaching is the only route to growth, so you better get good at it, or watch out for the meteorite that is coming your way.

Exploding the myths

And so here we are at the end of the beginning. And like any good story, this part should conclude with the myths having been shattered and the protagonists holding hands into the next instalment with their new enlightenment. So coaching is not soft and fluffy, in fact it is actually the toughest leadership style there is. But it's not us being tough on them, it's us helping them be tough on themselves. No it does not take longer to coach someone, in fact you can coach someone with a single question – sometimes even with a single raising of an eyebrow. It can be devastatingly fast. Teaching is teaching and it is vitally important.

Now we know how to coach, but we need to practise, practise, practise, and we need to never stop honing our skills. Now we know that we have actually not been coaching people, as we had previously told ourselves. And we do not need to wait until we are in the right frame of mind to coach, we simply need to coach to get ourselves in the right frame of mind.

So now we can start, and we can start to open up that rich world of possibility and fulfilment and enjoyment and achievement.

So go forth and be proud, clumsy coaches.

Section 2
Leadership

Chapter 6

Authentic leadership

Authentic leadership – it's not big and it's not clever

There's a great deal of rubbish written about 'authentic leadership' these days, and corporatism's pursuit of 'authentic leadership' has often been a cunning distraction. So this chapter outlines how to be genuinely authentic – a tautology I know, but we have to recognise the difference. Being authentic is pretty hard in a corporation, whatever level you're at, but authenticity is critical for a leader to be trusted… Authenticity does not of itself guarantee success for a leader. But without it, without being trusted, the leader is doomed to ultimate failure.

'Authentic leadership' must also contain elements of competency and ethics, of skills and principles, of context and personal strategies. An authentic leader is the right leader, in the right role, at the right time. The leader must be right for the role at the precise moment in the organisation's journey, but the role must also be right for the person, at the precise moment in their own personal career journey. And genuine authenticity means doing the right and moral thing, even when tradition or common practice or even the law or regulations would legitimise us in doing something very different.

Corporate cultures do not allow people to be human – it's inconvenient. Humans are messy, flawed, unreliable, inconsistent, uncontrollable, deceitful, manipulative and disloyal. (Characteristics that can, of course, be quite convenient when utilised in pursuit of the company's objectives.) They can be easily distracted by external stimuli, and they get sick, get pregnant and progressively acquire dependent relatives. They have to sleep and have holidays. Bring on the bots, I say.

Of course, humans are also beautiful, fabulous, richly and inexhaustibly talented, diverse, creative, passionate, committed, dedicated, supportive of each other and fun to work with.

So many corporate cultures betray their frustration at the 'negatives' to the extent that most employees do their very best not to appear human. They pretend to be confident when they are not. They look like they're going fast when actually they are not moving at all. They work at home and on holiday way more than is healthy or conducive to loving, long-term relationships. Ricardo Semler said that we've all learned to do emails on a Saturday, but no one can go to a movie on a Monday afternoon. How many of us have had to apologise for missing our kids' nativity plays?

As corporate leaders, working in ever-more competitive markets, and pressured to constantly return 'above trend' growth and positive like-for-likes, we often lose our way and, in the process, our integrity. We then forget to run our operations and manage our people by proven and ethical (boring?) strategies of sticking to our core products, serving genuine customers at fair prices, knowing the detail of our operations and checking every day that people are OK.

We come to believe that we have to be superhuman and in total control. How absurd. The pressure then becomes almost unbearable, as we exercise more and more energy and effort on pretending to be something we so clearly are not – infallible.

Go into most corporations and listen to all the business-speak conversations transacted between managers who are all desperately pretending to be calm, in control, knowing all the answers and great bosses. The pressure is enormous.

But the alternative feels truly scary, since it will involve admitting that we are not in control and that we cannot guarantee to hit the targets we have been set. Being ourselves, rather than pretending to be something that others want us to be, seems to involve falling back on faith, trust and instinct. We know that we are actually at our best, our greatest, our most influential and powerful, when we come from this place of authenticity. But it feels like a cop out. My colleague Martyn Haworth has a wonderful expression of how to be an authentic leader – *'Show up, and then see what shows up.'* We are profoundly at our best when we do this, but as a strategy it feels like we're not doing anything. Try explaining this strategy to your investors or even to your employees.

How should we behave if we stop pretending? What will we do instead of just trying to impress people all the time? What if we are simply not good enough? What if we get found out? What if we fail, looking foolish and naïve and letting people down in the process? Scary stuff indeed. These are understandable questions for us, but we need to ensure we do not allow them to turn into crippling self-doubt.

So how do we do this? We do this by going back to good old-fashioned purpose, vision and values – for ourselves as leaders and for our organisations.

We need to work out who we really are – uncovering our core (some might say our 'soul'). When we communicate from this place of real honesty, then we are trust-worthy and we inspire others. Our core does not try and get other people to do things, or worse, to be something they are not. Our core simply lays out the mission, sees who turns up, and creates the adventure. And what results will come, will come. Leaders build missions and environments where people choose to try to do the extraordinary.

And when I communicate from my core, you may well give me a glimpse of *your* core. Once this channel is open, and we are communicating core to core, life (and business) works. No pretence, no bullshit and no nonsense. The incredible thing about communicating from our core (being authentic) is that we attain that truly magical combination of attributes, humility and confidence. The good news is that we know how to do this stuff, but somehow along the way we have forgotten.

Authenticity demands leadership

Lots of us are capable of opening core-to-core channels with other individual human beings, but leaders need structures to move a whole community. Leaders need to be conscious that it is what they focus their attention on that actually dictates the behaviour of others. If we focus on trying to 'get' our employees to 'be' like we want them to be – bright, compliant, energetic, responsible, communicative, dedicated, enthusiastic, right, pacey, successful – then we inevitably stand in judgement over them, and set up that destructive dynamic where they will try and please us.

When people feel judged they defend themselves and are motivated to survive and stay safe, as opposed to being motivated to take responsibility. Since we humans are hardwired to survive, rather than being hardwired to flourish, when we commune together under a judgemental manager, we collude to survive, to stay firmly in our comfort zones, and in so doing we create a corporate comfort zone – a culture.

If, however, we focus on how our people 'are' and work with them to be at their very best, then we have the capacity to achieve extraordinary things. This all demands leadership. Since unconscious and habitual behaviours are coming from pretence at the moment, leaders have to break the cycle with feedback, making this conscious and giving awareness to people so that they have a chance to choose a conscious strategy. It's all part of focusing on people and not pushing for results – trusting that if we do the right things the best possible results will come.

Leaders who are pretending to be polished, competent and perfect have real difficulty in handling behaviour that does not conform. However, rarely does true authenticity come in a beautiful package. It can often be awkward, clumsy and overemotional. Who we really are as human beings is both beautiful and ugly; both perfect and flawed. And if leaders are only prepared to sit with the beautiful and perfect, sending strong signals that the ugly and flawed bits are unacceptable, then people will go back to pretending again.

if leaders are only prepared to sit with the beautiful and perfect, sending strong signals that the ugly and flawed bits are unacceptable, then people will go back to pretending again.

I've seen many leaders earnestly try and 'be' authentic at work, going through a rather ridiculous process of 'manufacturing' an authentic version of themselves that they can roll out at work. I really do blame the business schools and the advanced leadership courses for this dynamic. I worked with a very senior VP client, and in our penultimate session gave him this feedback, that I felt he was working hard to manufacture his authenticity in his role, rather than gloriously allowing himself to be himself. I felt he had two versions – the 'clever' version that he'd cultivated and the 'human' version that he really didn't let anyone see. And yet he was a truly beautiful human being, with a wonderful family and profound artistic talents. I knew the feedback would hurt, but I judged that with one session to come, we had sufficient time to work through this to an accommodation that would be helpful for him.

He was offended by my feedback, and soon after ended our coaching relationship. Of course he did not tell me the truth. He merely got his PA to email me to say that he'd got everything he could from the coaching and did not need the final session. It was very polite and indeed positive, thanking me for what I'd done. But I knew he was angry with me. I could not leave things like that, and I managed to persuade him to do the final session. I started the session by repeating the feedback, and saying that I felt his response was a really good example of what I had observed. I asked him to be honest with me and tell me how he felt about my feedback. It took several goes but eventually he looked me in the eyes and told me that he was really pissed off with me. It was the first time he'd been really honest, and the effect on me was profound. I started to cry – the connection I felt with him because he'd finally been authentic was just incredibly moving. And he felt it too. We had a fantastic final session, very real and very authentic. He'd got it.

If we are really going to encourage people to be honest, say it how it is for them, come close to who they really are, then we need to accept that it will not be comfortable. Great leaders understand this and work with what's in front of them. They open the core-to-core channel, and then exploit them in pursuit of the purpose.

What is authenticity?

There's a knowing when a role has your name on it, when it seems almost designed perfectly for you at a precise moment. Of course this is the ideal, the perfect situation, and many times (maybe always) there will need to be compromises, but those compromises can only be clearly defined, accepted and navigated if both parties are clear on their own ideal position.

> *90% of the world's woe comes from people not knowing themselves, their abilities, their frailties, and even their real virtues. Most of us go almost all the way through life as complete strangers to ourselves.*
>
> Sydney J Harris

Most psychotherapists will tell you this is true. Astonishing isn't it? The person we live with every minute of every day since the moment we were born, and from whom we cannot escape, is very often a stranger to us. We are often unaware at a conscious level of our needs, our true strengths, our desires, our principles and our beliefs, residing instead in a world of denial, distraction and conformity. And in order to remain unaware on a conscious level, we actually have to expend effort in denying, controlling and blocking our emotions, our feelings and the expression of our needs.

How can it be, that the hardest question you can ask any human being is '*What do you really want?*' And yet ask anyone that question and watch as they squirm and become an inarticulate wreck, before they deflect in some way.

Corporations, however, are not places of psychotherapy, existential debate or philosophical enquiry. Actually I would hope that they are indeed places where these activities are honoured, but it is not the prime purpose of a corporation to do these things. A corporation is founded or created to achieve a tangible purpose – therapy, debate and enquiry are processes not objectives.

So why should a corporation be interested in people acting authentically? Why can't people simply follow the Frederick Taylor/Henry Ford type dynamic of simply following processes, rules and procedures and turning out the required goods? Well, while that dynamic arguably served the world well when it wanted mass-produced, cheap, uniform consumer products, today consumers want concepts, services and virtual or digital content. And these require a workforce that can think and create – which in turn means allowing people to be human. If we want their flair, their creativity, their passion, then we have to take the whole package, and that means also taking their worries, their troubles, their flaws and their messiness. All very inconvenient, but a necessary part of the package.

The real trick, of course, is not just to tolerate the flaws, since that implies a judgementalism that will come through in unconscious controlling behaviours. The real trick is to see human flaws as positive contributors to the whole creative process. We should celebrate our messiness as humans, rather than roll our eyes and tut.

The real opportunity for us within corporations is to create workplaces that are real communities of growth, learning, progress, innovation and achievement. If you are managing a workforce of automatons, command-and-control-style hierarchies work mechanically pretty well. But managing a workforce of human beings, with all their flaws, emotions and external distractions, requires something altogether more sophisticated and refined. It requires humanity – it requires leaders who are authentic human beings first.

managing a workforce of human beings, with all their flaws, emotions and external distractions, requires something altogether more sophisticated and refined. It requires humanity – it requires leaders who are authentic human beings first.

Look in the dictionary for definitions of 'authentic' and you come up with the following:

⊛ *Being faithful to internal rather than external ideas*

⊛ *The quality of being genuine*

⊛ *Not corrupted from the original*

⊛ *Undisputed credibility*

⊛ *Worthy of trust and reliance*

An authentic person is open, honest, true, real... and has integrity. Trying to be someone else is stressful and doomed. Striving to be the best version of ourselves is joyful and effortless, as long as we can be guided and coached not to sabotage ourselves through fear... as Marianne Williamson said in her oft-quoted poem, '*it is our light, not our darkness that most frightens us*'. It is bizarre, but we will often procrastinate and distract ourselves from doing what we love, or from following our heart, for fear that we may just achieve it – and then what? What on earth would we do if we were truly happy, truly fulfilled? We'd have no excuses left.

> *Always be a first rate version of yourself, not a second rate version of somebody else.*
> Judy Garland

When we try to be someone else, we are already setting up lies that we then have no choice but to perpetuate, and this is incredibly hard work, requiring a huge amount of effort even just to remember what we've said and to whom. But we are interested in authentic leaders, not just wonderful individual human beings.

An authentic leader has purpose and a vision, and will do what's right for the good of the cause. Entering a joint endeavour or enterprise where we can all pursue our authentic selves is the finest way to serve the world. So as long as the world needs what we have... and if it doesn't then it's only about money.

> We never get to the bottom of ourselves on our own. We discover who we are face to face and side by side with others in work, in love and in learning.
>
> Robert Bellah

So let us see our corporations as places where we can commune together for an important purpose or cause, and where we can grow and learn together.

Our Golden Core

We are born with a unique genetic make-up that gives us our physical characteristics and psychological preferences – our Golden Core, our 'soul'. We are truly unique; a one-off. There is no one else like us out there.

And then, in our earliest formative years, through the attachments we form and the care and guidance we receive, we take on beliefs, principles and values. And we start to display the talents and skills we possess and that are available to be nurtured. What Ken Robinson would call our 'Element'.

Our Golden Core is who we really are – the beautiful, flawed, vulnerable, somewhat unknown, irresistible human being we really are at our core

Our Golden Core is who we *really* are – the beautiful, flawed, vulnerable, somewhat unknown, irresistible human being we really are at our core. And we go through life as souls searching for human connection. Some philosophers argue that it is our life's journey to work out our purpose, guided as we are by a largely unconscious set of principles and beliefs – our core values.

When running workshops on this subject at this point I show a photograph of a butterfly with its wings closed. It is clearly a butterfly, but I really thought it impossible to tell what sort, since the wings are what I thought to be anonymously brown. Until I did the exercise with the senior management team at a client company and one of the managers piped up '*It's a peacock butterfly*', thus in one moment both spoiling my reveal (the next photograph reveals the peacock butterfly in all its stupendous glory – the point being that I wonder if Mr and Mrs Peacock Butterfly told Junior not to show off and therefore to keep his wings hidden in public) and proving how extraordinary people are. I was stunned by the manager's incredible powers of observation. Asking him about it afterwards and still unable to hide my stupification, he recounted stories of his childhood when he had been taught about butterflies by his father. It was a lovely human moment as he then told me that it was the first time in probably over 30 years that he had accessed his knowledge of butterflies, and I could see (and feel) his emotional connection to his childhood and his relationship with his father.

The person who is calm, centred, happy and fulfilled is the person who knows themselves, who is comfortable with every aspect of themselves, including their flaws and frailties, who has integrity in that they live by their core values, and who follows a meaningful purpose to their lives.

We automatically and unconsciously trust the Golden Core in others, since nothing is hidden, and since what is being communicated is honest. I may not like you, but I trust you. I may not follow you, but I trust you. Psychopaths are often totally trustworthy since they are being authentic, honest and predictable. You can trust that they will kill you if they get the chance, and so you can adopt the correct strategy in relating to them.

The most wonderful thing about a corporation is the potential for human beings to come together in a common purpose, but more of this later.

Our Shield of Pretence

Unfortunately, but quite understandably, as we grow up we are taught to modify and mould ourselves to the world around us. On one simple level this is fundamentally about our physical safety. Keeping your child safe as they learn how to navigate their way into a dangerous world means instructing them *not* to do certain things that might put them in peril, and instructing them to do things that will keep them safe. There is no point being the most authentic version of yourself and dying early because you'd not been taught about the threats out there.

The problem for parents, and then for teachers, and then for leaders, is to really differentiate between what is a genuine threat to physical safety or health, and what is a threat to psychological safety. Sending your five year-old child to school dressed to their own unique style, but very differently to all the other children, is not going to kill them. However, it might open them up to bullying. Being different at school can be really difficult for a child, and parents are naturally very protective and very sensitive on their offspring's behalf.

But often this turns into being overprotective, overanxious. Parents so want to save their children from any pain or discomfort, they often deny their children the opportunity to learn and grow from their own mistakes and misfortunes. And if the parents are themselves living a life of some anxiety – maybe for financial reasons, because of family or relationship difficulties, or because of some mental health issues somewhere in the home or extended family – then the child will be subject to this dynamic, may even be the unwitting victim of it.

'*Don't you go showing off, now*' is perhaps a familiar exhortation from many parents to their children. After all no one likes a show off. Many children are brought up *not* to be themselves, therefore not allowed to find out who they really are – discouraged from being who they really are, and actively encouraged to conform and look like everyone else; the most successful versions of 'everyone else', of course, and so starts the other damaging dynamic. Constantly measuring ourselves against others is one thing, but when that involves a desperate desire to be better than others, it's no wonder we have some screwed up people and some seriously screwed up organisations where competition is celebrated.

So many children grow up dealing with the shame of hiding who they really are, and dealing with the guilt of not being who their parents want them to be. We grow up living in pretence, building a solid shield around our Golden Core. We get so much practice and feedback living in this space, and we spend so much time constructing the shield, that we simply forget what's at our core. We come to believe that the shell or shield we've built is real, is how we *should* be, and since being this way requires constant effort and attention, we know no other way than to live with anxiety, shame, guilt and frustration. Since living with these unhealthy dynamics is painful, we develop ways of being able to ignore them, living in denial and developing a stunning lack of self-awareness.

> *Our Shield of Pretence really becomes who we pretend to be – adopting the beliefs of others so that they accept us, being interested and motivated by being liked more than we want to be respected for who we are.*

Our Shield of Pretence really becomes who we *pretend* to be – adopting the beliefs of others so that they accept us, being interested and motivated by being liked more than we want to be respected for who we are. We pretend to be strong and confident. We pretend to like people we don't. We pretend to believe the same things that everyone else believes. We pretend to be happy and content, when deep down we are not. We pretend to be someone we are not – someone else.

And it's hard work. The amount of effort we have to put into maintaining this means we are lacking in time and mental capacity to challenge what's happening to us.

The craziest thing about all of this is that everyone else is pretending too! Every interaction we have with another human being is with the version of that person that they are pretending to be! There is simply no honest dialogue going on, which is why most conversations you will overhear are really just meaningless drivel, and maybe why it is so easy for us to escape into the virtual or digital world where our avatar can perhaps be the representative of our Golden Core.

And then we go to work... and at work we learn very fast how things are done – what behaviours, attitudes, beliefs and strategies are acceptable and which ones are not. None of these guidelines are written down, of course; even if our new workplace has a stated set of values or principles, it is unlikely that they will be used exclusively or effectively (or even at all!) to guide employees. No, it is the unwritten guidelines we pick up on very quickly, by watching others and through the immediate positive and negative feedback we get to our initial actions. We learn the particular management-speak and euphemisms of the company, and we watch as no one wants to ever make a decision. The culture infects us and causes us to behave contrary to our own core values – since we've come away from these anyway, we don't really notice. And since we've lost a sense of true self, it is hugely attractive for us to be part of the Borg in our new company, and so we take on the cultural values and behaviours with relish.

So at work, we exacerbate the schism between our Golden Core and our Shield of Pretence by adding a whole new level of corporate culture conformity.

When we connect with another person's Golden Core, we connect emotionally with them and open up a channel whereby we can have a core-to-core communication, verbal and non-verbal. We build a relationship where we are not allowing fear to cause us to 'play small', and where we are prepared to show vulnerability, to expose our true self in all its glory and with all its messiness, to another human being.

And in our corporation, if we are the right person, in the right role, at the right time, we instinctively connect our core to our company and to our individual role. We connect our personal integrity and our talents to the cause. Our communications internally then become an honest discourse between adult, expert, specialist professionals. Problems are identified clearly and solutions designed and executed.

Directive v consensual leadership

I believe there are only two styles of leadership:

1. Autocratic

- Directive, solution-providing, paternalistic
- At best – clear, explicit, trustworthy, safe
- At worst – intimidating, over-controlling, disempowering

2. Consensual

- Inclusive, involving, facilitative, coaching, delegating
- At best – empowering, communal, creative
- At worst – abdicating, absolving from responsibility, anarchic

Authentic leadership is then...

- The best combination of autocratic and consensual
- True to ourselves and to the cause

I believe that authentic leaders are without question the most effective. There are times when a leader must be non-negotiable. At such times it is inefficient and dishonest to pretend that you are genuinely asking for an opinion or an option, when you are in fact unprepared to consider anything, when the decision is already made.

On a prosaic level, if you need a report by 10.30 tomorrow morning for a meeting, then asking your colleague when they could get it to you is just a cop out, hoping they'll give you the right answer and that you won't have to ask them to do something without giving them a choice – God forbid issuing them an instruction. Asking them if they are able to get it for you for 10.30 is OK, and potentially more polite (since the inference is they are busy and might not be able to arrange things differently), but again only if you are prepared to accept the situation if they say that they can't. If you are genuinely giving them no choice, then be honest and issue them an instruction. It is entirely possible to do this and not cause any offence. *'Forgive me Charlie, I'm aware this will disrupt your plan, but I need the report for 10.30 tomorrow morning. I apologise that I've not organised myself properly, but please have it ready for me by then.'* No problem – of course, if you do this to people several times a day then they'll get very frustrated, but do it very occasionally and exceptionally and it really is no problem.

On a different level, where the decision you've made will really impact the person's life (rather than just their morning) then you still need to be clear. If you've decided that the person is leaving the company or their role then communicate this clearly and in a non-negotiable manner, and then move immediately to supporting them as they navigate the change you've forced upon them. *'Charlie, I need to inform you that I'm taking you out of your role as of today. Forgive me that I'm not discussing this with you or giving you an option or control over this. I've made the decision and it is non-negotiable. Given that you are leaving your role today, I'd now like to start the process of working with you to work out what happens next for you...'*

By the way, if you feel this approach is brutal or sounds particularly callous then all I can say is that the alternative in my view is way worse. I believe it is fairer for people to leave a room hurt, upset, angry but completely clear on what is happening, than it is for them to leave a room confused, anxious, uncertain but hopeful that things will actually be OK.

I find it very frustrating the number of times I've had a manager tell me that although a particular direct report is underperforming, in the wrong role, completely unqualified for the job they've been persuaded to do and unhappy in themselves, they are 'hoping' that their direct report gets the message over time and then decides for themselves to find another job. I despise such weakness in the name of being kind to others or allowing them their own dignity. The reality is that the manager's decision/position is 100 per cent communicated energetically to the direct report, dooming them to both increased failure and unnecessary stress.

Consensual leadership is pretty cool, and arguably where we should spend the vast majority of our time as leaders. After all if the vision and values are clear, and we've pretty much got the right people in the right roles, then they know what to do and when they get stuck, they can talk to each other, refer to guidelines and work out solutions and strategies.

I am a huge fan of this style. As a CEO myself, one of my favourite sayings was *'That's not my decision to make'*, before going on to ask some questions and encourage the person to make the decision they truly believed was the right one.

> *I characterise this as the I trust you, my door's always open, call me if you need me... approach – in my book this is a total abdication of responsibility*

But this style is not *passive* – it's a huge mistake to believe that being a consensual leader means always letting others do what they think is right without any intervention on your part. I characterise this as the *'I trust you, my door's always open, call me if you need me...'* approach – in my book this is a total abdication of responsibility on the part of the leader – not their responsibility necessarily to the company or situation or precise problem at hand, but an abdication of their responsibility to the other human beings involved.

If someone comes to you as their boss, manager, leader, coach and asks for help or guidance, it is because that's what they need. They do not need to be told what to do, or precisely what solution to execute and precisely how to execute it (although they may present in that way). So the 'Let me tell you what you need to do...' approach, while something of a natural habit in us problem-solvers and puzzle-breakers, is not appropriate.

They're at the edge of their comfort zone. They've thought of and tried all the obvious stuff. They're bright. They know that whatever they do next will involve them stepping outside their comfort zone.

This is where leaders really come into their own – as coaches and facilitators. These skills are dealt with in depth earlier in this book, but suffice to say that the leader needs simply to walk with the other person as they go outside their comfort zone, then hold their hand as they learn and grow while they are out there, then help them reflect on the experience. 'Walking with them' might mean pushing them, maybe even forcing them out of their comfort zone; 'holding their hand' might mean barring them from retreating back into their comfort zone once they are out there; 'helping them reflect' might mean pushing them to commit to an action or decision – notice these are not passive roles. Being in a relationship with someone as they go outside their comfort zone will certainly also make you feel uncomfortable. But this is where the work is really done. This is where progress is made. This is where learning and growth are sourced. And this is where our most profound partnerships and relationships of trust are forged.

It is the combination, the intelligent balancing of autocratic and consensual styles, that really make an authentic leader effective. It is this constant watchfulness of what's required that is palpable for followers and that engenders trust. Authentic leaders ask themselves one overriding question when posed a problem by another person – '*What does this person need from me right here, right now? An arm round the shoulder or a kick up the arse? Is it my job right here, right now to make them feel safe, or to force them to confront their fear? And in choosing my approach with them in this moment, how will I communicate what I am doing and why?*'

> **Authentic leaders ask themselves one overriding question when posed a problem by another person – 'What does this person need from me right here, right now?'**

We've seen that people trust our Golden Core. We've seen that people mistrust us when we come from our Shield of Pretence. But again this is simple human relationship stuff without the context of being in a corporation together.

Trust within corporations comes through the same medium, knowing that the leader is an 'authentic' human being. However, in order to trust them within context, we need to trust their competency as well – not to know for sure that they are always right, but never to have to question their motives being completely genuine and selfless. As Jack Welch said (see more on this below):

> *Trust is crucial. When a leader is trying to promote a major initiative or lead through a crisis, people cannot be embroiled in a debate about their sincerity. People may disagree on the merits of the plan, but never on their motives.*

Authentic leaders are passionate about making a personal difference – since they know themselves well, are really in touch with their own Golden Core, catch and correct themselves when they come from their Shield of Pretence, and know and are confident and proud of their unique talents, they are trusted in being the right leader, at the right time. The personal difference they can make is absolutely channelled into the right role.

And the role is right because they are passionate about the company's purpose, vision and values. They have taken on a role that truly has their name on it.

The greatest example of this for me personally was when I was asked if I would be considered for chairman of Longwood Park. The invitation was one of many that have come over the years, most of which I've said no to because they didn't touch me. But with Longwood I knew not only was it the right role for me, but I was absolutely the right person for *it*, and I am aware as I write these words that I must sound arrogant, but I can only express what I feel to be true for me. Coming from my Golden Core, I'll take the risk that you will judge me as arrogant and take the risk that you might reject me as a result. Because it is my truth.

> *Authentic leaders subordinate themselves to the cause and to the responsibility they've accepted – not in a way that excludes or overrides family, friends or external interests, but in a way that overrides their own ego and immediate self-interest.*

Because the role is right, and because they are passionate about the company's purpose and *raison d'être*, authentic leaders subordinate themselves to the cause and to the responsibility they've accepted – not in a way that excludes or overrides family, friends or external interests, but in a way that overrides their own ego and immediate self-interest.

Authentic leaders have high self-esteem and high EQ and are thus comfortable in showing humility and vulnerability, and in accepting the inevitable risk of personal criticism. Again these are the human qualities irrespective of context, so in a corporation I would expand this to say that authentic leaders have high CEQ.

They balance autocratic and consensual styles with a confidence, grace and humility. In their strategies, because they are naturally trusting of other people's Golden Cores, and because they know that organisational success is most likely assured when all involved are coming from that core, they have no issue with the natural corporate dilemmas of people versus results, control versus ambiguity, and maximising performance versus targets and KPIs.

As strategies, they focus on people and process rather than results, they trust that people growth equals business growth, and they trust that teams (not individuals) can and will solve any problem.

I want to return to the issue of authentic leaders having to take personal risks. It is inevitable that we cannot please all of the people all of the time. Indeed to attempt to do so would require monumental effort to the detriment of all other enterprise, and the very act of seeking constant consensus would ultimately be futile.

But what are we risking?

- ⊛ Authentic leaders see possibilities that others do not see, or do not want to see, and have a knowing and a belief that is seemingly unshakeable. *Leaders risk being accused of arrogance.*

- ⊛ Authentic leaders ask people to do things and achieve things that they do not know how to do themselves; that may even seem impossible or be 'beyond reason'. *Leaders risk being accused of unreasonableness.*

- ⊛ Authentic leaders constantly hector people with the purpose and the vision and are overt and passionate living examples of the values. *Leaders risk being accused of evangelism.*

- ⊛ Authentic leaders touch people emotionally, sharing intimate moments of joy and elation as they inspire others to go beyond their wildest dreams of performance. *Leaders risk being accused of seeking adoration.*

- ⊛ Authentic leaders put themselves forward as the public face and voice of the mission and the message, and allow themselves to be the embodiment, at times the icon if appropriate, of the cause. *Leaders risk being accused of narcissism.*

Chapter 7

Establishing the leader version of ourselves

Understanding ourselves

In order to understand ourselves, in order to best appreciate what our own Golden Core is, we need to go on a simple journey of self-discovery. We need to 'enquire within'.

I've been through many self-reflection exercises over the years, designed to establish personal core values. They are all pretty much the same. However, in 2001 I attended a retreat in Switzerland and I went through what for me became my defining personal enquiry. The difference this time was just one simple aspect: there was a question that asked about the unique qualities of one's parents – their individual qualities as mother and father. The hypothesis being that we are the finest synthesis of those individual qualities – that we are at our core the best combination of our mother and father, and that we hold the potential within us of being the living embodiment of a created being holding the finest qualities of those two unique souls who came together to create us.

As with many examples of research, enquiry or learning I've done over the years, I need a 'key', a 'hook' that inspires me and draws me into the whole process, and this was it. So I was inspired then to throw myself into completing the questionnaire as fully and openly as I possibly could.

Here's what I wrote in the section about my parents:

> From my mum I gained my love of and for people – respect, courtesy, fun, equality, service. Mum was a Samaritan at a time when you were not allowed to tell people for fear that they would not use the service when and if they needed to in case they got through to you. I remember at a very early age admiring this enormously – that here was someone doing good work for others, and yet she could not tell anyone to gain personal glory from it.

> From my dad I gained a healthy distaste for abuse of authority and for pomposity and self-importance. Dad always felt unfulfilled in his work, and yet he is so bright. He always found himself working for people who were 'not up to the job' and who's behaviour was status-driven.

> So this is what I am – the combination of the destiny of my parents. I love people – I love my relationships with people. I am compassionate, and yet I believe that people have to struggle to fulfil themselves. I abhor injustice and I detest people who exercise power and authority over others for their own self-important or egotistical ends, rather than for the love and support of the individuals they are responsible for leading. I empathise with people's struggles, fears and pain, yet I am intolerant of those who seek to blame others for their plight or who cannot muster their own inner positive thinking and turn that into proactivity.

What really struck me when I wrote this, was what I 'discovered' about my father, or perhaps what I felt about my father. Growing up I'd always felt that my father was a very passive parent. I remember him coming to watch me play football for the school only once, and he was not the sort of father who played games with me, either indoors or outdoors. At my most unkind, I characterised my father as the guy who sat in the corner of the room reading his paper. It was easy for me to appreciate and to articulate what my mum had given me, since she was the 'active' parent – the one who hugged, who talked, who encouraged, who disciplined. So writing about what I'd gained from my mum was straightforward and gave me nothing new, no new insights. When it came to writing about my dad, however, I was forced to analyse his role, his beliefs, his passivity. And what a lot there was to be newly enlightened about. I realised that his passive nature, which I had frequently criticised as his not really caring or being interested, was a really powerful and constant presence in my life, and how I had mistaken his trust in me for ambivalence. How wrong I was, and writing about my dad not only opened up a true potential for me to be the finest synthesis of my parents (and wouldn't that be a very special person to aspire to be), but it also changed my relationship with him.

At that time my mum had been dead for some 12 years. I decided that I wanted to take the opportunity of this insight to communicate to my dad what he meant to me, what he'd given me and just how profoundly appreciative I was. But remember this was a man that I didn't really talk to – we talked of course, but we didn't *talk*. That was what Mum did – she did the emotional stuff; it always seemed to embarrass Dad, and I had no desire to embarrass him.

So I wrote him a letter, telling him about the core values process I'd been through and enclosing a full copy of my completed questionnaire, obviously with the paragraphs above within. I'm not sure what I expected in response, but getting absolutely no response at all was not a surprise to me. I was a bit miffed, and had a slight anxiety over whether he'd actually received it (but not enough to ask him), but it was entirely in character for my father simply not to acknowledge it.

Twelve years passed, and in June 2013 my father passed away at the age of 91. As my brother and I went through the much-dwindled number of personal items he left behind, we came across the only two documents he'd kept safe – his passport and his will. Well, you wouldn't have expected anything less from a former officer with the Executor and Trustee Department of the Midland Bank.

And then to my surprise, out of the folded-up will dropped the letter I'd written him and the copy of my core values questionnaire I'd sent him all those years earlier. Not only had he kept it, he'd kept it with his most important documents. It was another example for me of how my father communicated without ever saying anything. He communicated by action, by gesture and by sheer example. One of my personal core values is 'constancy' and my father had that quality in spades. Everything

Everything I had been given by my dad I had received energetically and unconsciously. So much more profound and meaningful than mere words.

I had been given by my dad I had received energetically and unconsciously. So much more profound and meaningful than mere words.

Over the years I've developed and refined a personal core values questionnaire. There is nothing much original about it but you will see the 'Parental synthesis' section.

Personal core values process

As we progress through our work and life with our guiding principles unambiguously in our awareness, we can have the benefit of added clarity and power in our choices and actions. When we formulate a picture of ourselves that is both wide and authentic, we are then able to draw on the true heights of our creative power as contributors and as leaders. Powerful leadership requires authenticity, and authenticity requires self-knowledge.

The following exercises are designed to provoke reflection. There are no right or wrong answers, as the responses reflect your unique inner drives and principles. Clarity on these issues will assist in creating the clearing for a common endeavour at work that is totally aligned with your personal values, as well as supporting your personal goals and aspirations.

The process is not scientific and is not meant to be perfect, but rather to bring to the forefront of your awareness a broad sense of what really matters to you. This process can simply end there and be for your own reflection, or it can, through sharing with a coach and perhaps even through dialogue with close colleagues, come to form the foundation for the setting of an ambitious and exhilarating personal and professional future.

These exercises can be completed in under 30 minutes, or the process can be spread over a few days. Your choice. Either way they should be a joy to complete. That is not to say that they will be easy or that you will not have to go through some discomfort to complete them. You may feel some boredom or frustration. You may have to show diligence and commitment to complete them, but don't be disheartened if you need to spread completion over several different times. Let your thoughts flow freely. Write everything down at first – you can always edit later!

You will be asked to complete eight exercises, as follows:

Exercise 1: Parental synthesis

Exercise 2: Mentors

Exercise 3: Core values

Exercise 4: Leadership

Exercise 5: Defining experience

Exercise 6: Core purpose

Exercise 7: Vision and goals

Exercise 8: Reflection and commitments

Exercise 1: Parental synthesis

Think about the unique qualities of each of your parents – the positive strengths they exhibited and the principles they believed in. Some people believe that we are in fact a synthesis of the combined best qualities inherited and learned from our mother and our father, even in cases where we may not have had an opportunity to know one or either of them well. If that were to be true in your case, what beliefs and characteristics have you inherited from each of your parents? You can, of course, make this section about your primary carer if you did not know or were not raised by your parents, although I would encourage you still to acknowledge the genetic component as much as the nurturing.

Exercise 2: Mentors

Think about key individuals that you remember from your formative years – maybe up to and including your current job. Often we are lucky enough to come across someone special – a teacher, a first boss, a relation who takes a special interest in us – whom we admire or whom we aspire to be like. Who were these people in your life, and what were the qualities they possessed and beliefs they held that inspired your development and shaped your aspirations?

Exercise 3: Core values

Core values are the inner beliefs we hold most sacred. They rarely, if ever, change. We live our lives by them, even though we may be unaware of what they really are. When we fail to live up to them we get stressed and feel dissatisfied with ourselves. We frequently make compromises on these values and then seek to manage the situations that we find ourselves in. We may never have articulated our values to ourselves, let alone others. Working out what they are can be challenging, but here are a series of questions that will lead you to uncover them.

- What makes you angry, frustrated and irritated with other people?

- What are you doing and what is happening around you when you are at your most excited/at your happiest?

- What are the social issues that you feel most strongly about – in the UK/in the world – and why?

- If you had only one lesson to teach your children for them to carry with them through their lives, what wisdom would you pass onto them?

Now, how would you summarise your own personal values under a few headings?

Exercise 4: Leadership

In leading others, we unconsciously call on beliefs and principles to guide us. Believe it or not we have a strategy for everything we do as leaders; we are usually simply unaware. When we are clear about these beliefs and principles, we are better placed to perform consistently as a leader at the very highest levels, including having the courage to act when we know it will not be popular, thus inspiring people to follow us and use us as role models.

These simple questions will assist you in gaining clarity on your leadership beliefs.

- What are your fundamental beliefs about people at work?

- What are your fundamental beliefs about leaders at work?

- Who are the three leaders (whether personally known to you or not) you admire most and why?

- What qualities do they share?

Exercise 5: Defining experience

Think back to an event or achievement in your life (personal or work-related) that you would say was the greatest example of you at the height of your powers. Analyse *how* you did what you did – the mix of raw instinct, courage, planning, intellect, etc. Realise that you have successful strategies within your repertoire. Think about the single instance of time that was the most intense physical and emotional result of that event. Recalling the event should instantly reconnect you with those physical and emotional sensations, allowing you to 'use' the event as a defining experience for you to call upon when you need to motivate or inspire yourself – to use the memory or reliving of it as a source of ignition or fuel for new action.

Exercise 6: Core purpose

Our core purpose is our guiding star for meaningful action. It frames the context of our contribution in life. We may have a strong belief in this concept, or indeed we may eschew such notions. Either way, we can work out what purpose we are seeking to pursue as we live our everyday lives. Answering these questions will help you clarify your purpose. Don't be too concerned if your purpose is still not clear at the end – some people believe that our purpose is to spend our whole lives seeking to answer just this one question!

- What is the purpose of your life?

- What were you, uniquely, put on earth to do?

- If you could change three things about the way your industry works or is seen by others, what would they be?

- At the end of your career, what do you want your legacy to look like?

- If you could 'retire' today with no financial considerations, where would you choose to focus your talents? Why?

Exercise 7: Vision and goals

We have now considered our values and our purpose. What about our vision or our goals? A vision is a picture of what one aspires to achieve or become. Goals are specific targets or objectives that we set ourselves as milestones or markers on our path to achieving our vision. Again, we may be unclear about our vision, and we may simply set very short-term goals that are related to the more material elements in our lives. Answering these questions will assist in clarifying your vision.

- What makes you happy?

- What is it you really want in your life?

- What do you want to be doing in five years' time? In ten years' time?

- If you knew you were going to die in six months' time, what would you want to achieve to get your affairs in order or to complete any 'unfinished' business?

- What goals have you/would you set for yourself in each of the following areas of your life:

  - Financial

  - Health

  - Family

  - Friends

  - Work

  - Leisure

  - Learning

  - Social or community contribution?

Exercise 8: Reflection and commitments

Now you have completed all the exercises, what have you learned about yourself? What is clearer for you now? What commitments are you going to make to change something about your life?

When we know what the best possible version of ourselves looks like and behaves like, then we can constantly hold ourselves to account. We can truly hold the possibility and vision of our most creative future potential. We can ensure we are always 'on purpose'.

Purpose and values

No man will ever accomplish anything excellent or commanding except when he listens to this whisper which is heard by him alone.

Ralph Waldo Emerson

The meaning of life is that life has addressed a question to me.

Carl Jung

What are your personal purpose and values? Here are mine.

My purpose

To inspire leaders to implement practical strategies to lead all in finding purpose and joy in their work.

I wish it could be pithier – I've played with various versions of this over the years, and I've often tried to make it more punchy. But I simply cannot leave any element out. This is what I was born to do – or at least this is what my particular unique path and set of experiences and talents brought me to. And notice it is solely about work. I take issue with people who say that their purpose in life is to be, for example, the best husband and parent – for two reasons, first of all this is *not* a unique purpose. There are millions of people all over the world that could give this as their purpose, and for me that's missing the point of the exercise. Second, if that's it then what are we to make of our talents and our passions? Why has one person been given the ability to move people emotionally with their singing voice, when most others have not? Random chance it may be in the first place but the world needs each of us to seek to fulfil our potential. Of course it's OK for someone not to do this, if that is their conscious choice, but it's not OK for everyone to 'cop out'. No judgement here, notice!

My purpose happens to be about work. Now of course I can (and have) at times allowed this purpose to be over-consuming. I suffer no doubt from workaholism, although I still maintain that I will stun my friends and family one day when I simply stop. For good.

And let's break it down.

I *inspire* people. I have a real talent for this. I can touch people emotionally, see them for who they are, accept their flaws and fears, challenge them to strive, encourage them and be with them as they come out of their comfort zone. It is a gift I have. And while I can inspire anyone, my real core playing field is the workplace, and my experiences, credibility and personal confidence mean I am uniquely equipped to inspire *leaders*. I am never fazed meeting someone very senior. They are simply another human being, and actually it is highly likely that everyone else around them is coming from pretence when they deal with them, through their reaction to being intimidated by that person's status, power or reputation. I don't suffer from being intimidated. So I come from my core when I meet very senior people, and thus they feel the difference instantly. I make instant connections. I can have a connected conversation with a senior leader, almost with a degree of intimacy, within minutes of meeting them.

Implementing practical strategies is vital. Inspiring people is one thing, but nothing changes without action, and I am an intensely logical and practical person. I have a desire for things to be simple and effective. I have a passion for efficiency, and a loathing of wasted effort and resource. So it's not enough for me to 'simply' inspire leaders, making them feel warm and fuzzy in the process. That's actually not that hard. The hard part is helping them turn inspiration into practical and effective action.

Leading all their people is important – not just some. Not just the ones who would follow naturally, the early adopters, the self-starters, the ambitious, the brightest and the naturally talented. But the cautious, the scared, the damaged, 'the stubborn and the dull' as St Benedict rather affectionately labelled some, the hidden gems, the rough diamonds, the surprisingly talented, Shackleton's 'ordinary individuals'.

94

Finding purpose is at the heart of my corporate strategic work. Dan Pink categorises 'meaning' as one of the three motivating forces for people at work (the other two being autonomy and mastery) and Victor Frankel's book *Man's Search for Meaning* is perhaps my favourite inspirational story – harrowing and deeply upsetting at times, but for a living example of the sheer life-force of finding meaning in every situation it cannot be bettered. Workplaces without a sense of purpose are soulless, dehumanising environments, so leaders have the unavoidable responsibility to lead their communities in an inspiring common endeavour.

And finding *joy* might seem a slightly odd choice of final outcome – surely effectiveness or success would be more appropriate. But I am a believer of process and input over results and outcomes, since these are the only dynamics we stand any chance of controlling. So I know and trust that if people are experiencing joy in their work, they are at their most creative and resourceful and at their most efficient and effective.

At work – for this is my playing field. The world of work; largely the world of the corporation, since that is where I have lived for 40 years.

So I am very clear about my purpose and this helps me in two ways. First of all, I know that I personally experience the greatest fulfilment and joy when I am 'on purpose'; when I am engaged in activities that serve this purpose. I also know that I experience stress and frustration when I am engaging in work/paid activities that are not serving this purpose. So when I am frustrated or stressed and when I'm starting to sense a physical anxiety about me, I can check in with what I am doing and make a change.

Actually, of course, the greatest value for me personally is to check in before I commit to a project or assignment, to really help me with my acid test, '*Does this have my name on it?*' A sense of purpose also therefore helps me know when I hear a calling...

> *A sense of purpose also therefore helps me know when I hear a calling...*

Second, I gain confidence from knowing that what I am engaged in is serving my purpose, since I can be reasonably sure that I'm ably qualified and competent to do what is asked of me, even when I'm feeling some self-doubt. It helps me to have the courage to lead a client when I'm meeting resistance – to position myself as the expert to be listened to when the client naturally and understandably questions whether the 'risk' I'm asking them to take is really necessary.

My core values

I've done a lot of work on these over the years, enquiring, researching within myself and constantly refining. Interestingly, while it feels like they've been hugely refined over the years, these are pretty much the same ones I wrote in Switzerland in 2001, the only difference being that 'constancy' has replaced 'truth' during that time, although even then the content under that heading is largely the same as before.

In arriving at my core values I learned that we do not choose them or select them for ourselves – they are given to us, through our genes and through our upbringing; actually through our brain chemistry as our brains develop in early childhood and

> *In arriving at my core values I learned that we do not choose them or select them for ourselves – they are given to us, through our genes and through our upbringing*

adolescence. And this increases the sense of duty and responsibility to use them wisely and consciously.

So here they are – again I offer these to you not as a stellar example, nor as a guide as to what your values should be, but simply as a guide to your own process of defining your own personal values, and in all humility to demonstrate that we have uniqueness in us all. If I can know that I come from a remarkably ordinary place and background, can feel wholly ordinary in myself, and yet know and that I am also completely extraordinary, and I can show you the process, then I believe I will have been of service.

❀ Courage

❀ Commitment

❀ Leadership

❀ Optimism

❀ Respect

❀ Constancy

❀ Service

Courage

I believe that while our talents and our core integrity should come naturally and almost effortlessly to us, we cannot ignore the fact that we live in a world of risk and constant change. While we may not be in constant survival mode as we were 100,000 years ago, we are unlikely to be so fortunate as to be financially independent or even secure, and we are also having to constantly negotiate the often choppy waters of personal and family relationships and

> *So often 'doing the right thing' involves some form of risk or overcoming some very palpable fear.*

dependencies. So often 'doing the right thing' involves some form of risk or overcoming some very palpable fear. The reality may well be that the greatest threat any of us faces in a corporation is that someone will get a bit miffed with us today; it is unlikely we'll lose our job, and certainly no one is going to die. But fear is relative, and corporations are often places of high anxiety due to the nature of the beast and the environment within which they exist. And so courage is vital. Knowing this and knowing that courage is one of my core values, I gravitate to situations where courage is going to be required; where my leadership will be the critical factor in jumping so there is no way back.

Commitment

Commitment is a binary thing. There is no such thing as being 90 per cent committed. You are either all in, or you are not committed and this hesitancy will communicate itself.

So I take courage and head on in. I am aware that sometimes this can give me a false bravado, that at times I may take a risk almost for the sake of it. There may even be times when if the 'drug' is absent, I may get bored. I am not perfect and I am as open to egotism and selfishness as the next man. But I am aware when this happens – I know. My body tells me even if my head is in denial.

> Until one is committed, there is hesitancy, the chance to draw back, always ineffectiveness. Concerning all acts of initiative (and creation), there is one elementary truth the ignorance of which kills countless ideas and splendid plans: that the moment one definitely commits oneself, then providence moves too. A whole stream of events issues from the decision, raising in one's favor all manner of unforeseen incidents, meetings and material assistance, which no man could have dreamt would have come his way.
>
> William Hutchinson Murray – leader of Himalayan expedition,
> but probably originally by Johann Wolfgang Von Goethe

Leadership

I have been a leader since my earliest memories. I can get others to follow me. I love the limelight, I love performing. Ask me to stand up and speak in front of 1,000 people and my adrenaline will start flowing as I excitedly contemplate the sheer egotism of having the attention of a crowd. Whatever job I've done I've been given greater and greater responsibility within a few moments of starting. My first recollection was at age six being asked by my teacher to sit next to Ian Bushnell, a rather scruffy child in our class whose behaviour was disruptive. I didn't like him – not really because he was disruptive, but because I was angry that he was disrespecting the environment (OK I was six so I'm probably mythologising, but I believe that was what was going on for me). My teacher asked me to take some responsibility for him, and to help him engage. I took to my task with alacrity and suddenly I was able to muster some compassion for a kid who was struggling.

My teacher asked me to take some responsibility for him, and to help him engage. I took to my task with alacrity and suddenly I was able to muster some compassion for a kid who was struggling.

Working in a greengrocer's at the age of 12 and being allowed to take money from customers (my dream job was to place the brown bag of vegetables on the scales and then 'twirl' the bag closed with a flamboyant flourish of showmanship). Working summer holidays in a factory as a student and being asked to be a supervisor of a team of full-timers within a week; being a CFO with 60 people under me at 25; being a CEO at 32; being a plc chairman at 46.

And for the last 18 years I've supported hundreds of senior leaders in their own journeys of self-discovery and strategic development and execution. Leadership is my field of expertise but I also have profound beliefs about leadership, and a profound belief in how critical it is to changing the world for the better.

Optimism

I am not good with pessimists. I really struggle to hide my frustration with them. While I know that some people are born with cautious preferences, and/or have been through experiences that have caused them to be almost pathologically nervous and untrusting, I really struggle. For me, and remember I am an atheist, it is almost a blasphemy to be more focused on what's wrong or what could go wrong, than on what's beautiful or what's creatively and joyfully possible. They say that optimists believe we live in the best of all possible worlds, and pessimists fear this is indeed the case. Well I believe the world is a place of stunning beauty and potential, and that people are truly extraordinary. Yes the world is full of risk and constant change, and yes some people behave badly. But when I meet a pessimist I just feel like asking them why they bother? What's the point if all they see is risk? Having optimism as a stated core value helps me to be clear that I choose not to have pessimists around me, and helps me to not feel guilty about this. I love optimists. Optimists can make the wrong decision and still make things turn out well. Optimists know there is a solution, it's just that we've not found it yet. They turn every situation to their advantage, they see the silver lining in every cloud, they spot the diamond in every 'ordinary' human being, they see the potential for positive change in every crisis, and they accept that bad things will happen, that events will sometimes go against us, that random chaos will sometimes cause us to have to change course, but navigate those dynamics with an energy and enthusiasm for life that is infectious and inspirational.

> *For me, and remember I am an atheist, it is almost a blasphemy to be more focused on what's wrong or what could go wrong, than on what's beautiful or what's creatively and joyfully possible.*

Respect

One of the ways in which you can work out what your core values are is to pay attention to the things that make you angry. I abhor people disrespecting others. I am completely cool with disagreement, and I have no issue with someone who holds diametrically opposed views to me, as long as they hold those views honestly and without prejudice or malice or subjugation. So I have no issue with people of different political persuasions, since I can see that they hold their beliefs genuinely and sincerely. In my eyes, everyone is equal – we are all human beings, we just happen to have different skills, we just happen to have had differing opportunities, we just happen to have different market rates for our skills and talents. But we are no different, no better or worse than each other. I believe courtesy is a huge part of showing respect for another person. Taking conscious care not to harm or hurt them in any way, and in a more active manner, taking care to greet them and be in relationship with them in a courteous and respectful manner. There is never any excuse for rudeness or seeking to belittle someone – yes, of course, at times some people deserve this, and I have at times been guilty of indulging myself in delivering some searing, witty put-down, but I've always paid a price afterwards – that horrible self-loathing that comes from knowing that I've offended my own values.

I have at times been guilty of indulging myself in delivering some searing, witty put-down, but I've always paid a price afterwards

Constancy

When I first wrote my values in 2001, this value was labelled 'truth'. It contained stuff about honesty and reliability stemming from discovering and communicating the truth. But as time went on I knew that I actually had a bit of an issue with the word 'truth', since to have it as a value would mean that I was unable to lie, or not tell the truth and stay in integrity, and I believe there are times when the 'truth' is not appropriate, may even be wholly self-serving. And what is 'the truth'? What is a fact? In reality there is my view of a situation and there is your view, and believing in absolute truth can also lead us into arguments of 'right and wrong'. So I began to dig into what was really at the core of this for me, and I discovered that it was really about my being a constant presence, force or influence in people's lives. Reliable, but more than that – constant. Being a force for safety and sanctuary for people I care about, so they know they can rely on me 100 per cent, which is not about being 100 per cent truthful with them 100 per cent of the time, but is about absolute trust and reliability, meaning they have access to that power even if they choose not to ask something tangible of me or even speak with me. The greatest example of this for me is my relationship with my children. I want Steph and Tom, and more latterly Duncan and Leonie, to know in their bones that I am there supporting and encouraging them even when I am thousands of miles away or we've not spoken for some time. They know that this is nothing to do with money, or bailing them out or rescuing them; I hope they know it's about what I would say if they asked my opinion, what I would think of them if they acted in a certain way, how I would be positive and encouraging and accepting of them no matter what situation they find themselves in,

Being a force for safety and sanctuary for people I care about, so they know they can rely on me 100 per cent, which is not about being 100 per cent truthful with them 100 per cent of the time, but is about absolute trust and reliability, meaning they have access to that power even if they choose not to ask something tangible of me or even speak with me.

so I am a constant and unshakeable force in their lives. And I try to bring this to my client relationships. I want my clients to know the level of care I feel for them and that I exercise towards them, that is available for them to call on whether tangibly or unconsciously and energetically. This is why I have become very much more 'choosy' over the years as to who I will work with, because I want to work with people I care about or can come to care about. There is also something in constancy for me about continuous improvement – that I must continually learn and seek knowledge and experience and be constantly better at everything I have responsibility for.

Service

This is probably the value where I get closest to a form of religious zealotry. I am an atheist, but I feel incredibly spiritual. There is not 1 per cent of me that even entertains the possibility that we were created by a superior intelligence who is still pulling all the strings. And yet I have a profound belief in human and natural connection, and in the responsibility in all of us to understand and utilise our talents for the good of humanity and the whole natural world. I am enormously grateful, humbled by how fortunate I am – to be who I am, where I am and when. I am mightily blessed, and I profoundly believe this endows me with a responsibility to give of myself. One way I believe I can show my gratitude is to give service to others, indeed to look at every situation as an opportunity to be of service. From small random acts of kindness (often cited as the most effective form of therapy) to taking on commitments. I am here to help others to get the best out of themselves and to feel the joy of striving to fulfil themselves – I am here to serve. Thus it offends me when I see someone with privileges wasting the talents they've been given, and I find it abhorrent when hugely blessed individuals use all their efforts to shut others off from their wealth in all its guises.

I am acutely aware that I've just described a cross between Mother Teresa and Nelson Mandela, and that you may well be thinking *'What an arrogant ****'*. I'll take that risk in expressing my innermost beliefs and thoughts. I offer my personal example to you as a guide of process, not content. And please understand that I am not trying to tell you that I live 100 per cent by these values. I am human, I am flawed, I have an ego, I can be selfish, lazy and mischievous. There are times when if you observed me you might say my values were in fact pedantry, revenge, one-upmanship and egotism. And you'd be right (I am a pedant and proud).

> **I am human, I am flawed, I have an ego, I can be selfish, lazy and mischievous. There are times when if you observed me you might say my values were in fact pedantry, revenge, one-upmanship and egotism.**

The real point for me is that I am acutely aware when I slip, and so my values really help me to live a life, not of a saint, but of someone who is much better these days at being calm, anxiety-free and able to live with myself. Knowing my values so intimately also means that I can make conscious decisions on compromises, and then act accordingly, often meaning I am able to communicate clearly with people in advance of action or in anticipation of predictable difficulties that will arise.

You'll notice that an oft-quoted favourite value 'integrity' is not listed above. There's a good reason for this in that many people cite 'integrity' as one of their core values or principles, and I find myself taking issue with them, since integrity is not in itself a core value. Acting with integrity is of course incredibly important, but for me it's a given – a prerequisite for actually communicating a set of values in the first place. Why communicate values unless you have the intention of adhering to them or at the very least striving to be true to them?

Integrity is, according to the Oxford English Dictionary, *'Uncompromising adherence to a code of moral values'*. So for me it's about acting with integrity, whatever your values may be. And I believe this is when we are trusted – when we are coming from our Golden Core and acting in line with our core values. I believe we have a natural and instinctive ability to detect this, through the unconscious energetic communication that passes between us. Sometimes this is pheromones, and sometimes this is brain chemistry such as adrenaline or dopamine.

I believe that when I am acting in integrity I am emitting positive energy to everyone I come into contact with and that they feel better about themselves; that I am emitting encouragement that helps people to feel that whatever is before them is possible and worth going for; that I am emitting an enthusiasm that is infectious and fuels them to act.

My Golden Core and my values are my source of self-esteem and self-confidence, and I know that whatever I do with confidence, with style, flair and panache, is highly likely to succeed.

Establishing the 'leader' version of ourselves

There's a running debate as to whether leaders are born or made. This question is usually posed by people who are in the business of selling leadership training, and therefore their answer is invariably that leaders can be trained.

While I would not wish to denigrate the practice of leadership development, I believe it plays into the old model of leadership being located only in certain individuals (and by definition, therefore, only at certain hierarchical levels or roles), and of leadership requiring some form of rational or intellectual component – that leadership is about making decisions and getting others to follow. I believe everyone has leadership capabilities given the right circumstances and situations. Everyone is at times a leader. Everyone at times needs to be a leader.

And I believe that while leadership often requires a considered decision to be made and executed, it is actually more often about changing the course of a single moment or situation. We understand leadership in the example of a powerful individual making a decision and then getting people to carry out the necessary ensuing actions. But leadership is also the quiet person in a meeting finally holding their hand up, saying they disagree with the direction the meeting is going in, holding a moment's silence, and then watching as every other person comes to the realisation that they are right. That person may not speak again that day – but at the moment they intervened, they were exercising leadership. They changed the course of events.

> *while leadership often requires a considered decision to be made and executed, it is actually more often about changing the course of a single moment or situation.*

Here are the leadership principles and beliefs of four very varied leaders. But before I present these four examples to you, I want to offer a disclaimer:

✪ Three of the four examples are male. So while this is not completely gender-balanced, this ratio does represent the gender ratio of my personal experience with leaders in the corporate world. Also only one of the four examples is personally known to me, and that leader is female.

- Since two of the examples are from a bygone era, the language is not gender neutral – I ask you to accept the language in good faith.

- There are many religious references, and predominantly Christian at that. I am aware there are other religions, but I am not a 'tokenist' and as such I did not search for a more balanced sample.

And to this illustrious four, I've then added my own – not because I hold myself in the same league, but since I am able to use myself as an example through the process I am outlining for readers, without sounding pious, as an example of how us ordinary mortals can still become extraordinary as leaders if we can only work out who we are, what we believe and how we will behave.

Jack Welch

While I am by no means Jack Welch's biggest fan, and history is perhaps still taking stock of whether he was great or not, I still love the clarity and pragmatism of his principles as stated here. And he is the author of one of my very favourite quotes, when he said of empowerment:

If you teach a bear to dance, you better be ready to dance until the bear gets tired.

I often quote this to leaders looking to empower their employees or workforces, as a form of warning to them: don't start unless you are willing to see it through to the end, because it's like a bungee jump – once you've launched there is absolutely no going back. You will be out of control – so only jump if you are serious and know what you are letting yourself in for.

Authenticity

- Trust is crucial. When a leader is trying to promote a major initiative or lead through a crisis, people cannot be embroiled in a debate about their sincerity. People may disagree on the merits of the plan, but never on their motives.

The vision thing

- Leaders must know when to improvise, but ultimately a clearly conceived, inspirational mission is critical. It means making the case, until your tonsils bleed, with a story that says, '*Here's how our destination will make life better for our customers and for you personally*'.

Hire great people

- Not just hire them but utilise them; challenge them for new ideas and deeper insights. Leaders also need the courage to dispatch managers who fall short, whatever the risk to the short-term results.

Resilience

- The capacity to bounce back after defeat without feeling defeated. Leaders regularly get the wind knocked out of them. The best leaders learn from their mistakes and get right back into the saddle.

See around corners

- Leaders need to anticipate unforeseen events. Leaders can feel market shifts in their fingertips. They need to act quickly, influencing the blind and galvanising support from all stakeholders.

Execute

- It doesn't matter whether a leader generates action or channels it through others. What matters is that promises get kept and plans get completed.

Giavania, Nobel Peace Prize nominee

I had the great fortune of meeting Giavania in 2005 in her own community, a small town some 400 miles into the heart of the semi-arid desert region of north-east Brazil, founded 200 years ago by a small group of slaves who escaped their captivity. In order to get there, we had to take an overnight bus ride and it was quite disconcerting to leave the almost Caribbean atmosphere of Orlinda early one evening, and wake up some ten hours later in a scene from a spaghetti western. The first thing I saw getting off the bus was tumbleweed blowing down a dusty mud road in the approach to the town. I swear I heard the Sergio Leone whistle from *The Good, the Bad and the Ugly* in my head.

The community had grown to a small town of several hundred people, carving a dusty and meagre existence from the parched land. Giavania, a young woman in her late twenties, was the elected leader – she had been sent away by the village elders to Sao Paulo for her education, in readiness for the fight ahead – a fight against powerful landowners encroaching inexorably on the borders of the town. The night before we arrived, for example, some land on the edge of the town had been stripped of its crops, simply as an act of sabotage and intimidation. Giavania, through an amazing simultaneous interpreter, told us that she had to constantly seek the support of central government to protect their land. It was election time, and there were posters with her face on stuck up throughout the village. She had to deal with political realities as well as external forces, and she often slipped into sounding very much the consummate politician.

> *Giavania, a young woman in her late twenties, was the elected leader – she had been sent away by the village elders to Sao Paulo for her education, in readiness for the fight ahead*

I asked her what she believed was the secret of success for a leader, and she responded without hesitation – I guessed afterwards that as a Nobel Peace Prize nominee, she had probably had to rehearse her responses to such questions, but I was also struck by the politician's skill of oratory and rhetoric. I loved the simplicity and the emotion of what she said, but also the wisdom.

Set the historical context

🌐 It's not enough to tell people where you are going, you have to honour where they have come from.

Share leadership

🌐 Don't do everything yourself – ensure others take responsibility.

Fall in love with your cause

🌐 Love is unreasonable; it is only this that will give you the courage to do what is needed.

Ernest Shackleton

In many people's eyes, of course, Shackleton was a failure, albeit a rather glorious one in that rather British underdog sort of way. In 2000 I read Caroline Alexander's account of Shackleton's Antarctic expedition and I was struck by three things. First the sheer scale of his endeavours and efforts to save his men once their mission to get to the South Pole was abandoned. What they achieved as a team was both Herculean in proportion and near-miraculous in outcome. Second, his experience of feeling the presence of God with him at the lowest moment of his journey is probably the closest this atheist has come to considering that just maybe there is some intelligent force bigger than us. Finally his principles and beliefs just connected so deeply with my own.

Shackleton's popularity among those he led was due to the fact that he was not the sort of man who could do only big and spectacular things. When occasion demanded he would attend personally to the smallest details. Sometimes it would appear to the thoughtless that his care amounted almost to fussiness, and it was only afterwards that we understood the supreme importance of his ceaseless watchfulness. Behind every calculated word and gesture lay the single-minded determination to do what was best for his men. At the core of Shackleton's gift for leadership in crisis was an adamantine conviction that quite ordinary individuals were capable of heroic feats if the circumstances required; the weak and the strong could and must survive together. The mystique that Shackleton acquired as a leader may be partly attributed to the fact that he elicited from his men strength and endurance they had never imagined they possessed. He ennobled them.

> **At the core of Shackleton's gift for leadership in crisis was an adamantine conviction that quite ordinary individuals were capable of heroic feats if the circumstances required**

St Benedict

Finally, I give you St Benedict from 1,500 years ago. There are remarkably few religious leaders that I would offer up as great examples. However, in 2001 I spent a few days at a Benedictine monastery courtesy of Father Dermot Tredgett. I liked Dermot the moment I met him, as he had to interrupt our initial discussion to take a business call on his mobile phone. Father Dermot, as well as being a practising Benedictine monk and peripatetic parish priest, was an advocate for spirituality in business, and spent time working in the business community presenting on the subject, running leadership workshops and inviting business leaders to residential retreats within the monastic community.

Father Dermot introduced me to the rules of St Benedict, in particular the 'Qualities of the Abbot' – a set of guidelines for the election of a new abbot from within the ranks of the brothers, since that is how abbots are elected. When Father Dermot took me through these (and the ones I've transcribed here are simply a small extract – the best ones, I believe, however), again I was inspired by the poetry, the pragmatism, the wisdom and the sheer ordinariness considering the lofty elevation of the role in question in terms of both hierarchy and closeness to the divine.

> *I was inspired by the poetry, the pragmatism, the wisdom and the sheer ordinariness considering the lofty elevation of the role in question in terms of both hierarchy and closeness to the divine.*

- He must point out to them all that is good and holy more by example than by words, proposing the commandments of the Lord to receptive disciples with words, but demonstrating God's instructions to the stubborn and the dull by a living example.

- He must vary with circumstances, threatening and coaxing by turns, stern as a taskmaster, devoted and tender as only a father can be.

- Goodness of life and wisdom in teaching must be the criteria for choosing the one to be made abbot.

- His goal must be profit for the monks, not pre-eminence for himself.

- Excitable, anxious, extreme, obstinate, jealous or over-suspicious he must not be – such a man is never at rest.

- He must so arrange everything that the strong have something to yearn for and the weak nothing to run from.

Nearly 1,500 years on, I think if every leader took cognisance of these six principles, they wouldn't go far wrong!

And now for my own

- Act like you just took over

- Trust employees with the truth

- Set ambitious goals

- Don't rescue people from events

- Stamp out 'them' and 'us'

- Radical comes before drastic

- Be a game-changer, not a seat-filler

- The vision is the boss

- Celebrate mistakes

- Point people at process

While these may not be the most poetic in the world, they have been refined and refined and refined over the years, and so they really feel like they've been tested and proven. And they really are mine – very personal to me.

Act like you just took over

All leaders know that their replacement would come in with new energy, fresh perspective and absolutely no emotional baggage. Leaders often get bogged down the longer they're in post – the experience, history and sheer knowledge they learn and accumulate in the role are clear advantages, of course; however, the longer they are in the role, the more problems leaders feel responsible for, and the less objectivity they seem capable of. The new guy, of course, would have the luxury of a honeymoon period, and of being able to criticise the past mistakes and obvious strategic flaws. So what would your immediate successor do? What would they immediately suspend or cancel? What changes would they make to strategy or structure? And in answering these questions, notice how easily the responses come. And then notice how hard it is to contemplate making these decisions yourself, for all the emotional reasons that come up. But if it's right...

I sometimes play a game with execs I am coaching. I ask them what's happening within their business that they might deem 'unacceptable'. They can often tell me without much thought or reflection, since invariably there are things happening that should not be, and things happening that consistently frustrate them. They may even volunteer the phrase '*and that was/is completely unacceptable*' without me having to initiate it. I then simply ask them why they are indeed accepting it. This elicits the fatuous response of either '*I'm not...*' or '*Well, when I say unacceptable...*' The first is dishonest and the second is denial.

- What is happening on your watch that you would acknowledge to be 'unacceptable'?

- So why are you in fact accepting this? What fear is stopping you from tackling this?

- Why if this is 'unacceptable' to you, is it not just non-negotiable?

You see, your successor would have no issue in stamping this out or firing the person, or at the very least making it explicitly clear that this was *never* to happen again. So what's stopping you? Railing against something within the business that you lead is an illegitimate indulgence. Sort it out.

Trust employees with the truth

I see many leaders seeking to hide the truth from their followers. They mistakenly believe that it is their job to protect their people from things that they don't need to know, to keep secret information that would only cause people anxiety if they were to know, that might even create panic or flight. This is a very dangerous thin end to a catastrophic wedge. It all comes down to two things – not trusting people and not wanting to be personally uncomfortable. So the argument goes like this – if we tell people, they'll leave and so we cannot take that risk. If we tell people, they'll blab and so we cannot take that risk. If we tell people, they won't understand anyway so there really is no point. Leaders convince themselves, believing it is part of the 'burden' and loneliness of leadership, and justifying their withholding of information on commercial grounds. If leaders have put 'professional' support executives around them, these voices may well be advising them to keep secrets, and as a leader should you not trust the people you've appointed to those posts? You cannot go around overruling your chosen professional advisers all the time. So your HR director may earnestly and in many ways correctly advise that giving the employees information about an impending round of redundancies is simply not in line with employment law. Your company secretary may advise that informing the employees of a forthcoming investment before announcing this to investors and analysts is not in line with the combined code (corporate governance). And yet the right thing to do is treat people as human beings and give them the information. People are amazing. Tell them the truth and let them start to help change the situation or solve the problem. They won't leave, and any that do leave were not going to be effective anyway. They won't blab, and any that do won't necessarily be heeded anyway.

Leaders convince themselves, believing it is part of the 'burden' and loneliness of leadership

A few years ago I was coaching a senior executive with a national retailer, and he was about to announce the closure of a distribution depot employing 2,000 people. His human instinct was to stand in front of these 2,000 people and tell them the truth. His HR advisers, however, told him he could not do it that way because of employment law. His company secretarial advisers told him he had to legally announce to the City first. These were powerful and really compelling voices. They were not to be denied. They carried the weight of the law. But my client's values and leadership won the day. He told his advisers that he *would* stand in front of 2,000 people and tell them the truth, and that it was up to them to design and arrange everything else in the process to keep the company legal.

The result? A remarkably smooth change. Not devoid of pain and hurt of course, but the vast majority of the 2,000 people affected stayed and assisted the process. They kept their dignity, and they behaved as reasonable human beings. And my client was received like some sort of messiah! They loved him for the care he had taken. The reality was that the announcement of the closure was not a surprise to anyone. All 2,000 people had pretty much been expecting the news, so while they still suffered the shock of it now being final, and still had to navigate the hurt and uncertainty, they were able to appreciate being able to plan, and to appreciate that, for once, someone had treated them like human beings and had trusted them with the truth.

In 15 years of inviting factory floor workers to attend board meetings, I have not ONE instance of them breaking confidentiality. I wish I could say the same of my fellow Directors.

Pehr Gyllenhammar

Gyllenhammar would say, why would a factory floor worker betray company secrets? These guys make Volvos and are proud of making Volvos. They've done it for years, their father may also have done it, their son may do it one day. They want nothing more than for Volvo to survive, succeed and thrive, and they will do whatever they can to support this. These guys are almost akin to owners, with a stake, an investment in the future. They would never betray a confidentiality. Directors, on the other hand, are more like hired guns who can sell their professional services to anyone, and who frequently decide to do just that. They are often more interested in their own status, ego or CV than in the true good of the company. They would betray a confidence in a heartbeat if able to justify it to themselves for the most spurious of excuses.

In my very first CEO role, I set up a 'Foreman's Meeting' – chaired by one of their own group, and tasked with keeping us senior managers sane. Everything we wanted to do was run past this group first. And they were encouraged to bring things to us that they believed were important to change or pay attention to. They ran the day-to-day business, leaving the senior managers to focus on culture, strategy and growth.

As a plc divisional MD, when doing monthly dealership accounts reviews at the various outlets, I started a practice of inviting two employees from the dealership to be in attendance in rotation. Nothing was hidden. I would sit next to them and take time during meetings to explain certain things to them. I banned management-speak and so we talked in plain English. At times we had to work to not patronise, and there is always a risk in setting up a potentially patronising environment. But it's a risk worth taking. I'd rather have to apologise for being patronising than not try and explain something.

So while leaders will frequently use 'commercial confidentiality' as their excuse, the second aspect of leaders not telling employees the truth is the real one – leaders simply don't want the discomfort involved. They fear the reaction, not in commercial terms, but in human terms.

Get over it – it goes with the territory. I learned very early on that many people would think I was an idiot. If I was going to be a change agent, my decisions would upset people along the way. I would have to accept that I would be the lightning rod for the very real and understandable emotions that are released as people navigate change and loss. Thankfully I also learned very early on not to put energy into a futile and fatuous attempt to win the respect of people that I did not respect myself.

Set ambitious goals

There's no real point in working for an enterprise that's got no vision or ambition. People want to work for a company that they can be proud of and that has plans and ambitions for the future. So having and being able to communicate a vision is critically important, as this is the emotional story that people attach to. But you need also to set a goal, an ambitious goal, something that is an icon or symbol of the vision or mission we've signed up for.

Kennedy's 'man on the moon' goal was a terrific example. While massive in itself, it simply focused on one small area of American progress – space exploration. It was nothing to do with health, education, equality or peace. And yet it caught the mood and became the icon or symbol of all other aspects of American life. It unified the country. It communicated on so many aspects of life that were troubling America at that time. It was an extraordinary goal to set, and it's not outrageous to suggest that it was a huge factor in America's ultimate success.

People love to work for a leader who has ambition and a confidence around that ambition. People love to work for an organisation that has ambition. When asked who they work for, all people need is a story they can tell that makes them proud. And part of this is instant recognition – '*I work for company X, we are the people who make Y*' – and part of it is future inspiration – '*I work for company X, we are the people who are working to…*'

The trick is to pick something that on first hearing causes people to react with surprise, uncertainty and even hesitancy, characterised by a '*Wow, really? That seems impossible. You really think we could do that?*', but after a moment's reflection sets up a connection to a logical or rational thought, characterised by a '*But actually why not? It makes sense for us to be the ones who could go for that. Maybe we could achieve it. Wow, let's start!*'

Don't rescue people from events

There will be '*events, dear boy, events*' (Harold Macmillan) that are completely outside of our control as leaders… And these events will require us to make major shifts in our strategies and plans that will in turn affect the working lives of our people.

These things are not our fault. Of course, we may bear culpability for not predicting the obvious, or for not having contingency plans, but if the environment we are in suffers a cataclysmic and wholly unpredictable event, we are not personally to blame, and we should not seek to protect people from the uncontrollable. I remember as a very young manager meeting someone on holiday that I had met the previous year in the same resort. He'd been made redundant and when I asked him about it he said that it had been a terrible shock and had made him depressed. He was scathing about management. I asked him what the company did and he replied that they had made pit props (this was the mid-1980s). I remember thinking, well if you didn't see that one coming… He might well have been correct to be critical of management, and he had every right to feel sadness and anxiety over the event, but I couldn't help thinking that the whole company must have been in collective denial, from top to bottom.

If something happens that is outside your control that is going to impact your employees, it is not your job to rescue them. It is your job to lead them, but it is also their responsibility to look after themselves, by making changes in their own lives to handle the impact of the event and the change.

> *If something happens that is outside your control that is going to impact your employees, it is not your job to rescue them. It is your job to lead them*

Stamp out 'them' and 'us'

Of the myriad things that can happen in an organisation, not much makes me angry. But this one does. I cannot stand people who seek to divide us into 'them' and 'us' and I *will* stamp this out. I am very clear that this is non-negotiable for me. As a manager, this will get you fired if you persist. On its largest and most obvious scale, this will present as management versus employees, or sales versus marketing, or supply chain versus procurement, or head office versus sites. It is a classic distraction tool for people to blame others, and since naming actual human beings might involve having to take action, it's so much easier to generalise. I cannot tell you the number of times I will hear some intangible entity blamed – 'group', 'finance', 'HR', 'head office', 'the States'.

My reaction is to ask a simple question – *'Who?'* I'm looking for a name, since once you give me a name, I can ask you what conversation you've had with that person, that human being. But if you tell me that a building, or a town, or a group of people have done this to you, you can both apportion blame for your misfortune and absolve yourself of any responsibility for changing, since there is clearly nothing to be done.

The most insidious use of this excuse is where it is used in advance. This is where the person hasn't even asked the question, since they feel they know that the answer would be no. *'Head office would never allow it.'* My blood is now boiling. I have countless examples where 'they' have been set up in someone's mind to be such ogres on absolutely no evidence whatsoever. I have some sympathy with people if they fear a reaction from someone who intimidates them, but so often where I have challenged the fear with questions such as *'And what happened the last time you went to them with such a request?'* or *'What's the most recent example of that person doing that to you?'*, I am told that there are no examples. It is simply a fear – what I would call a spectre in this case: a *'mental representation of a haunting experience'*, according to the dictionary. In other words, a convenient illusion of fear.

And this can easily become a cultural collusion – if we all agree with each other that head office are the bad guys, then we will collude with each other to make it so, and we will sympathise with each other at every example of their stupidity and intransigence. So much easier than taking responsibility and changing things.

Radical comes before drastic

As leaders we often have to take big decisions. In some ways this is our greatest calling, since on a day-to-day basis the managers and employees are far better at running the company, solving the problems, continuously innovating and improving, delighting the customers and generally executing the plan. Interestingly some people really come into their own in a crisis. You see, in a crisis, we have no choice but to act, to take some risks, to break some china, to go on raw instinct rather than overthink things. And some leaders will cheerfully (albeit often unconsciously) create a crisis so they can ride in and save the day. In a crisis we have no choice, and so it's quite convenient to have a crisis every now and again to give ourselves the excuse of acting. When drastic action is required, we often have no problem acting drastically. But for me this is lazy and melodramatic. The danger with waiting for a crisis is that it will come too late. The danger in creating one is that it will be based on a lie and people will know this and mistrust the situation (and you).

So I believe that radical comes before drastic. Radical is the time period just before drastic action might become necessary. The beauty of acting radically rather than drastically is that a) we can make a coherent and well researched and tested plan and b) we have the oppor- tunity to be creative and to therefore generate a great

Radical is the time period just before drastic action might become necessary.

deal of positive energy for the change. Drastic means operating from fear and on adrenaline. Radical means operating from excitement and on endorphins. I believe it is a major job of the leader to be constantly scanning the horizon for threats and opportunities, and then to bring options to the table for radical strategies and actions.

Be a game-changer, not a seat-filler

I love the concept of stewardship as a leader. More on this below, but there is only one person in your role at this moment in time – you are *it*. And the role is important and demands to be discharged to the very best of your ability. And it is a leader- ship role – a role, therefore, by definition that involves you instigating and certainly navigating change. There is no place for someone to simply occupy the role. Who went before you? What stage of the journey must you steward your part of the organisation through? Change things, make progress, innovate, do your best. Do not

get seduced by the status of the role, nor the trappings of the office. Do not play cautious and safe on the basis that as long as you do no harm and leave things organised and ordered, you'll have done OK. An empty chair can do that. Are you earning the return on invest- ment the company is making in your role, or would the company be better off saving the money and allowing your deputies to simply do their best without a leader? I often ask my clients '*What would happen if you didn't do anything?*'; in other words '*What difference are you*

Do not play cautious and safe on the basis that as long as you do no harm and leave things organised and ordered, you'll have done OK. An empty chair can do that.

making?' Now I'm really happy if you don't interfere in the day-to-day, so in answer to my question, please don't respond with a litany of micro-management tasks you are involved in personally. That's just doing the job of the people below you, which is expensive and massively inefficient. No, bring me back to the purpose of your role – to why this area of the business needs a steward. And go change the game – do not sit on your arse and take the money.

The vision is the boss

I am acutely aware that much of what I believe and write about on the subject of leadership could be said to play into a rather old-fashioned view of leaders being powerful, charismatic and indispensable individuals, without whom the world would fall apart. I am wary of this, since I know only too well the risk of corruption (in the truest sense of that word) that goes with this dynamic. Who am I to say I'm right when I decide something that affects thousands of employees? Who am

I to autocratically impose change on other human beings that will seriously affect their livelihoods and even maybe their health and their whole futures? Who am I to exercise such God-like power? What makes *me* right? What *gives* me the right? I've been round this loop so many times, and all I keep concluding is that leadership *is* vital.

Therefore, it must be placed in the hands of those who can best exercise the power and responsibility that goes with it, which comes back to the right person, for the right role, at the right time.

But we can also put some governance structures around the leader to keep that leader honest and to keep them safe from the temptations that will come their way. A proper chairman, a proper board of non-executives or trustees (a proper coach?) and a written mandate that states the leader's responsibility. I deal with the construction and design of vision and values statements in another section, but suffice to say here that the leader needs a clear vision, not just to be able to communicate this and inspire followers to action, but to be held accountable to.

> *Because the CEO is not the boss – the CEO is simply the steward of the mission for a period of time. The vision is the boss. It's the vision we all serve, not a single individual, however charismatic or inspirational they may be.*

Because the CEO is not the boss – the CEO is simply the steward of the mission for a period of time. The vision is the boss. It's the vision we all serve, not a single individual, however charismatic or inspirational they may be. Don't act because I'm asking you to, don't act because you need to show you're busy; act only in service of the vision. If what you are about to do does not serve the vision, don't do it. And if a manager uses personal persuasion to get you to do something that you feel is wrong, check against the vision, and if it doesn't pass the test, push back. Have the courage to say to your manager that you believe you are being asked to do something that goes contrary to the vision.

And as leader be careful of asking people to do things *for you*, because they should never be motivated in that way. The vision is the boss, it's the vision we serve. As a leader I'm always striving to be 'on purpose' which both helps me with my self-regulation in being consciously intentional in my dealings with people, and helps me always remember it is the cause that I serve, and that all around me are doing their passionate best to serve also. This harks back to my beliefs on authentic leadership, being the combination, the synthesis of the right person at the right time. Of being authentic as a human being, of knowing the leader version of ourselves and being clear on the organisation's mission and purpose. Always being 'on purpose' is about always being true to one's own personal purpose and values, and always serving the purpose of the organisation.

You'll see the Banbury Therapy Centre's vision quoted in a section later on. We worked hard to create the vision when we founded the organisation so we had something bigger than the individual founders. We use the vision actively. I read an article in a local business magazine recently featuring the centre, and some of the employees had been interviewed. None of the founders were interviewed. And there it was in the article – the quote from one of the employees talking about the centre's vision, with the words '*as we always say at the Centre, the vision is the boss – this is what we all serve*'. A proud moment.

Celebrate mistakes

I've talked earlier about my own profound learnings from teachers, mentors and bosses who have handled my mistakes with grace, acceptance and humour. As leaders we should actively look for people making mistakes, and reward them instantly for their striving and their courage and their creativity. There will be instances where people make mistakes through carelessness and negligence and when they will therefore need strong feedback and even consequences. But if we've built the environment correctly, these instances will be rare, and even then only come about because people are exhausted or overwhelmed, and they must be met with compassion and understanding.

Point people at process

We will have worked hard to design and refine sound processes within the business – from information systems, to production processes, to people management, to monitoring systems, to values, to coaching. All we have to do is make sure that people are using the processes. If they use the processes, the business will work beautifully. So a favourite question of mine when presented by someone with a problem is to ask about the process. Frequently the question in itself is sufficient to get them going away reflecting on what the process is and how they can best engage in using it. If the answer they give is that the process does not work, I can challenge them to make it work by using it, or I can ask them what the process is for changing the process – because there will be an agreed way in which we improve or redesign processes continually and consistently, so all they have to do is use the process. My major learning from Tony Barnes and from Toyota was that when everyone uses the process, not only does the organisation run smoothly and efficiently, but people are then liberated to use their flair, their humanity and their creativity on the important things like customer service, colleague learning and development, product innovations and even revolutions, and looking further ahead than our competitors to see what the market might need and want from us.

These principles are like my values in their usefulness as a guide for my behaviour, my actions, my decisions and my communications. But the additional value for me in 'knowing' my leadership principles on an almost cellular level, and in being able to articulate them, mantra-like, using the words and phrases above, is that I can bring them to my daily leadership practice. I can use these phrases when I am coaching others. And since these phrases will become known to my team and to the people I lead, they can also use them as a silent guide. I am often asked by my clients running organisations of thousands of people, how can I touch or inspire people when I simply cannot visit every store and I certainly cannot know each individual? Well, you can ensure that every communication is consistent and contains some mantras. People love mantras – notice how often people will repeat an advertising jingle they've heard, or a favourite comedian's *it's not important (not possible) for you to know 50,000 people individually. What's important is that they feel they know you.*

catchphrase. There is safety in repetition, and it's not important (not possible) for you to know 50,000 people individually. What's important is that they feel they know you.

Chapter 8
Matching ourselves to our roles

When we match ourselves to our roles, we will notice that the fit is not perfect. It may be near perfect, and we should certainly strive to always make it so, for ourselves and for our followers, since this will produce the best results at the lowest cost. But the reality is there are bound to be areas where we will have to make some compromises. So we start by being crystal clear on who we are, our Golden Core, our purpose and our values. We then establish the leader version of ourselves through gaining clarity on our leadership beliefs and principles.

All we need to do now is be equally clear on the role we are taking on. So we need clarity on the purpose of the role, the stage of stewardship, the company founding and enduring values, the leadership buckets of the role, and the results, outcomes or objectives that are pre-set and non-changeable.

Stewardship

Whenever the president of the United States is introduced, they are not just introduced as the president, but as a number in an illustrious sequence. Donald Trump is the 45th president of the United States. In that simple and consistent communication is conveyed a weight of history, tradition and grandeur, with an immediate emotional equation to Lincoln, Washington and whoever else may be your favourite from down the years. What a fabulous way of communicating the gravitas and tradition of the role.

When you enter a church, stop for a moment and find the board that lists the incumbent priests down the years. The church itself may be several hundred years old, and the board might go back a similar time. You will see a list of names and dates. You will notice how few priests there have been over such a long period of time. You will wonder at how old some of them must have been when they finally retired.

Of course one problem with this concept in the twenty-first century of digital tech start-ups and megalithic corporations that come from nowhere at the speed of a bullet, is that you may be taking up a role that simply has no history or indeed no predecessors. New roles are very often old roles with fancy new titles, in which case it's still possible to trace a heritage, but the role may genuinely be new – never before held down or discharged in that business.

So be George Washington, be Pope Marcellinus, be Neil Armstrong, be Sean Connery. Set the foundations, leave a legacy for others to follow, strive to be the one that history remembers not only as the first but as the founding father.

Stewardship questions

- When was your role founded?
- Who came before you and what characterised their stewardship?
- Who before you in the role is universally acknowledged as the greatest ever? Why is that?

- If the role is brand new (and you are therefore the first), what foundations will you lay?

- How long is the next steward required for and what is required of them?

- Where will the organisation be at the end of the next chapter?

- When they carve your name and dates up on the board, what will your legacy and reputation be?

Remember, are you a seat-filler or a game-changer? Leadership is about change – it's about taking something from A to B. And when we are clear on our stewardship, we can get out of bed in the morning knowing where we are on the journey and that what we do *matters*.

Now, what is the purpose of the role?

It is vital that you are crystal clear on this, and not just from your own understanding, but in agreement with your investors or governors. Here are the questions to ask:

- Why does the role exist?

- What is the overriding objective?

- What would happen if no one performed the role?

- What is the vision? What are the goals?

- What is your personal return on investment?

- What would the finest possible candidate be doing differently?

- Where are you in the 'life'/the journey of the role?

- What will characterise your stewardship?

- When will it be right to hand it on or even eliminate the role?

It may not be possible to be crystal clear on all these questions – the point is not to achieve total clarity since you must have freedom to create along the way; the point is to be aware, to be conscious, to be ever-mindful of these important questions and have them as a constant bedfellow, available to guide you as you deliberate and as you make decisions between hugely conflicting tensions and pressures and possibilities.

So now we start the process of matching, of aligning ourselves with the role. We start this process by looking at how our values align. This is not an academic exercise of matching two columns of words or even a conceptual exercise of trying to harmonise our respective lists. Here are the questions to ask:

- How do your personal values align?

- Where do you need to have more courage to insist upon what you *know* to be right?

- Where do you need to submit yourself to the company line?

⊛ Where do you need to compromise on your own personal values?

⊛ Where do you need to be more cognisant of/more supportive of the company values?

So you can see this is a *practical* exercise – if we do this academically or conceptually we can convince ourselves that we are 100 per cent aligned. Ask any executive to recite their company's values and they will probably struggle. Recite them back to them and they will nod furiously in agreement, and then tell you that they don't need to be able to recite them, since by and large the list is the same as their own personal values, so all they do is come to work every day and use their own values as a guide. Now if that were true I'd have some sympathy with them, I may even have a sneaking admiration, but in my experience it *won't* be the truth. First of all very few executives I've met are completely clear on their own personal values and, second, even where they are, they have not been through a practical exercise of matching, aligning and working out the areas of compromise. The only thing of practical importance in compromising is where as a leader we need to confidently get off the fence and make a stand one way or the other – to say no to something asked of us by the role, or to consciously and deliberately act out of integrity (ie, against) our own core values. Being completely realistic, it is unavoidable that there will be situations where we will have to do one

> *very few executives I've met are completely clear on their own personal values and, second, even where they are, they have not been through a practical exercise of matching, aligning and working out the areas of compromise.*

or the other, maybe many times during our stewardship. One of the reasons I chose 'constancy' as my core value over truth or trust, is that in order to best discharge my responsibilities, I may have to change my mind, go back on my word even. And if I do that, all I can ask is that you know that I do this in service of others not myself, and that I do so after proper reflection and internal (and possibly external) enquiry and debate. If I am ever going to let you down, and I might, then you must at least be confident that no one could say '*he knows not what he does*'.

Strategies and behaviours

So now let's get truly practical and look at some of the strategies and behaviours to adopt as an authentic leader. I love the simplicity of the following mantra:

Lead, follow, or get out of the way.

You'll notice throughout my writings that I am at one moment waxing lyrically about spirituality and values, and the next about logic and practicality. I believe that when we've done the work on the former, we are then truly and most effective when we engage with the latter. In my work with Toyota I came to really appreciate the value of the 'Toyota Way' – a whole cultural guide based on five core values. When you join Toyota you are schooled, almost drilled, in the 'Toyota Way'. If you work for Toyota, there is no other way than the 'Toyota Way'. It borders on being cultish, and it is by no means for everyone. As with every strong and almost intolerant corporate culture, people joining can suffer a huge cultural shock in that it appears to them that they simply are not allowed to think for themselves. They rail against the culture, and refuse to subsume themselves with a sort of '*I am not a number, I am a free man*'-type defiance. But they miss the point, which is that the cultural values are there not to confine or imprison us, but to free us to use our unique talents and flair, for which we've been hired, and to ensure that everyone's efforts are genuinely in support of the company mission. Instead of producing automatons and clones, the finest corporate cultures are environments of creativity and individuality. Adherence to the corporate values becomes the common language and safety that allow us to truly trust each other. So if I see you act in a strange way, instead of automatically thinking you are an idiot, I can know there is method and integrity behind your actions. And instead of criticising you and maybe even fighting against you, I seek to enquire and then to support.

When we know ourselves, when we know each other, and when we are clear on and willing to subordinate ourselves to the mission, we can act, and we can change things and achieve things fast. No great need for meetings – sharing information is important, as is creative discussion and debate, but action is *most* important.

I use a metaphor of 'leadership buckets' – a mental picture of buckets into which you can categorise and organise your responsibilities and your time and your activities. You could call these your key responsibilities or prime results areas. And my guidance would be to have a small number – between four and six. It should be no fewer than four in my view, because as a leader you have some responsibility for at least four distinct areas:

⊛ Something to do with innovation and growth – sales, design, acquisitions

⊛ Something to do with use of resources – costs, efficiency

⊛ Something to do with people – cultural leadership, executive development

⊛ Something to do with governance – strategy development, investor relations

Your specific role may have one or two other truly separate buckets, or it may be most efficient for you to organise yourself by splitting one of the above into two parts. But I would strongly advise you not to have more than six, and that four is best!

What are your leadership buckets?

⊛ What are your prime responsibilities?

⊛ What will you be held accountable for?

⊛ What results are you expected to produce?

⊛ What measures will key stakeholders (investors, analysts, advisers, board members, commentators, colleagues, followers, family) use to determine whether they think you are successful?

⊛ What responsibility does the role specifically have in the area of growth?

⊛ What responsibility does the role specifically have in the area of resources?

- What responsibility does the role specifically have in the area of culture development?
- What responsibility does the role specifically have in the area of external advocacy?

How will you organise yourself?

Once you are clear on your leadership buckets (and you should check these out with your stakeholders to 'contract' them in), then you can set about organising yourself. And again I offer the clarity and digital nature of these structures not to keep you bound tightly, but to free you to perform to the very best of your individual personality and flair. When you have a firm structure to rely on, to hold on to, to trust without having to constantly check, then you can act in the moment with confidence.

There is only one of you, and everyone will want a piece. The demands on your time and attention will far outweigh what you will have or make available. You will have no choice but to ration yourself. How on earth will you know how best to do this without going through some form of analysis and planning first?

If you are going to indulge yourself, by the way, then don't skulk about, bunk off or try and label an activity as something it's not. Go and indulge yourself – you are human and you need refreshment and respite on occasions, but the reality is you are at your best when you are engaged in an activity that you love and that gives you energy and joy, and so you are highly unlikely to 'waste' time in any 'indulgent' activities. As a leader, you do not have the luxury of pandering to any feelings of guilt you may experience. Get over it.

If you are going to indulge yourself, by the way, then don't skulk about, bunk off or try and label an activity as something it's not. Go and indulge yourself – you are human and you need refreshment and respite on occasions

So what activities must you engage in to perform the role under each of the buckets? What is the optimum time allocation between buckets? The best way to answer this question is to pretend that your successor has asked for guidance on the same question.

What activities could you easily be drawn into that you really need to avoid? What *must* you get others doing? These last two questions are likely to occur around activities or whole subjects where you have deep prior experience or knowledge, but where you now have an able lieutenant with a mind of their own. You simply cannot second-guess your senior managers nor interfere in any way. You can challenge of course; you can enquire and you can check.

ACRC

As a young manager I was introduced to the 'new' concept of MBWA – management by walking about. Revolutionary. As a leader, this activity should be a regular part of your regime, otherwise how do you keep your finger on the pulse of the organisation? How will you *feel* what's really happening and what your people are thinking, feeling and prioritising?

In an earlier book I outlined my own process for this, ACRC:

- ⊛ Awareness
- ⊛ Checking
- ⊛ Recognition
- ⊛ Challenge

So rather than walk round the factory or store or lab, only 'bumping into' those people you feel comfortable with and rather than awkwardly trying to insert yourself into their personal world for an instant, by asking them about their weekend or the football or the picture of the cat on their desk, follow ACRC.

Do some preparation, even if it's only 30 seconds of private thoughts as you go in. What's happening in this place? What are they working on? What pressures are they under? What's likely to be the content of their water-cooler conversations about the company? What successes and achievements have they had recently? What should they rightly feel proud of? Who do you need to recognise today? Who in particular has something special happening right now?

And you should always be prepared, since an opportunity to inspire a person could come across your path any moment. 'Are you ready for your 30 seconds with the president?' If you knew in advance you were going to encounter the president for 30 seconds, you could prepare. You could practise your breathing to control your nerves and take as much wobble out of your voice as possible, and you could rehearse your elevator pitch to be able to communicate your message clearly, succinctly and confidently. And of course the prime preparation is done in the form of purpose, values, role and buckets, but you should be constantly aware and watchful for the mood of the moment. Don't be a leader who can be accused of being out of touch.

> **Ask them what they would like you to 'notice' as you go round.**

Ask the host or senior site manager what they feel you should know in advance. Ask them what they would like you to 'notice' as you go round. Ask them what value they would like you to add today. Ask them what they would like people saying when you leave.

'Who's got a birthday today? Who's got a work anniversary? Who's the longest server? Whose daughter is getting married at the weekend? Who is struggling at the moment and could do with a boost? Who needs congratulating? Who's going on a training course in the next few days? Who's got a big external presentation coming up?'

It blows people away when you 'know' something about them. It makes them feel incredibly special, and remember as leaders we cannot shy away from the huge impact we can have on people simply by paying them some individual attention. We do not have the luxury of false humility, of playing small so that the world does not judge us as arrogant. So this 'technique' may sound manipulative to you, in that we seem only to be engaging in an activity to deliberately make someone *feel* something. But my definition of manipulation is when we get another person to do or feel something that is in *our* selfish interests, not through open request or clear instruction, but by making them believe it was their idea. I see an enormous amount of this being done in the name of 'coaching' within companies. Indeed it has become part of the 'corporapathology'.

Trust yourself to know when you are being manipulative – and the clearer you are on your values and your role, the less likely you will be to operate from any such place. As long as you are motivated by what's in your heart, you cannot go wrong. So setting out to inspire people, to make them feel proud, loved, needed, important, accepted, witnessed, human, trusted, enthusiastic, creative and courageous is part of your job as a leader. While of course you expect your lieutenants to do this too, you cannot delegate or outsource this aspect. You cannot be anonymous. You cannot hide. It's OK to be introverted and it is not about being charismatic, it is about caring enough to do what's required of the role, and finding ways of being comfortable in this particular bucket.

And all we have to do having asked the questions is to notice the response. And I don't mean just listen – I mean notice. They may say they're looking forward to a forthcoming training course, but their body language, their non-verbal communication, might indicate some anxiety. If so, I can follow up with a question that I could never have rehearsed or prepared for today, but that is perfect for the moment. *'What's going to be the biggest challenge for you in attending the training? What are you hoping the training will give you? How are you managing your family commitments while you're away from home? What more support could we be giving you?'*

And notice all I am doing now is being human. Talking to another person I care about, even if this is the first time we've met. And I know that the impact will be huge…

Now, is that manipulative? Am I only doing this in order to create a workforce that will work like dogs for me and make me personally wealthy; a workforce I would cut in a heartbeat if I needed to? Yes, it is manipulation if that is my motivation.

But that is *not* my motivation. My motivation is genuinely to lead all to find purpose and joy in their work. I passionately and profoundly believe that if I act in this way, the very best results will flow. I may not be able to forecast those results correctly. Some of the results may in fact be inconvenient for me in the short term. Some results will be simply stunning and completely out of my wildest dreams or predictions. When I converse with people on my walk-rounds, I am in my element. I luxuriate in the human connections. I feel deeply blessed to have an environment where so many people will let me in.

So the success criteria for a store visit is simple – did you leave the store manager feeling what they need to feel in order to move forward? I used to say *'Did you leave the store manager feeling 10 feet tall?'*, but there are moments in any performer's journey when actually what they need is to go through some self-doubt, some self-reproach, even some despair. I am acutely aware of not wanting to leave a store manager feeling so low

So the success criteria for a store visit is simple – did you leave the store manager feeling what they need to feel in order to move forward?

that they cannot pick themselves up again, but I am not afraid to engage with them honestly and give them the respect they deserve, and if that means an honest conversation about underperformance and where they are letting themselves and the team down, then that's what I will do. Respect is one of my core values, and I won't lie to someone to make everyone feel better. I will give people the professional respect they deserve. A store manager demands the respect of being treated like a great store manager, or at the very least a store manager with huge potential. So if something is wrong, I'll not shirk from discussing it.

However, in my discussions, I will use every fibre of my being to communicate my support for them. I may need to leave them feeling flat, criticised even, but I cannot leave them feeling condemned, for there is no way back from that. It's also my guidance on giving people feedback in general – *truly great feedback hurts* – to try not to pass judgement in your feedback, focusing as much as possible on facts and data, or the way their behaviour is experienced, or the risk you believe they are running if they persist, but sometimes in our correct priority to give feedback in the moment, we will be clumsy and may betray our judgement. Don't worry too much about that – people can take it and they can take being criticised. The mortal blow is when we condemn them, when we leave them feeling not just judged but condemned, for that feels like no way back for them, and their actions from that moment forward will be all about survival and defending themselves.

What are you working on at the moment?

> My favourite question on meeting someone new on a walk round is simply 'What are you working on at the moment?'

So on a walk-round I would want to know as much as possible – not necessarily in advance, because I can ask questions as I go round. My favourite question on meeting someone new on a walk round is simply 'What are you working on at the moment?' It's a fabulous question. First of all it contains positive presuppositions – that the person has a brain, has talent and has autonomy. Second, it invites them to tell me about something that is both current and relevant for them, giving them licence to offer up what they're pleased or proud of in their work, and to offer up a glimpse of where they may be struggling.

Struggle is good remember, struggle is great. Nothing of worth will be achieved without a struggle, and anyone working on stuff that does not involve them in struggle will be bored very quickly, meaning they will turn their brain off and simply get through the day.

OK, so far we've done the AC part of ACRC. We made ourselves aware and we've checked. Before we leave the person, however, we are going to complete the process by adding value. We are going to recognise them and we are going to challenge them.

Recognition can be part of a process or whole conversation with an individual. For example, in the training programme conversation, having noticed and honoured their response to my initial questions, I might then make a couple of statements of recognition – '*I'm really pleased you're going on the training as I think you'll add a lot to the other participants/you'll represent your department really well*', etc. Or it can simply be an end in itself, recognising someone or something special. '*I understand that you completed 25 years' service with us last week, and coming here today I wanted to seek you out to congratulate you and say thank you. Your name was mentioned at a board meeting last week for winning a design award and I wanted to personally congratulate you and thank you for the amazing work you are doing.*'

And remember the power of ritual in recognition. If every Friday at 12pm is pizza discussion group, then drop in, eat pizza, discuss. Show them the rituals can be trusted. In setting up champions' surgeries in a factory a couple of years back, where one of the champions would sit at a desk in a corner of the factory for one hour at a certain time each week to hear ideas, gripes and gossip, I told them that it would take some weeks before the process would actually be used and to not be surprised if no one came for the first few weeks. People need to trust a process before they'll use it. So be aware of the formal rituals (and the informal ones if appropriate) within your business and honour them by showing you support them. If you expect others to behave in a certain way, you should role model this.

But there is a final step, and this is where we add real value. This is where we earn the invite to come back any time. We leave people with a challenge.

> **But there is a final step, and this is where we add real value. This is where we earn the invite to come back any time. We leave people with a challenge.**

If you know me, if you believe in me, then you have earned the right to challenge me. I love challenge. I don't want to be told what to do or how to think. But for someone who cares about me enough to really know me, and for someone who cares enough to believe in me, I will do whatever they ask of me – I will follow them unhesitatingly.

Leave people with a challenge – which could be a direct request, asking something of them, or it could be in the form of a question for them to ruminate on and find their own answer to. So in our training programme example, we might finish the conversation by saying '*Do me a favour, please give the trainer the most honest and truthful feedback you can to help them improve the training – thank you.*' Or we might say '*How will you ensure that your own workload is covered in your absence? I don't need to know now, but I encourage you to think about that and have a clear plan.*'

A bit clumsy maybe, but human and relevant. And the time to challenge people is when they are at their most open, receptive, positive and confident – so get them to this place through your coaching, and then leave them with a challenge.

Fernando – nobleman or fool?

In Cuba in 2016 I had the good fortune to spend a day with Fernando, a Cuban farmer. With a degree in agronomy from the University of Amsterdam, he had returned to Cuba and had created a thriving farm from 16 acres of 'barren' land. Using only traditional rustic skills and processes, he had experienced all the difficulties, all the crises that only nature can throw at the artisan, but he had equally experienced the joys of building something with his bare hands, of learning skills, and of working with others in a common endeavour of physical challenge and solving problems. After five years, he was proud that the farm now supported the livelihoods of several families, and had achieved a semblance of true sustainability.

Fernando was an intelligent, articulate, educated man who if he were living in the West, might well be motivated to build personal wealth and to progressively employ others to do the dirty work. He might look to build branded products to make more profit, rather than simply sell his entire production to the government. He might look to protect 'his' land for himself and his progeny, with trust funds to avoid tax and actions to stop potentially damaging developments on adjacent land. But Fernando is Cuban. He is not motivated by personal profit. He is motivated by community. Since he gains everything he needs on a daily basis from his daily work, and is therefore 'happy', his medium- and long-term motivation is the development of the environment and the community that his children will grow up in and inhabit.

His resistance to wanting an alternative to selling his entire production to the government also has the wonderfully positive benefit of protecting him from the anxiety that goes along with entering a competitive arena. It's easy to say that he could successfully build brands to make more profit, but those brands have then to be nurtured and cared for, including fighting the competitive brands that would try and take his market share. Selling all his production for a fair price to the government doesn't just outsource that anxiety to others, it eradicates it. Only greed or a misplaced sense of unfairness could possibly cause Fernando to be dissatisfied with getting a fair price for his entire production.

Here is my question to you. Is Fernando a fool or a nobleman? Is he gloriously and perhaps vainly naïve and foolish in his beliefs and his practices or is he to be admired for his altruism, his heroism even? Well, in my view Fernando is neither. He is certainly no fool – he's intelligent, self-aware, self-determining, proud, loved and happy. Sounds pretty cool to me. Bring it on. But neither in my view is he a nobleman, for that would endow him with a piety and a hubris that he does not possess in any measure. To be noble is also potentially to be patronising, to set oneself up as being better than others, and to demonstrate by one's actions that one is in search of plaudits and adoration. No, Fernando is no more and no less than that glorious combination of being both ordinary and extraordinary. Fernando is simply a man. He has taken his God-given talents, his genetic blessings, his parental gifts and put them to the best possible use he can. He is truly living out his purpose and his destiny – hence, I suspect, his happiness.

Section 3
Teams

Chapter 9

Teams

When is a team a team and not merely a group?

There are groups of individuals, and then there are teams. A group is simply a collection of people that I have no collective responsibility to. If I am a 'member' of a group, I can be an individual going about my own work the best way I can, and serving my company, customers and direct reports ably and maybe even exceptionally – it just happens to serve a purpose for me to commune with the group on occasions to share information and knowledge, and maybe to give input to a creative debate. A team, however, is a unit with collective responsibility – we live or die together. If I succeed in hitting my objectives or performing my part of the bargain perfectly, but the overall objective is not achieved, then we've all failed. *I* have failed. A team is a group of people with specific roles and therefore people specifically formed into a unified force to lead the business or one part of it. If I am a member of the team, I owe it my allegiance and my loyalty – it is bigger than me, and I must be prepared to subordinate my own views and interests to it in the name of the cause.

If I am a member of the team, I owe it my allegiance and my loyalty – it is bigger than me, and I must be prepared to subordinate my own views and interests to it in the name of the cause.

So how do we first determine which are groups and which must be teams, and second, how do we then create the genuine high-performance team, with that sublime and synergistic blend of individual contribution with group collaborative endeavour? This chapter outlines the ten characteristics of high-performing teams, and describes the strategies and practical processes for the achievement of that desired sublime state.

Coaching teams (aka facilitation)

People often ask me, in that way we have when we want someone to confirm that we are right, '*Don't you think it's only possible to coach one-to-one?*', to which my response is always '*No*'. (It is a closed question after all, and in my book, closed questions get a one-word answer.)

While I see a dearth of genuine coaching skills in companies, I see an even greater paucity of facilitation skills. It's as if the anxiety over self-worth and the overwhelming desire to 'help' people get to the solution is magnified tenfold when faced with a group of people rather than a single individual. If a single person seemingly rejects us and our coaching, giving us that look that says '*Don't just ask me questions, tell me what you think*', then we can recover our composure and our authority quite easily. We can win back control and reassert our credibility. But if a pack turns on us…

But coaching a group can be an almost exponentially more effective way forward than coaching a single individual, since you only have to communicate the non-negotiables once (and everyone hears precisely the same message) and since you can make the group coach itself when it appears to get stuck. Let's just reflect for a moment on how our coaching skills are so critical here. Here's my definition of facilitation:

> *The facilitator is there to guarantee a quality, depth and honesty of discussion that is wholly targeted at the problem at hand, and that would simply never take place without them.*

The facilitator is there to guarantee a quality, depth and honesty of discussion that is wholly targeted at the problem at hand, and that would simply never take place without them.

Just as there is a structure for one-to-one coaching, here are the five steps that need to be followed in order to provide great facilitation or team coaching:

1. Plan the session

   - Ensure you are totally clear on the objectives for the meeting
   - Pose the clearest possible questions for the group to answer
   - What do you want people to *know*, *think*, *feel* and *do* as a result of the meeting?
   - Make sure the session has pre-prepared questions that 'force' them to:

     Bring out any negative views and feelings

     Absorb and accept any non-negotiables

     Create ideas to populate strategies or plans

     Reflect on personal behaviour changes they will need to make

     Own the plan and commit to personal actions

2. Guide the process

   - Guide towards clear and practical outputs
   - Constantly bring the group back to their task
   - Point out where they may be ignoring additional factors
   - Take 'time-outs' when you sense the team has shifted
   - Change pace, subject matter, style, etc, when needed
   - Control humour and banter – make them stay professional and adult

3. Reinforce vision and values

   - Point out when behaviour steps out of line with values
   - Bring the group back to vision and values when they struggle
   - De-personalise authority – the vision is the real boss
   - Get them to check commitments against the vision

128

4. Challenge thinking

- ⊕ Control the loudmouths and insist that the quiet contribute
- ⊕ Coach for passion and energy
- ⊕ Coach people to be specific
- ⊕ Watch the body language for frustration and disagreement and then bring it out

5. Recognise individuals

- ⊕ Notice their strengths, weaknesses and preferences
- ⊕ Accept contributions without judgement
- ⊕ Coach them to go further in saying what they *really* think
- ⊕ Protect people who take real risks
- ⊕ Passively reward desired behaviour – a smile, nodding, encouragement
- ⊕ Actively reward behaviours outside comfort zones – praise, positive feedback, publicly acknowledging their courage

Coaching teams is different to coaching individuals, but actually the trick is to treat the team as a single organism. Many managers fall into what I call the 'hub and spoke' trap. This is where in meetings, the boss has a series of one-to-one transactions with individual team members, thus reinforcing their control culture and communicating that they need to be involved in everything.

Many managers fall into what I call the 'hub and spoke' trap.

My technique is to keep the conversation or the issue out at the perimeter, to get the team members helping each other – relying on each other rather than me. So in a meeting I will encourage people to converse with each other and not with me; to challenge each other and not to wait to see which side of the judgemental fence I am going to jump down on.

Often when chairing a meeting, or facilitating a group, I will drop my eye contact to the floor after throwing a question out to the group. I am now communicating that it is the group's turn to speak – that I will not rescue them. I may sit back and have a sip of coffee, demonstrating that I am under no pressure at all. The key however is that the group must *know* they have been asked a question. Therefore you will need to ask a very specifically worded question, not simply make an observation that sort of invites a response but could be avoided!

Peer group coaching

My mission when I undertake a coaching programme within a company is to see peer group coaching embedded into the culture. Then I know it's going to stick and to grow. I have been described as a virus in the past, and that's fine with me.

> *the best way to create and develop teams is to work on the relationships of trust and respect between members*

I believe that teams operate better than individuals. Teams can achieve more – it's the old 2 + 2 = 5 syndrome. And the best way to create and develop teams is to work on the relationships of trust and respect between members. This cannot be done by simply telling people to trust and respect each other or even just agreeing that we all *do*; it *has* to be facilitated. And it is peer group coaching that does this. Psychometrics and 360-degree feedback processes are great to create a basis and a foundation or understanding, acceptance and mutual support, but it is peer group coaching that makes it all come alive.

All this means is that instead of struggling alone with an issue, or taking it to our boss, we ask one of our colleagues to coach us through it. And who should we pick? Well, let's pick the person who is least like us, because then we will get the clearest difference in approach. Or we could go to the one who will challenge us the most, or the one with the characteristics we most need – courage, humility, people appreciation, commerciality.

Again this is one of those common-sense things that we all agree is great and that we will do, and then we don't do it. I'll leave it to you to decide.

> *When team members understand the differences between them, it encourages acceptance over judgement, thereby facilitating a supportive and genuinely collaborative culture over one of competitive and ultimate division.*

Profiling and 360-degree feedback allow team members to understand each other and give a wonderful coded language for feedback. When team members understand the differences between them, it encourages acceptance over judgement, thereby facilitating a supportive and genuinely collaborative culture over one of competitive and ultimate division.

The trick is to create an environment where the team is bigger than the individual – not just a personal subordination to the mission or purpose, or even to the value, but to my team. And when peer group coaching is established, people go to their peers with an issue, rather than automatically taking it to their boss like some needy child wanting Mum or Dad to make it better.

In fact, when it's really in the culture, people will go to the peer who will challenge them the most, which might well be the one whose characteristics are most different. True diversity is not about what has become the 'politically correct' view of gender, ethnicity, sexual orientation or physical and mental capacity (although equality of opportunity and access is of paramount importance), it's about honouring difference as the most amazing source of innovation, efficiency, execution and support.

The first question I ask people when they say they want an offsite or a team development day is '*Why do you want to be a team? What makes a team? Why not just call yourself a group and meet when you need to, to share information or simply come together on an ad hoc basis when the group needs to concur on a decision?*'

The purpose of teams within a business

- Senior teams set the direction and make transformational decisions
- Middle management teams design the processes and manage the change
- Employee teams operate kaizen and make continuous incremental improvements

What can only teams do?

Only a team can achieve a quantum leap, which is defined by the Oxford English Dictionary as *'A change in status from one set of circumstances to another set of circumstances, that takes place immediately without passing through the circumstances in between.'* Individuals can achieve breakthroughs, but in an organisation then comes the cementing of those breakthroughs into something that executes consistently and is ultimately sustainable. Individual success in an organisation is only relative – I succeed only in relation to others around me, and how they react and build on my personal achievement. Only a team can guarantee success.

Individual versus team accountability

I profoundly believe that only teams can truly be held accountable for results, and only teams can solve any problem. Individuals must be held accountable for actions, but only teams can be held accountable for outcomes.

A team is made up of individuals, and their performance and actions are what make up the combined energy and output of the team, but if we are to truly harness the exponential power, the synergy that only a team can produce, then we must be clear on what makes a great team.

If a star salesperson hits a personal sales target, it's easy to laud them to the exclusion of the mere 'support' staff. But the only way that salesperson was able to hit their target was because the contracts teams got all the legal stuff done properly, the admin team ensured all the paperwork was accurate, the warehouse had the right stock in the right place, the delivery team got the products out on time and ensured a smooth delivery to the customer, and the accounts teams collected the money professionally. Is there really any such thing as individual success in a corporation? Of course the 'star' salesperson is probably going to get the most plaudits, and will most likely earn the most money, but people can accept this as part of the 'natural' order of things in a business at the whim of market forces. Most 'support' staff occasionally eye the commission payments with some envy, but none would swap places and suffer the constant rejection.

How can we balance the pressures we are under as managers to hit short-term targets, yet deliver sustainable long-term growth? Are we striving to make people accountable for achieving a specific result or for maximising their personal potential? Are we acting solely for short-term results or acting only in the long-term

Are we striving to make people accountable for achieving a specific result or for maximising their personal potential?

interest? Are we in reality acting in self-interest for our own personal gain or acting in the interests of the team for overall company benefit?

The place for targets

Individual targets are OK, but must be backed by coaching, not 'absentee' performance management.

A soccer coach might set the star striker a target of one goal per game, but he does not rely on that target as the sole motivator. He would not call the striker in to remind him that he hadn't scored for three games, remind him he was paid to score goals and then tell him to go and do better. He would first look at the overall performance and results of the team, and the performance of the striker in relation to this. If the striker had made three assists and the team had won every game, why change anything?

Second, the coach would work both one-to-one with the striker and with the whole team, to practise and train to improve both individual and team performance. The only important thing is not whether the striker scores 40 goals that season, but whether the team wins the league. In this example, the target is simply a tool – to give the striker a personal target to stretch his performance and aid self-belief and motivation, and also to act as a guide and structure on which to build a strategy for winning the league.

Unfortunately, when seeking greater personal accountability, too many managers fall back on the old 'command and control' ways. They ensure that all macro-financial targets are broken down into smaller numbers, and 'owned' by salespeople and, in turn, sales managers. Targets are then used as the main weapon to motivate and manage individual performance. Sales management then often rely on the approach of *'I pay you to hit targets. You have an adequate sales area and a great product. You've been through the sales training. I trust you, I am not going to do it for you, I believe in you – now go and do it.'*

When the pressure's on (and when isn't it?) individuals do what is best for themselves and not the team.

This breeds individual success as being more important than team success. When the pressure's on (and when isn't it?) individuals do what is best for themselves and not the team. The star striker shoots through a field of defenders from 18 yards out, rather than passing to an unmarked teammate on the edge of the six-yard box. The salesperson goes for the small order that would count towards his own target, rather than choosing to 'notice' the chance to forego the order and pass a much greater opportunity to a colleague from another division.

In the old world of individual sales performance being paramount, it is not unusual for salespeople to reach a comfort level of earnings and activity, usually at a level well below that needed for the company to achieve its overall corporate revenue targets. The battleground in this scenario, instead of being customer development, product penetration or new business wins, becomes internally focused, excuse-based conversations, with the salesperson blaming poor marketing, old product, excessive pricing or unrealistic targets, and the sales manager (who may well agree with some of what is being said) wavering between manfully defending the company, and empathising with the salesperson, particularly when they are having similar conversations with the sales director. And we wonder why we lack focus on the customer sometimes.

Account management

Structure first, or structure as a guide/support? Matrix structures only fail when the organisation says one thing (in its values, in its communications about how the structure works, in laid-down guidelines for passing leads, in exhortations from managers about co-operation across geographic, functional or account divisions) and does another.

For example, leaders say things like 'We want an organisation that is customer-focused', 'We put the needs of the customer first', 'We want to build long-term relationships with our customers', 'We want our salespeople to work in the best long-term interests of the company, passing leads and business to colleagues in another division where appropriate.'

Fine and noble words, and structures can be designed around these sentiments. Dotted lines, cross-functional team meetings, virtual teams, etc. And then they go and behave like before – managing salespeople who are short of their targets with old-fashioned tools. In other words, the reality is that our focus is on ourselves, not the customer – our focus is on individuals who are underperforming, not on the teams as complete units. We actually show that we value salespeople hitting their individual targets more than we value their collaboration.

This is because it is 'easier' for a manager to exercise control over an individual than it is over a number of people grouped together. The fear is that unless one person, or a series of people dealt with one by one, can be 'motivated' and held accountable, then management have no effective control. In reality the reverse is true. Motivating an individual to raise his or her performance when they are struggling personally requires professional coaching, which is undoubtedly best dealt with one-to-one; however, most managers are highly unskilled as coaches, and therefore revert to old-fashioned fear-based tools. These tools often 'work' of course, leading to improved individual performance, but damaging the culture.

However, the real difficulty comes when trying to deal one-to-one with an individual who is actually performing exceptionally (doing everything they have been exhorted to do by the words of the leadership) and yet is falling short of the personal performance target set. Old-fashioned techniques in this case are highly dangerous, because not only do they damage the culture but they also do not work on the individual, due to the frustration and disillusionment caused.

Collaborative working demands a focus on the team before the individual. Team targets and team performance must come before individuals.

Collaborative working demands a focus on the team before the individual. Team targets and team performance must come before individuals. There is nothing wrong with setting individual targets, just as there is nothing wrong with communicating what looks like a relatively fixed organisation structure. These should, however, be for the purpose of assisting individuals and their coaches to work to maximise individual performance against both personal potential and the needs of the unit, and to inspire exceptional performance.

The three-dimensional matrix

Today there are many organisations wrestling with strategies for the most effective management of multilayered objectives. It is not untypical for companies to be operating across many continents and countries, leading to a need for a high element of local leadership, experience, knowledge and accountability. Yet at the same time these companies have grown successful by vertically integrating, possibly even through merger and acquisition (M&A) activity, gaining advancement from the specialisation of functional experts in areas such as research, manufacturing, finance and marketing.

It is also more and more common for large multinationals to have become horizontally integrated, thus adding often exponential growth, but leading to a potentially fragmented sales approach to major customers, with many different points of contact for a customer, at a time when the customers may well have rationalised their supply chain management.

So modern multinationals have to construct not just a matrix organisation structure but a three-dimensional one!

It is hard enough to communicate and effectively operate a two-dimensional matrix, but it can be done and it is increasingly being achieved – often with a mix of old-world 'command and control' tools and more modern leadership and coaching methods. Often the professional and intellectual background of the employees affected by the restructuring makes things work, almost in spite of management's efforts! The company steals a march in the marketplace and success breeds high motivation internally, fuelling collaborative working and a productive and innovative atmosphere. The danger here, however, is that the moment the competitive pressures build up and those employees see layoffs being put through, or tougher and more stretching productivity objectives being imposed, management become the enemy again, and things start to disintegrate.

But now we are talking about a three-dimensional matrix, with a salesperson covering country A, who is specialist in product X, having three reporting lines – one to their local sales manager (often a country general manager), one to their central product sales manager (often the central VP of sales), and one to the major account coordinator for the client he or she is dealing with at that moment.

There are three specialisations, and therefore three potential points of focus. We must have local geographic specialists involved, due to the sometimes extreme and sometimes subtle (but always critical) differences between countries and regions, and because many customers demand to be dealt with by people whom they perceive to be more empathetic and in tune with their needs (or can at least speak the same language!).

We must also have functional expertise, due to the absolute need to stay at the leading edge of thinking and research in the area concerned, and because the most cost-effective and productive way to deliver this is to have dedicated teams of specialists working together, probably grouped centrally or regionally.

Finally we must have co-ordination of sales activities across major global accounts, with management at the very highest level of that account, preferably CEO, being absolutely paramount. This is particularly important where we have customers who mirror our scale and global reach, for they will have organised supply-chain management as a specialist function. Thus a disparate collection of local sales initiatives, however professionally managed – unless the product is a quantum step ahead of the competition – will ultimately result in zero sales, as central negotiation and purchasing dictates that sales are given to a competitor.

Relying on structure, process and performance management will simply not work in this new world. The new structures will only work if leadership behaviour changes.

The fine words must be backed with consistent and highly visible action. Employees and customers will judge leadership by actions not intentions. If the customer is the desired focus, then *act* that way. Take the focus off the individual's personal results as measured against their target, and place it on their performance within the team. Given that salespeople will be part of any one of three different teams at various times, the leadership, co-ordination and facilitation of those teams are critical.

Structures need to change to facilitate the working of a three-dimensional matrix, but any element of rigidity should only be communicated when there is a need to dramatically change the fortunes of the organisation. Otherwise structure is simply a guide – to help people know why and how, just as the company values are a guide to what people should do in certain unscripted or unpredicted circumstances, and a guide as to how they should behave.

The reality of most reorganisations is that 99 per cent of employee activities remain 99 per cent the same. They may acquire a different boss, but they probably still engage in their old job. However, if the 1 per cent change is critical, then the change must be communicated as being radical and dramatic. Structure allows guidance, order, certainty of systems that must always be consistent and replicable. If leaned on too rigidly, the structure becomes the arbiter of success or failure, which is daft considering it does not physically exist.

The bottom line is that when performance needs to be raised and results improved, it is infinitely more effective to call a group together and let the creativity and collective accountability loose than it is to exhort individuals to work harder or do more to hit their individual targets. Creating a three-dimensional matrix necessitates a step change in leadership. And thank God for that.

when performance needs to be raised and results improved, it is infinitely more effective to call a group together and let the creativity and collective accountability loose than it is to exhort individuals to work harder or do more to hit their individual targets.

Tuckman and Lencioni

Patrick Lencioni's five dysfunctions of a team

One of the reasons I like Patrick Lencioni's work is that he unashamedly focuses on the eradication of negatives, rather than putting an ideal up and telling us to aim for it. Of course he lets us work out what the ideal is – by definition the opposite of the negative – but in allowing us to create our own ideal, and in tapping into the change energy of moving away from pain, he is incredibly effective as a provoker of change.

The five dysfunctions are:

1. Inattention to results

2. Avoidance of accountability

3. Lack of commitment

4. Fear of commitment

5. Absence of trust

Many companies use this model to support them in team development work, particularly some of the large US corporations I've worked with. My issue with this framework is that while I applaud the use of negatives to provoke change, these dynamics only hint at what to do about these dysfunctions, whereas what teams need is specific guidance or templates to adopt. Lencioni may be a great provoker of change, and analyst of what is wrong, but he's not a great guide, teacher or coach. If you read his books, or work with him personally (although God knows what that would cost you – stick a zero on the end of what I would charge probably), then he goes into these aspects, but the dysfunctions themselves are not of much practical help. Notice that all these dysfunctions, apart from the last one, are really criticisms of individual behaviours, which therefore only individuals can attend to – the key is to find characteristics or principles and then strategies and tactics that the whole team must adopt and execute.

Tuckman's five stages of team development

The most commonly cited team development theory was developed in the 1960s by Bruce Tuckman – the classic 'Forming, Storming, Norming' model. It still holds good today. The five stages are:

1. Forming

2. Storming

3. Norming

4. Performing

5. Transforming

The reason this model has stood the test of time is because it is psychologically sound. These *are* the natural stages and this *is* how people behave in groups the more they work together, irrespective of their consciousness around team theory.

The five stages are logical and progressive. All stages are inevitable, necessary and desirable. Teams will often fall back to earlier stages, and teams can go through the cycle many times as they react to changing circumstances.

Like any model, the greater the awareness, the more choice and control is opened up. And so a team that has an awareness of Tuckman's model is already in a great place to maximise their efficiency as a unit.

Stage 1: Forming

The team learns about the opportunity and the challenges and agrees on the objectives and goals. They then begin to tackle the task with team members largely behaving independently at this stage – motivated, but still relatively uninformed. Everyone is on their best behaviour, but still focused on themselves – how they feel and how they are being received by their new colleagues. The more 'mature' members start to role-model behaviours, but of course this does not mean they are modelling the behaviours that are right or needed for the task.

Stage 2: Storming

In this phase, different ideas and styles start to compete for space, and if there is no overt team development debate or process now, then individual competitiveness is likely to win the day, meaning a vast amount of energy is spent jockeying for position. Some team members will want to prove how much they know and will try and 'convince' others. Some will focus on minutiae to evade change. The team needs to be challenged on *how* the team will work together, where team members open out to each other and confront each other's ideas and viewpoints. This stage can be contentious and uncomfortable, and will even be painful to those averse to conflict. But this stage is critical, and if the development work is done at too superficial a level then the team may never actually proceed out of this phase.

Stage 3: Norming

Team members start to adjust, and be seen to adjust, their behaviour to each other, developing new work habits that then come to feel more natural and fluid. Agreement is reached on values, rules, professional behaviour, codes of conduct, working tools – even taboos. Given enough time, agreements can of course be reached naturally and without overt awareness or development work but it is likely that time will run out way before this happens 'naturally'. So through an overt development process we speed things up – trust builds and motivation increases, comfort rituals start to solidify.

Stage 4: Performing

The team starts to hit objectives and achieve success, truly functioning as a unit. Team members are motivated, knowledgeable, individually competent and autonomous and they make decisions without supervision – team members have become interdependent. Dissent is not only expected, it is encouraged as part of the creative growth process, but allowed only if channelled in accordance with team culture created in prior phases. The trick in this phase is to watch out for the collective comfort zone, and to continually check in to ensure maximum effectiveness.

Stage 5: Transforming

And so we achieve the state and real opportunity for the team to transcend into a transformational stage of performance, stretching beyond the original remit and achieving truly extraordinary results. Within the team there is exceptional synergy and apparent effortlessness, with a huge unspoken communication and strong emotional connections. The team has become massively attractive to outsiders and can exploit the opportunity of how easy it is to get people to follow. If the task is completed, the team enters the 'adjourning' phase where it will consider its future remit and existence. Maybe it's time to break up, and if so the team will enter the 'mourning' phase, where individuals both within and without the team support each other through their sense of loss.

Adapting theoretical models

In the early 1970s Procter & Gamble adopted 'Cog's Ladder', which is very similar to Tuckman's model – their five stages were:

1. The polite stage
2. The why we are here stage
3. The power stage
4. The co-operation stage
5. The esprit stage

Notice that all P&G did was to translate a solid and reliable model or theory into a language that fitted their culture a little better, and this is another important factor when dealing with theoretical models – mould them to the culture, practice and language of the particular organisation so that people can accept and adopt the structural assistance more easily. Don't deny or neuter the theory in a way that makes it more comfortable – for example, don't delete the 'storming' phase believing you can do without it. You can't, and if you seek to over-sanitise something to reduce or avoid discomfort for people, you are making a huge mistake.

Chapter 10

The characteristics of high-performance teams

I've encountered, researched and witnessed and had experience of many versions of answers to this question. There are, of course, some accepted classics as we've seen. But my own experience and practice have led me to the following:

1. Common purpose, inspiring vision, shared values, ambitious goals, great strategy

2. Clear structure of roles and responsibilities

3. Utter respect for each other as expert specialist professionals

4. Acceptance of individual idiosyncrasies and personal circumstances

5. Conflict embraced and used as a creative force

6. Honesty valued as the most precious commodity

7. Space honoured for rehearsal and celebration

8. Team is individuals' place of sanctuary and solace

9. A leader who is an honest coach and facilitator

10. 100 per cent commitment and personal subordination to the plan

I believe in the fundamental truths of how human beings are wired to behave, whether through genetics or environment. So theoretical models are of profound value, in which case we may as well access the healthiest and most aspirational of those models. But I also believe in practical application, in tools and techniques and processes that actually work in the day-to-day realities of the modern corporation.

What you will notice about my ten characteristics therefore is, first, they are all action-oriented – each one exhorts you to do something active to be a better team. Second, while there are undoubtedly some old favourites here, elements that you would find in any half-decent list of what great teams are or what they do, you will also see some that may be somewhat new or unusual to you. Good.

Let's consider them one by one – and in doing so I'll leave you to your own conclusions about the degree to which they are naturally sequential. My advice would be to take 1 first, then do 2 but after that I'm not sure there's any advantage in finding a logical or rational sequence.

1. Common purpose, inspiring vision, shared values, ambitious goals, great strategy

Many lists will break these down into their separate elements, and I see the argument for separating the *why*, the *what* and the *how*. Why are we forming a team (purpose), what are we looking to do (vision and goals) and how are we going to go about this (values and strategy), but for me they are aspects of the same fundamental question, and we need to allow some blurring between these elements. I've seen teams get incredibly hung up on semantics at this stage, with discussions that predictably degenerate into committee-style generalisations and platitudes.

When we treat these elements as a single topic, we force the debate on priorities, not in the sense of actions and timescales but of what is truly non-negotiable for us before we even commence the quest: the conscious agreement of what's important and how the elements relate to each other. This starts the process of breaking any unconscious Newtonian thinking right at the start – the flawed thinking that we can have one thing at the expense of another, or indeed that we can have absolutely everything all at once.

We need to have a debate, and know that we are in a process of design and flow as much as we are in a process of control. We may have to change the plan along the way – if we are so wedded to elements of the plan, we may be guilty of culpable inflexibility at a future date. External events are bound to knock us off course; so we need to know our true north, our guiding star – the thing that transcends all other considerations. And this might be encapsulated in the purpose, or the vision, or the values, or in a single iconic goal.

> *External events are bound to knock us off course; so we need to know our true north, our guiding star – the thing that transcends all other considerations. And this might be encapsulated in the purpose, or the vision, or the values, or in a single iconic goal.*

So this section *has* to be taken as one. By all means break it down to make the task easier, but don't break it down in such a way that the outcome is already prejudiced or even dictated by that process. Do the work – do it well and do it diligently without shirking from the hard work involved.

2. Clear structure of roles and responsibilities

This step might in reality have been decided in advance. How do we really decide who is going to be on the team unless we've been through a process of reviewing what roles are required, what skills or attributes the task demands? In a corporation, the team may well pick itself according to hierarchical levels as much as functional expertise or responsibility. But this does not mean we can take anything for granted as we assemble our players. We still need to go through the process of understanding and then collectively agreeing the roles each person will take, and the responsibilities that go with that role. Partly this is an exercise in breaking down the bigger team goals and strategies into departmental or role-specific smaller chunks, but mostly it's an exercise in each individual team member gaining an understanding and appreciation of not just their colleagues' roles, but more importantly their challenges and the risks they run in not meeting their commitments.

> *Nothing kills team unity and effectiveness as fast as a team member unconsciously colluding with criticism of one of their colleagues.*

Nothing kills team unity and effectiveness as fast as a team member unconsciously colluding with criticism of one of their colleagues. And we are bound to hear criticisms – we are putting the organisation through change, which means putting people through discomfort, and people often defend themselves by blaming others, in a *'You'll never guess what Department X have done now'* manner. When we hear criticisms of one of our colleagues we must respond like adults and be very careful not to collude with the criticisms, even if we may have some sympathy with them. And we avoid this by first of all being able to refer the complainer to the strategy being implemented by the person or department they are complaining of, forcing them to engage with the fact that they are in fact only experiencing the predictable fallout from the agreed strategy being implemented, and second, by coaching the complainer to take personal responsibility and to challenge the correct person, rather than taking the lazy route of whingeing. It's the same issue as dealing with a 'them and us' energy or behaviour. To be stamped out.

And this brings me to the subject of a team dynamic that's come to be known as 'fortress mentality' whereby teams can become strong and arguably highly effective units by creating a culture of an 'enemy without'. The philosophy is that if we demonise other people or teams we give ourselves a huge advantage by harnessing and focusing our energy on protecting our own and attacking those who stand in our way. I've seen a lot of this in corporations, in fact I've seen it feted and promoted as a legitimate technique. Where it is aimed at a competitor, I'm not going to argue too strongly against it. I would still not advocate it as a positive strategy, since it will only serve to elicit a like response, and we will end up in a war that will destroy margins for the whole industry. We should be in a more collaborative mindset even where our competition is concerned – our legitimate position in the supply chain is not always strengthened when a competitor is weakened. Often we are better served when our competition is strong and successful, assuming there is a legitimate place for all. Who wants 100 per cent market share? It wouldn't last anyway, and a monopoly position only guarantees strong profits in the very short term. But I'm not overly critical of a company that chooses to focus energy on fighting the competition. I would just not advocate it positively.

The real problem, and I've seen this dynamic many times, is where the aggressive energy created by a fortress mentality is aimed at another department within the same company! And you would think that this would not be tolerated, but never underestimate the power of machismo and testosterone within a business where looking and sounding tough is celebrated and rewarded, and where, conversely, sounding weak and naïve is criticised and even belittled. So beware of this false God.

Perhaps my favourite line in the Nestlé values is *'Nestlé people base relations on trust, expecting mutual integrity and rejecting intrigue'* – the establishment and common knowledge and ownership of the roles and responsibilities will really serve to make the rejection of *intrigue* both possible and more obvious.

3. Utter respect for each other as expert specialist professionals

The amount of second-guessing that goes on in organisations is staggering and it is both inefficient (a total waste of time and energy) and divisive (causing frustration and often retribution). It is an entirely natural human dynamic to want to have input in and even control over things that happen around you and that impact upon your own plan. It's frustrating when something happens to divert you, especially when it feels as though it only happened because someone was lazy or incompetent or both. So when you look around the table at your teammates, to what degree do you judge them as being experts in their field, true specialists and complete professionals? Or are you guilty of judging them as 'less than' – as people who are not as good in their area as you are in yours; as people who are OK, but not as good as they need to be in order for the team to succeed; maybe even as people that you will need to 'carry'? (And how are they looking at you?)

Having respect for someone does not mean falsely judging that they are a superstar when they are not. It does not mean hiding your legitimate concerns about their competence, experience, strategy and performance. It *does* mean being honest with them in your views and opinions, being openly inquisitive and utterly supportive of their growth and success, and being wholly reciprocal in all humility for them to properly respect you back.

I often encounter a dynamic where a team leader will earnestly tell me that they cannot talk openly about each team member's strengths and weaknesses in front of the whole team, for fear of embarrassing anyone. It's as if there is something shameful about not possessing 100 per cent skill or competency in a role, or in exhibiting a trait or habit that is getting in the way of peak performance. This is ridiculous in my view. First of all it sets up an unhealthy and inefficient dynamic whereby only the leader possesses certain 'sensitive' information (and yet one of the team values might well be 'absolute honesty'!) and therefore the leader is burdened with expending energy on keeping confidences and having to handle individuals personally and in sequence. Second, it means that only the leader can support individuals in their growth and development, and then they have to attempt this in total isolation. Can you imagine trying to manage a football team in this way, where you have to keep 'private and confidential' the fact that the goalkeeper is struggling to perform to an adequate level? In a football team this would be inconceivable and simply ludicrous. First of all, everyone knows when a person is underperforming so there is no point in pretending there is no issue. Second, when it's in the open, all team members can be part of the correction. The only way the goalkeeper improves, conquers the obstacles raised and offers consistent high performance is if the whole team plays their part – protecting, then encouraging, then challenging, but ultimately believing.

Respecting someone means that we may have to communicate our disagreement, our frustration even. It means not allowing someone to fail needlessly. It means being prepared to be in conflict with someone and handling the unsettling feelings that come with this state. And it means trusting that they will do the same for us. When this exists, the team has the best possible chance of assessing a situation or event honestly and reaching the finest decision. If a team fails to do this, it will procrastinate, prevaricate and fudge the issue – it will then expend energy on justifying the flawed strategy. Number 5 below has more on conflict specifically.

One of the pitfalls I've seen many times is where team members adopt a safe and convenient mindset before a team meeting, rather than remembering consciously that they need to trust each other and not shirk the potential tensions and discomfort from a passionate and emotional debate. When we respect each other as expert, specialist professionals, we know and trust that each of us will come and advocate *our* area of responsibility. Rather than each of us coming and advocating the 'safe' aspect, we each come with the 'risky' aspect – and I don't mean 'safe' or 'risky' in the business or commercial sense, I mean it in the emotional sense. Here's how it plays out.

Team dynamics							
(1) Safe	a b c		X		d e f		**Risky**
(2) Safe	a	b	c	X	d	e f	**Risky**

Often the culture of team meetings is to debate 'safe' topics and arrive at 'business as usual' decisions. When the time comes for more strategic discussions, maybe at times of key scrutiny, the team might need to consider much more radical options. How do they go about this?

The cultural dynamic may be for individual team members to come well prepared to meetings and put fully formed ideas on the table, usually ones where they have 'laid the ground' with the CEO in advance. After all, the fear is that a 'poor' showing at a critical strategic meeting could be career-limiting.

What they will *not* do, unless they are very brave, is to come with a half-formed idea – something that has been niggling away at them as an option that the company might just have to consider.

So at (1) in the figure, individuals (a, b, c, d, e and f) put their 'positions' on the table and the team arrives at decision X, either by a genuine consensus or, more likely, on a tight deadline to end the meeting, after a summing-up by the CEO.

This looks like a very satisfactory decision-making process, and has the surface appearance of a team that is trusting, open and honest, if a little deferent to the CEO.

The awful reality, however, is that the team has not in fact reached a decision to which all are committed, and potentially has reached a decision to which none are committed. Individuals have put relatively 'safe' views forward, and have thus not been satisfied by being able to truly 'debate' the options.

This lack of commitment manifests in a conversation when one manager gets back to their office, to be greeted by their number two with the typical, *'How was the meeting?'*, and responds, *'Well, I am just not sure we are doing the right thing...'* And thus the rot starts.

At (2) in the figure, those same individuals put their true views on the table, or possibly 'risk' airing a half-formed idea, with the effect that on the surface the team looks like it is at times in irreconcilable conflict. Yet, because the fundamental respect is in place, and because the culture here is for individuals to feel safe in airing their passionate views, even though they are not always sure about what they really think and are genuinely open to persuasion, the quality of the debate is at its very highest potential.

> *Each individual then goes away emotionally and commercially wedded to the decision reached, and willing to put aside their own preconceptions and judgements*

The CEO in this scenario is a true facilitator, and brings the decision-making process to a close, exhorting the individuals to remember that team unity comes before 'being right'. Each individual then goes away emotionally and commercially wedded to the decision reached, and willing to put aside their own preconceptions and judgements for the good of the unity of the team and the unity of purpose of the company.

This is a true high-performance team. So in preparation for a meeting, do you work out what you think you can get or persuade others of and go in with pre-sanitised options and recommendations? Or do you work out what you truly believe to be best for your area of the company – for your customers, for your people – and prepare yourself to put those views forward passionately, to listen openly to others and to be truly open to adopting an entirely different option than that which you've argued?

So here are some questions that can be given to people to get them to prepare for a key meeting:

❋ *Although you may not be sure, what radical option do you think the company ought to at least be considering at the moment?*

❋ *Why do you think that?*

❋ *What would your worry be in raising that now?*

❋ *The acid test is this – can I as an individual go to a team meeting, engage in an open and honest debate, give my views and opinions with all the passion I have for them and listen respectfully to the differing views of my colleagues (without shirking from the discomfort of the conflict), watch as the team reach a different conclusion to me, and then go out and enthusiastically action the decision, as if it were my own?*

I often ask '*What's the size of the boardroom table?*' Have you ever noticed that boardroom tables are often huge – way bigger than any table we would ever have in our own home. And have you ever noticed the small scale of the debates that go on around such tables – when we respect each other as expert, specialist professionals, we can use the whole of the table, not just the safe and comfortable bit in the middle.

Why is it that Olympic athletes fall into each other's arms immediately after they have been trying their utmost to beat each other? Because of professional respect which turns into brotherhood when the battle is over. Do not be afraid of hurting someone's feelings or of appearing arrogant. If you are respected as a fellow professional striving for the finish line then you have nothing to fear. More than this, you have the potential for fellowship. But the gateway to fellowship is not politeness or sociability. The gateway is not being dishonest no matter what positive or caring motive that drives this. The gateway is being truly yourself. The gateway is discharging the totality of your responsibilities to the very maximum of your potential.

Be the expert specialist champion. Be the strident advocate for your area, your customers, your staff. Be their voice. Don't compromise in advance or sanitise your views to make them more acceptable or more likely to be approved or to make yourself more liked. You do not have that luxury. You *are* the head. You are the *one*. Live up to the responsibility that you have been given. It is a privilege to hold the office you have been given and every moment and every interaction is precious. Do not choke on the edge of the diving board. You have one chance. Every day you have one chance. Every day is your Olympic final. Be at your peak every day. To do this you will need the team's support, and you will feel that they should get an equal share of the glory as you. But take the glory and let them bask in your success. They want to work for someone who wins, not a nice guy who always come second.

When we describe our journey is it honoured or judged? If we had a frustrating time with traffic delays, do people say we were stupid to take the motorway or leave late, or do they accept the situation and ask what we need to get us back on time and feeling positive?

High-performance means being courageous enough to be a performer. Unapologetically the best you can be. Believing in yourself. Not hesitant, or holding back. When we hold back for fear our passion will hurt or offend others then we deny them the opportunity to be inspired and join us in our mission. Leave people changed, yet do not try and control their path.

Criticising a colleague for not *being* something is not a constructive act. Our job in supporting colleagues within a team is to help them be the very best they can be, using all their talents and passions. Then we should determine, with their agreement and input, how to support them by filling the gaps they will leave in their wake. It's called teamwork.

And while we are on the subject of respect for professionals, let's ask ourselves 'What is our reputation as a team?' Team unity is vital, but so is our reputation as a leadership team. People need to follow us even when we are not around. So how do we get our message out? How do we manage our own PR through internal communications and peer advocacy? Are we a team to be proud of? Are we a team to be copied? Are we a team to aspire to join? There are times when it's not just about the quality of the chocolates, it's also about the attractiveness of the packaging. Brain research has shown that if we are attracted by the quality of the packaging, the product within tastes sweeter to us. It may have the precise same chemical make-up as the product in the dull packaging that's fetching a tenth of the price, but whereas that product will taste at best OK and at worst terrible, our product will taste great. Same taste and yet not the same – our brains experience a different taste because our brain chemistry has been affected by our expectations. As a great team we want people to emulate us in our absence, and the best way to achieve this is, having got the product right first, of course, to focus on communicating expectations of quality, and ensuring that brain chemistry is working for us not against us – because the opposite is also true.

4. Acceptance of individual idiosyncrasies and personal circumstances

One of the themes running through this book, and perhaps the underpinning of corporate emotional intelligence, is to remember and then honour the fact that we are human. We are not machines, with the ability to pound out hour after hour of utterly consistent productivity with no rest and without getting sick. Neither are we prisoners, forced to live 24 hours a day, seven days a week, 52 weeks a year in sole service of our corporate roles and goals. And neither are we Vulcans with the ability to control our emotions to the extent that we behave rationally at all times.

We are human – beautiful, flawed geniuses all of us. Humans get sick. Humans have private lives. Humans are irrational. Humans make mistakes. There's a lot of 'messiness' and inefficiency that goes along with being human. If we focus on that aspect, bemoaning it and using both positive and negative forces to change it, we will fail and not only that, we will damage people along the way. So rather than wishing people were perfect, let's celebrate their messiness and see it as the critical creative factor that it really has the potential to be.

> *This is the true value of diversity – not the politically correct misinterpretation given to that term where we end up focusing on outputs (of gender or ethnicity balance, for example), but where we truly understand differences and proactively use these as creative forces.*

Thank God we are all different. It is our differences that will create the synergy of the team. This is the true value of diversity – not the politically correct misinterpretation given to that term where we end up focusing on outputs (of gender or ethnicity balance, for example), but where we truly understand differences and proactively use these as creative forces.

So when I encounter a colleague who possesses habits that irritate me, do I judge them as wrong, or bad or, worst of all, inferior to me? If this is my reaction, then first of all they will know this however hard I work to hide it, and second, I invite them to sit in judgement over me in return.

Since I am human, I may not be able to stop myself being irritated by their habits, but what I do have control over is how I react. So the real question is how we manage these reactions in each other within the team, and how we build an environment (a culture) and relationships of mutual respect, where we focus first and foremost on each other's strengths and skills and talents. Where we focus on their genius, not their flaws.

The use of psychometrics can be very helpful here. Psychometric profiling allows individual team members to understand each other and therefore accept each other. Profiling gives a language for honest and direct feedback and we can therefore learn not just to tolerate each other's idiosyncrasies, but to positively embrace them. We can consciously encourage acceptance over judgement, thus building a supportive culture not a competitive one.

It is also vital that we accept and support each other's unique personal circumstances. If there is a single male in the team, that individual may just be 'lucky' enough to have no responsibilities outside work (it being so inconvenient that people have private lives that frequently encroach on their work time and focus, that occasionally even deliver massive emotional changes that severely affect performance for many days or even weeks). But increasingly we will have care responsibilities outside work – children, aged parents – and these must be genuinely honoured.

Remembering that EQ has two parts – awareness and performance – it is fantastic for us to develop awareness and acceptance around these factors, but the truly great team goes beyond awareness and 'tolerance of', and is brave enough to pro-actively work to add value, deliberately and consciously using the differences to make things even better.

And this is where coaching comes in again – where we can practise peer group coaching, coaching each other and seeking each other out for coaching. First of all this assists the process of 'relieving' the leader of automatically being used as the sole coach. Second, it opens up the possibility of being coached by the 'best' person for that issue.

Who do you go to for coaching? You may, of course, naturally go to your boss, but they might not be the best person for you with the issue at hand – they have an agenda and may not be able to stop themselves from moving into rescuing or directing. More likely you will gravitate naturally to someone you trust, someone who knows you well, someone who is like you and thinks the same way, someone who shares the same beliefs (and who will therefore give advice that you could see yourself following quite comfortably), someone who will be kind and sympathetic, someone who may even offer to help out.

In the high-performing team, the opportunity is there to go to someone who is different to you – someone who will come from a completely different angle, someone who may give advice that is uncomfortable to contemplate, someone who isn't like you and who believes very different things, someone who will be really honest.

So go to your peers with an issue; go to the one who will challenge you most; go to the one with the characteristics you most need.

5. Conflict embraced and used as a creative force

We do not like conflict (well, OK there are some who do, but they are probably on the psychopathic or sociopathic spectrum). We find conflict uncomfortable. We experience anxiety as we anticipate conflict. Conflict leaves us feeling unsettled. It disturbs us to know or to feel that someone thinks badly of us. These are very powerful forces in a corporation and massive amounts of energy are wasted managing these forces, particularly since so many of them are hidden away like dirty secrets.

We like harmony. We love the comfort and security that accompany a sense of everyone being in agreement and of us all liking each other. Now I'm not going to undervalue liking each other. I want to work with people I like and frankly I find it stressful working with people I don't like. If I don't like someone, it's probably because they have different core values to me. If I like you, I am far more likely to be motivated to expend effort to support you, and far more likely to cheer when you have a personal success. But it's *how* we come to like each other that's really interesting.

There's an old saying: '*Set out to be liked and you'll end up being disrespected. Set out to be respected and you'll end up being liked.*' I really believe this and I've seen huge amounts of evidence to support it. My experience in corporations is that the people that I come to like the most, dare I say come to love even, are the people with whom very often I've had the biggest battles, the people that I've been in conflict with many times. But since they've always demonstrated their integrity, and they've accepted mine in return, we've come to a place of true mutual respect, and then the camaraderie is open to us, even the friendship.

I am not scared of making friends at work. Peter Thompson, who was the first CEO of the National Freight Corporation (NFC) when it was privatised in the early 1980s, said that it was the friendships within NFC that got him and the team through the difficult times. I believe that to be so scared of making and having friends at work (on the basis that I might have to fire you one day, therefore it's not appropriate nor efficient for me to make friends of my teammates) is another way we deny our humanity. Of course we are going to make friends at work. We may not use that collective noun when we talk of them, but actually why not? What are we so scared of? I will go to the end of the earth for a friend.

> *I believe that to be so scared of making and having friends at work (on the basis that I might have to fire you one day, therefore it's not appropriate nor efficient for me to make friends of my teammates) is another way we deny our humanity.*

Here's our problem – conflict is inevitable. And harmony is often an illusion. That's not to say that harmony is totally undesirable – listen to the harmonies of a male voice choir or a fabulous acapella group, and you'll be moved and entranced by the way the voices fit and complement each other. But look at any stable object under a microscope and see the vibrations going on, see the atoms and molecules bouncing off each other – so we may experience a sense of harmony and this is a great state, but often in corporations we achieve a false harmony – a passive harmony, a harmony of lies in actual fact. Which, of course, is no harmony at all.

Conflict is inevitable because there is more than one of us. And the more there are of us, the more open we are to being in conflict. And in a corporation we organise ourselves in structures by specialisms or geography. And we have limited resources. So we create conflict merely by communing together and trying to organise ourselves efficiently. There are, therefore, natural points of tension in any organisation. Sales are in conflict with admin if they've judged that the prospective customer cannot in fact pay; design are in conflict with production if they've judged that the product cannot physically be made in that way by a machine; marketing are in conflict with legal if they've judged that a claim for a major benefit of the product cannot be substantiated; France are in conflict with the people in the UK if they've judged that there is insufficient demand in France to launch the sexy new product there; distribution are in conflict with HR if they've judged that a star applicant has too chequered an employment record.

The very fact that we organise ourselves into specialisms actually guarantees that we will be in conflict with each other. So we better a) get used to it and b) embrace it. We must see conflict as a positive – as a source of creative energy to get us to the best possible result. Remember the example of 'What's the size of the board-room table?' from characteristic 3 above. So if we are discussing something and there is no apparent con-flict – stop and check. I know that the temptation will be to put it in the bank and carry on, and as a leader we are wary of being constantly accused of going and

> *We must see conflict as a positive – as a source of creative energy to get us to the best possible result.*

looking for trouble when it's not there, but if there is no apparent conflict, either we could be heading for a fall, or we could be doing something that is irrelevant to the cause. If there's no apparent conflict it will be either because the true conflict is being hidden (possibly not deliberately but due to a lack of really thinking some-thing through in how it will actually affect the people 'below' us who will have to execute the plan) or because no one actually cares, in which case why are we even bothering?

Tension is inevitable in a business organised by function and specialism, where expert professionals are each fighting for their own interests. Then we add the inner tension in each individual between what one has already achieved and what one still ought to accomplish. So be prepared for conflict. Embrace it, and don't shy away from the sometimes difficult emotions that go with it – anger, frustration, impatience.

'Sometimes I only know how passionately I feel about an issue when I get angry with someone who disagrees with me. And if I don't get angry, and I don't feel passionate, then why can't I just fall in behind...?'

6. Honesty valued as the most precious commodity

'Teams rely on one overriding commodity to be truly effective – complete honesty. And if a team is going to progress to a new level, the natural points of tension and conflict need to be explored and exploited. It's not that executives seek to hide things from each other, or even deliberately avoid conflict, but often an individual feels pressured to conform or to be the one that brings harmony back to an uncomfort-able situation.'

Fear of saying the 'wrong' thing can cripple a team, and nothing destroys progress within an organisation quicker than disunity among the senior team. In my experience, the manifestation of this is where individual directors communicate one thing within the team, and something

> *Fear of saying the 'wrong' thing can cripple a team*

different in the wider organisation. But why would a director say one thing in a board meeting and another outside? Simply, they do not hold absolute honesty to be the *most* valuable commodity that binds them together as a single cohesive unit.

Since none of us would say that individual directors deliberately lie to each other, or mischievously act in conspiracy with cynics lower down the organisation, what exactly am I talking about? I am talking about situations where an individual director chooses in a meeting with their co-directors to communicate (whether overtly in words, or subtly through body language, or indeed simply through omission – doing nothing) that they are in agreement with a decision, but then goes out and behaves in a way that communicates that they do *not* agree.

Take the case of a board agreeing that each director will allocate one member of their staff to a central task force. And let's say this decision is taken in October. So how can it arise that four months later only two of the directors have actioned the decision and the rest are still querying whether it's really necessary. How can this happen? Was the decision made or wasn't it? What has stopped the three non-conforming directors from actioning the decision? Why has the CEO allowed the situation to go unchallenged? Are they all in fact in a conspiracy with each other? *Something* is not right, so what is it?

There are a number of reasons why as an individual director, we might choose to say one thing and then do another.

Fear is a very powerful motivator. If we fear that communicating our disagreement will cause a negative reaction from either the CEO or indeed any of our colleagues, then we may not be courageous enough to voice our views honestly, especially where we may have gone along with the thinking to date. The fear of evoking that look of judgement from a colleague across the table that says '*How can you be raising this now, after what you said to me last week?*' or perhaps even worse, the look from the CEO that says '*How can you possibly believe what you are saying?*' might be enough to stop us from going against the decision. Maybe we just don't want to be seen as over-pedantic or cautious.

Care is another very powerful motivator. If we know that saying no to the CEO or to a colleague will disappoint that person, then we may be tempted to go along with a decision. Maybe we feel that to really be honest, we have to risk making one of our colleagues look foolish. We can often allow personal sensitivities to get in the way of true honesty.

Hope is a much-used but unpublicised strategy. Sometimes we may disagree, but we actually tell ourselves that it will probably work out OK, and that maybe we shouldn't rock the boat. After all, who are we to stand against our colleagues? We then persuade ourselves that they are probably right and we then hope that it will all work out. Or maybe we just hope that we can say yes and then no one will actually follow up?

But maybe its simpler than all the reasons above. Maybe we just have a *culture* whereby we are actually all in conspiracy with each other – where we can all go along with the CEO, but that experience has taught us that we can get away with not actually doing anything about it, especially where we can obfuscate with a mountain of excuses. If I know from experience that the team will accept my not achieving something or not having acted on something by the deadline, then why would I put myself under pressure?

There are many forces at work that could stop a team from being completely honest. However, as individuals, if we are going to 'go along' with a team decision, are we then going to go out and wholeheartedly work to make the decision a success? Or are we going to go out and effectively do nothing? Worse – are we going to go out and betray our disagreement by the way in which we behave? Employees are very cute readers of body language, and know instinctively when we are not behind something.

We work incredibly hard in our organisations to minimise cost and waste, and to maximise productivity and efficiency. And these things are clearly measurable when it comes to employees, equipment and money. However, all the gains we can make in these areas pale into insignificance when put against 'management' efficiency. If we can achieve maximum efficiency in management, we gain on many fronts – fewer managers (and therefore lower costs), speedier decisions and actions (and therefore faster growth) and more involved and motivated employees (and therefore higher quality).

And the way to maximise management efficiency is to ensure that absolute honesty sits at the heart of the team culture around the boardroom table.

When a senior team have mutual trust and respect at the heart of their relationships, and when honesty is the most valued commodity, then a company truly harnesses the power of the whole being greater than the sum of the parts.

7. Space honoured for rehearsal and celebration

Sports teams spend 95 per cent of their working time training. Orchestras spend 95 per cent of their time rehearsing. Business teams on the other hand, spend 100 per cent of their time performing (even when we are practising we are concerned with how we look!). In other words when performance is the most critical thing, teams spend huge amounts of time and energy on training, practice, rehearsal and experimentation so that they can perform to their very best. They create environments and activities where they have full licence and permission to experiment, improvise, try new ways, make duff shots, hit bum notes and generally look foolish in the process. And this is the true creative process. This is where excellence is honed, iterated and refined. We learn and grow not by an intellectual process of acquiring knowledge or theory, but through a process of repetition, iteration and constant refinement. We hone our performance until the basic and fundamental techniques are in our muscle memory, so that we can do it without engaging our conscious mind, so our body does it for us, and then we are free to use our conscious mind in reaction to the dance that is going on around us in the moment. We are free to use our flair, our instinct, our essence, our soul. Wow. What a performance!

So how does your team do this? What are the critical performances that you give? A team meeting is not a performance; it's training and preparation. A presentation to a major client is a performance – *that's* where we have to be at our very best. An all hands or town hall meeting with the employees – *that's* a performance and a place where we need to have fully prepared ourselves in advance.

A team meeting is not a performance; it's training and preparation. A presentation to a major client is a performance – that's where we have to be at our very best. An all hands or town hall meeting with the employees – that's a performance

And by performance I don't mean putting on an act. I don't mean pretending to be someone or something we are not. I mean striving to be the best we can at that moment in whatever we are doing and whatever role we are playing. If I consciously think about myself as a father, think about what I do wrong and what I could do to be a better father, and if I then seek to consciously do those things, I'm not acting, I'm just trying to be the best dad I can be for my children. I am seeking to perform my role as a father the best way I possibly can. This for me is the difference between acting and performing. So although I understand Tony Robbins' exhortation to 'Fake it before you make it', and I might even seem to advocate this at times (when asked 'How do I become a director?', my advice is always 'Behave like one first'), for me there is a critical difference between acting and performing.

I sometimes hear the argument that says 'if I rehearse then I won't be spontaneous', but this is a cop-out uttered by someone who can't be bothered to put the work in. Would you make your wedding vows up on the spot or would you at the very least have thought through the essence of what you wanted to communicate to your new spouse and all your friends and family congregated? Would you go for the most important interview of your life without doing any preparation? Then you won't get the job.

So if we would naturally prepare for critical performances, why would we not prepare for 'smaller' performances? As a leader we do not have the luxury of playing to small theatres where it really doesn't matter. We are always on stage and every action and inaction is judged. This is tyrannical and exhausting – there is no hiding place – but it is the responsibility that goes with the privilege.

I'm amazed at how managers don't observe their direct reports performing as a matter of standard management practice. How as a sales manager can you give accurate and effective, nay inspiring, feedback and guidance to one of your sales guys, if you do not observe them in the spotlight and under the pressure of the sales calls they make to customers? And yet I often hear that managers don't want to put their people off, and don't want to be accused of not trusting their people.

The trick is to make the prospect of your observation exciting, so it is eagerly anticipated. When the store colleagues see your car pull up in the customer car park, do they feel a thrill of positive anticipation or are they filled with dread?

Have you noticed how salespeople hate failure – fear it? And have you noticed how engineers love it – invite it? Why is this? Well for salespeople their experience is that failure (to win the deal, get the order, achieve the price increase, hit the target, etc) is punished, either overtly in missing out on financial rewards or promotions, or in that dreadful passive aggressive sort of way emotionally where they suffer the disappointment of their boss and maybe their colleagues. For a salesperson, failure is horrible and potentially final. It is to be avoided at all costs, and if suffered, it is to be deflected as much as possible. This is why we have to be so careful in our use of targets and in how we set objectives.

But for engineers, failure is inevitable and necessary, and provides incredibly valuable data – it is simply one amazingly useful step along the way to perfection. An engineer is dissatisfied and suspicious if something works first time, since that *had* to be luck. Engineers will test things to destruction – this is what they trust and then they know how to replicate the product or situation reliably and predictably, which means we can scale it and allow others to get involved. But salespeople will often take the first order, the easy sale, and get out quick. Weak salespeople miss so many opportunities.

Do you play video games? How do you learn the game? Do you studiously read the instructions, or do you simply experiment and learn as you go along? I'm no expert but even I've noticed that video games no longer come with instructions. There may be some tutorial modules to equip us with the basic console techniques, but after that we'll learn as we go. And in the combat games, we learn by dying. We may die hundreds of times before we successfully progress to the next level – and every time we die we learn something, and have new data to inform small changes in our strategies and techniques. So if we can do this when we play…

We have to let people play at work, for this is where we will create the finest arena for creativity and learning and improvement and growth. Our team meetings are the classic medium for rehearsal and practice, so we must create the culture that gives licence and permission for people to play, and then have structures and devices we can implement when we are all being too serious. One of my clients created what he called a '*Jumpers for Goalposts*' rule in meetings. He recalled that as a boy walking home from school (he lived in the Dickensian era), he and his mates would often stop on a small piece of waste ground and put their jumpers or school bags down as goalposts and have an impromptu football match. They all knew it wasn't real and it certainly wasn't perfect, but it worked. Ten minutes later the posts had been collected up and they continued home. So the rule in his meetings was that anyone, at any time, could literally call out '*Jumpers for goalposts*', and the team would metaphorically kick a ball about for ten minutes. During that ten minutes, the rules of the game changed from having to be right, or serious or even respectful, and the team members were allowed to be childish, wrong, crazy, politically incorrect, human… just for ten minutes. It was an amazingly powerful device and would often have a dramatic impact on the team performance and output.

> *We have to let people play at work, for this is where we will create the finest arena for creativity and learning and improvement and growth.*

8. Team is individuals' place of sanctuary and solace

In all the work I've done on team dynamics and in all the team rules, characteristics, etc, that I've witnessed, I've never seen this noted as something of vital importance. It is sometimes cited as a bonus, but for me it is an absolutely critical element of a great team. There are going to be times when I feel shit, when my performance is awful, when I am overwhelmed with responsibilities and tasks. Where do I go for support? Where do I go for solace? Where can I go for sanctuary? If my team does not perform this role for me, then the chances are I will not access what I need, and thus I will suffer harder and longer than I need to, and certainly harder and longer than is effective for me to deliver on my commitments. I have to know and trust that my team is the place I can go – for understanding, for sympathy or TLC, for support, for succour, for refreshment, for rejuvenation. I don't need much – the smallest dose has exponential power – and I don't need it often, but I do need it when I need it. And if it's not available, then I will suffer. And then I have to expend vast amounts of emotional energy on treating and healing myself.

And again the leader needs to set the tone here in their role modelling. It's fabulous working for someone who is open enough to come to the team and say that they haven't got a clue what to do. It's inspiring working for someone who is courageous enough to show their vulnerability and to expose their weaknesses and flaws. This means it's OK to be human in this team.

If you know the answer to everything and could do everyone else's job better than them, then what's the point of me?

Working for a boss who works hard to be invulnerable is exhausting and debilitating. If you know the answer to everything and could do everyone else's job better than them, then what's the point of me? How do I genuinely contribute and be seen as an individual star in my own right, if I can never surprise or delight you?

Always start a team meeting with a check-in. This is vital for one very simple reason – it brings human beings back into the room, whereas it was their corporapathic avatars who entered at first. If I go to a meeting focused on my own anxieties, objectives and motives, then all I will want is for you to have done what you committed to. And if you haven't, I'll be pissed off with you – I may or may not express this verbally, but you will know. Indeed you will be anticipating my reaction of frustration (anger) and so you'll be nervous and potentially defensive. Not very helpful.

But at a check-in you get a chance to say where you are and how you are. And if the reality is that you're not in a good place, then you get a chance to express that and have it witnessed and accepted. You are human after all. What happened is that you had every intention of completing the piece of work in time for the meeting, but you made the mistake of leaving it to the weekend knowing our team meeting was on the Monday. Then your dad had a fall in his care home (again) and you spent all day Saturday at the hospital, and all day Sunday helping reorient him back into the care home, which he had forgotten he lived in, even in just 24 short hours away. Although he's been in the care home for two years, he still occasionally gets disorientated and believes he is in fact in a mental hospital (the polite version of what he actually calls it), being held against his will. When you got back home at 10pm Sunday night, drained and upset, you were simply unable to write the report you'd committed to completing.

Because we have a check-in, I now see you as human – I see you as the beautiful, flawed genius that you are. My heart goes out to you as you tell us the story of your weekend, and my compassion thankfully wins the days. I am no longer annoyed at you, nor critical of you, nor do I condemn you silently as a jerk. Quite the opposite – I tell you not to worry, that I can either do the work myself or safely proceed without it or safely wait another week for it, and then ask you what I can do to support you in any other way.

What a difference.

154

9. A leader who is an honest coach and facilitator

The leader's role is critical – 'forcing' behaviours where necessary through great coaching, being ruthlessly consistent on boundaries, with a huge use of non-verbal rewards and sanctions, and a martyr-like willingness to stand apart when necessary.

The leader is the one who picks people up at their lowest point, who reminds them how privileged they are to be on the team when they are at their most self-absorbed.

Remember what Caroline Alexander said about Shackleton:

> When occasion demanded he would attend personally to the smallest details. Sometimes it would appear to the thoughtless that his care amounted almost to fussiness, and it was only afterwards that we understood the supreme importance of his ceaseless watchfulness.

The leader is the one who picks people up at their lowest point, who reminds them how privileged they are to be on the team when they are at their most self-absorbed.

Remember St Benedict's words about the abbot:

> He must vary with circumstances, threatening and coaxing by turns, stern as a taskmaster, devoted and tender as only a father can be.

The leader's role is vital – and since the team leader is conventionally the most senior manager, that leader needs to be supremely self-aware and wary of falling into the hierarchical power trap, as this can kill great team-working stone dead in a heartbeat.

One seemingly innocuous example of how leaders often fail to discharge their responsibility to the team is what I referred to earlier as the 'hub and spoke' model of running a team. This is where the leader positions themselves metaphorically at the centre of their direct reports, making themselves the hub through which all discussion and change must pass, with the direct reports merely the spokes on the wheel.

Typically in this scenario, people attend meetings for the most part for the boss's benefit. The boss gets updated, re-establishes personal control and gives input on issues and problems they care about. As a subordinate of this type of leader, you have to prepare for the meeting using your best telepathic powers to predict what the leader will want and what they will be interested in and focus on, and then endure the experience of watching as your colleagues 'get their turn' being grilled on what's going wrong in their area of the business. Unfortunately in this scenario, instead of using your creativity and energy to support your colleagues as they strive to perform their roles and meet their commitments to the team, your focus is on protecting yourself from the impending onslaught winging its way round the table as the boss's focus inexorably creeps your way. It is likely that your overall workload increases while you are in the meeting, both from all the things you are unable to physically attend while you are not at your desk, and from the additional tasks and changes that the leader asks of you in the meeting.

Depending upon what business you are in, your company will have its own version of the weekly update meeting. In retail it will be the often gladiatorial Monday trading meeting reviewing last week's numbers. In B2B it might be the Friday review of the week's numbers. The weekly update meeting has become the corporate colosseum, where Caesar watches as grown men and women fight to the death, and then delivers his verdict on the stressed individuals in front of him – 'thumbs up' for a *'Well done and you're OK until next week'* verdict, or 'thumbs down' for the condemnation of *'Your results have let the team down and you better deliver next week'*. And people wonder why the forecast is often missed week after week.

Part of the reason leaders get so stressed, and therefore can behave in the ludicrous and inhuman way I've described above, is that they very often believe that it is absolutely their job to sit at the hub of the wheel. They don't see this as control freakery, which is what it is, they simply don't know any other way. So they put themselves under enormous pressure, setting themselves up for an impossible task and superhuman responsibilities.

The leader must be the keeper of the sanctity of the meeting. Why do we meet? When do we meet? What's the agenda? What's a manageable and appropriate time for us to devote to it? What must it achieve? How do we ensure that our team meetings are positively anticipated rather than dreaded?

> *Notice, however, that I don't insist that the leader must be a 'great' facilitator, just an 'honest' one. It's the honesty that's critical, not the precise level of mastery of the skill.*

The leader *must* be a coach and facilitator – this is *their* role in the team. Notice, however, that I don't insist that the leader must be a 'great' facilitator, just an 'honest' one. It's the honesty that's critical, not the precise level of mastery of the skill. Like coaching, the most critical factor is being prepared to be clumsy with the skill, thereby demonstrating vulnerability and letting others in the team help out.

This is why, when we dealt with authentic leadership, I suggested that one of the 'buckets' of a leader must be the development of the senior team. This a crucial aspect of the leader's role. They may be the leader because they were the founder of the company. They may be a professional general manager recruited from the marketplace into the CEO role, in which case they may have been chosen primarily for their experience, their vision or their strategic prowess. While their competence in coaching and facilitation might have been a factor in their success in being given the role, it will not be the prime reason. But it is crucial, and may well be the most important aspect of personal development work that the leader undertakes.

10. 100 per cent commitment and personal subordination to the plan

Team unity around purpose is important, but not as important as unity around a plan. Under pressure, it's not that important *why* people do the things they do, as long as they follow the plan. We can sort of rely on the fact that we're bound together by some commonality of personal values and integrity. I don't care what is motivating you in the moment you need to act, I just care that you meet your commitment to the team.

An individual can choose to slack off or throw a sickie since they only have themselves to be accountable to, but in a team you do not have the luxury of acting through sheer self-interest. The benefit, of course, is the support. You are not alone and isolated, and although at times it is convenient, even comforting, to climb under the duvet and wish the world would go away, ultimately there is no satisfaction and fulfilment there.

The reason I place this characteristic last is that it presupposes that all other characteristics are in place, and if they are then this works brilliantly. Because all the preparation has led to this moment – when we are underway and there's no turning back. When the train has left the station. When we are 'all in'.

Chapter 11

Self-managed teams (SMTs)

Principles of self-managed teams

I've actively promoted self-managed teams (SMTs) as much as possible in the companies I've led, chaired and advised. For me the self-managed team is the ultimate expression of my whole corporate culture philosophy.

the self-managed team is the ultimate expression of my whole corporate culture philosophy

So many managers, when given power and authority over other people, fall into the trap of being both over-controlling and over-paternalistic. No wonder people stay safe and small and end up frustrating us. The more we try and control them, the more they defend themselves. The more we shepherd, the more they sheep.

But setting up SMTs is undoubtedly the scariest thing leaders have to contemplate. Giving 'our' power over to a potentially unruly and disorganised mob? Wow, that's truly scary. How do you 'manage' a team once you've told them they must in fact manage themselves from this point forwards? Surely in pushing the start button, you've relinquished power and authority to them? And to try to take it back will only serve to demonstrate that you never really meant it in the first place, or only went along with it as some sort of leadership fad for as long as the team did pretty much what you would have told them to do anyway.

Once SMTs have been launched, there can be no going back, and yet there are powerful forces that will naturally cause you as the leader to want to cling onto control, and to 'rescue' members of SMTs, however much they relish the new autonomy and however much they protest that they do not want to return to the old world.

There are principles that underpin the effective establishment and operation of SMTs – many of these will now be familiar to you from other parts of this book. Leaders have to be clear, resolute and utterly committed to the following:

1. A profound belief that SMTs lead directly to exceptional performance across the whole range of metrics, for all stakeholders

2. The setting of a few, high-level non-negotiables – around purpose, vision, values and goals

3. The absolute philosophy that 'the vision is the boss' – people should not seek to serve individual leaders, but strive always to serve the cause

4. A personal commitment to self-development, vulnerability and learning as role models

5. A collective commitment to coaching as the predominant cultural management methodology

6. An acceptance of the nature of human beings as both fabulous and flawed, both talented and frustrating

Having initiated the change to SMTs, there are some structural processes, rules and boundaries that are vital to install and reinforce:

1. The constant, mantra-like communication of the vision and the ritualisation of messages and disciplines

2. Enforcing 100 per cent compliance to non-negotiable processes – there must be agreed and enforced consequences for non-compliance

3. The setting and agreement of goals, objectives and KPIs

4. Constant watchfulness for positive and desired behaviours, and strong positive recognition of same

5. Similarly constant watchfulness for negative and undesired behaviours, and appropriate sanctioning of same

6. A step-changed regime of the highest quality of communications of results, metrics and comparatives of same to past periods, to plan and to best in class

7. Consistent coaching based on the questions *What do you think?* and *What decision will you make?*

8. Leaders investing all their time in education and facilitation

Ultimately, leaders have to know what they are letting themselves in for and go willingly into the unknown – more scarily into the 'out of control'.

One of the phenomena to watch out for is the 'Animal Farm' effect – how SMTs seem to want to exercise power and control over others as soon as they start to flex that which has been given to them! I've seen this happen every time I've launched SMTs in a business. It's just human nature, and so leaders have to be on hand observing to be able to give feedback and offer guidance.

The SMT conundrum is just a mirror of the conundrum of leadership in general. People in a team, a group or a community can and will work together over a period of time. But do they work for the good of the group, or do they work for individual ends? Do the more talented, more resourceful, more driven individuals stick with the team through thick and thin, or do they run for the hills when things get tough, or when they start to feel that things are unfair (for them!).

Leadership is an inevitable dynamic in any group – certain characters will exercise power and influence over others (consciously or unconsciously) and certain characters will eschew taking responsibility. So in any group there is a power dynamic playing out and organisations have simply found ways of harnessing this to ensure that leadership is exercised for the achievement of specified goals, rather than unspecified ones. Hierarchical leadership has proven popular because it has been a hugely effective way of legitimising leadership in pursuit of goals. The leaders have their power and authority formalised and then backed up with an array of rewards and punishments.

I believe that leadership is an essential dynamic for groups to attain positive goals and/or to achieve future states that benefit the whole rather than benefiting individuals. But here is the conundrum – if leadership is really about the greater good and the achievement of group or community goals that would simply not occur *without* leadership, then how is leadership formalised, institutionalised or personi-fied? How is one individual selected or appointed? Endowing one individual with power and authority over others is a dangerous dynamic. And yet leadership must at times involve a single individual espousing a unilat-eral and even autocratic decision as to what is right. This is so much easier when there is a single formally appointed leader with a recognised authority. But who the hell is that single individual to hold themselves in such a position of power over others? How do they judge *when* is the time or situation that they must dictate? And who monitors them?

> *Endowing one individual with power and authority over others is a dangerous dynamic. And yet leadership must at times involve a single individual espousing a unilateral and even autocratic decision as to what is right.*

We can strive to ensure that as leaders we are authentic, 'servant', consensual, collegiate, open, transparent, democratic, etc, but leadership also has to mean, at times, being dictatorial. So for me there are two foundations that must hold true for leaders to be truly effective:

1. Their motivation must be pure

A leader's actions and behaviours may be clumsy, difficult to receive, inappropriate even, but as long as their behaviours are motivated by both a purity of intention and serving the cause, the mission, the purpose and the achievement of the common unifying goals or ambitions, then they will be effective because their followers will feel their leadership to be completely authentic and thus completely trustworthy. It's why it often feels safer (although not more comfortable) to work for a well-intentioned bully than it does to work for a wishy-washy nice guy.

2. Their skills must be developing

Particularly in coaching and facilitation. When it is clear that the leader is learning and developing, striving visibly to be a better facilitator, followers are much more free to experiment, to be human and vulnerable, and also to challenge the leader with feedback and with contrary opinions and strategies.

When I'm asked to assess the effectiveness of managers within an organisation, especially as a cohort, the first question I will ask is *'What would happen if there were no managers?'* and it's amazing how hard some leaders find this question. Inevitably they come to list things that would go wrong if the managers were not there to check or control. I inevitably look at the list and find it unbelievable. In many organisations I honestly believe that employees' effectiveness and performance would go *up* if there were no managers – and this is where SMTs come in. Given guidance, information, some non-negotiable rules and processes, and some facili-tation, teams are wonderfully capable of managing themselves to achieve fantastic goals. What a team cannot do without some 'leadership' is raise itself to ever-higher plains of ambition and performance.

Before we end, let's look at one final aspect of team development and the question I will pose here is: What can we learn from animals? Animals communicate non-verbally; they are connected energetically – 'spiritually' even. And they can survive *only* by acting together. They instinctively know this and therefore they do not try and deny it.

Why don't fish bump into each other?

I have often been entranced by the beauty of a shoal of fish moving as if dancing like a single organism. I also recall a truly incredible display of a flock of starlings above the M40 last year that almost brought the motorway to a standstill. So when the BBC announced a new two-part series on swarms, I knew that I wanted to catch it – partly to revel in the beauty that I knew the camera teams would have captured, but mainly to learn more about *how* swarms behave and how those incredible effects are achieved. That critical question '*Why don't fish bump into each other?*' has haunted me for some time.

'One Million Heads, One Beautiful Mind' was the subtitle of the second part of the BBC programme. The title telegraphed the conclusions around collective intelligence. The programme duly delivered some breath-taking cinematography that left me incredulous as to the sheer 'intelligence' of the rest of the animal kingdom, and I could not fail but juxtapose the stupidity of us humans. For all our arrogant strutting at the top of the evolutionary tree, mere insects make us look Neanderthal. We may be the only animals on the planet to have developed consciousness, but as we have learned language to communicate, politics to organise ourselves and trade to exchange our skills, we seem to have lost our *collective* intelligence.

Seven lions are gathered around a water hole in Namibia at dusk. Six are drinking and one is listening. The lion who is on listening duty hears a wildebeest a half mile away. Forty seconds later, the wildebeest is dead, and all seven lions are eating. There was no verbal communication, no argument, no hesitation. No meetings, no politics, no research. The six lions knew instinctively when the listening lion moved that they had to go too. These animals cannot communicate with the same sophistication as us, they do not possess the intellect to organise themselves efficiently, and yet they operate as a team and *ruthlessly* achieve their objectives.

This everyday story of Mr and Mrs Lion and their extended family – their trials and tribulations, hopes and dreams – is often used to highlight how teams in business could operate, if only they trusted each other, respected each other's roles, and had that most precious of all corporate commodities, a common purpose.

Now we could spend time researching just how the animals, insects, birds and fish communicate and achieve such seamless collective effort. We could analyse what they do that is different to what we do. Some of us might even get religion in the search. Seeking to learn how the animals do it would be the typical way humans seem to want to make progress these days – looking for the new way, the latest fad, the 'answer' that will rescue us. Or we could just acknowledge the stupidity of how we humans currently behave, and focus on the interactions we have with each other as, in fact, mere animals. How much easier it is to simply focus on what *we* do wrong.

Humans do three things that animals don't:

1. We rely solely on words, ignoring non-verbal communications

2. We never say what we really mean

3. We break our agreements

Cesar Millan, the ubiquitous 'Dog Whisperer', tells us that humans are the only animals that will follow an unstable leader!

We talk too much

Our habit when we want someone to do something is to use words, and if they seem resistant, we talk slower and louder. You see, our words have become *all* that we have to motivate others. We humans are fantastically skilled at reading body language, yet we ignore it most of the time. We humans *are* connected to each other (I'll refrain from banging on about quantum mechanics here), and yet we are so cynical of anything 'spiritual' that we again ignore any ability we have to communicate through our very connection as human animals. But the problem is that when we rely on words, we invite resistance and procrastination from others through greater verbal gymnastics. Our love of debate, of dialogue and discourse, has become a major block on meaningful action. How many meetings did you attend last year where the same issues were discussed again and again, with necessary actions 'parked' as no consensus could be reached?

> *Our love of debate, of dialogue and discourse, has become a major block on meaningful action. How many meetings did you attend last year where the same issues were discussed again and again, with necessary actions 'parked' as no consensus could be reached?*

We are not honest and direct

It would also help greatly if we were courageous enough to say what we really meant, but we have become so fearful in organisations of hurting people's feelings or of being thought of as arrogant, that we pre-censor everything that we say. So we end up having conversations with people at work that are superficial and not honest – what Martin Heidegger called 'idle talk'. Organisational thinking of the past 20 years seems to have been preoccupied with creating cultures of harmony and consensus, but harmony is not a state that exists in nature, and Mr and Mrs Lion would laugh like hyenas at the notion of consensus on the issue of wildebeest hunting and sheer survival.

We say 'yes' when we mean 'no'

Finally we have learned the survival method of saying 'yes', when we actually mean either 'no' or 'maybe'. We so want to please others and look good, busy and helpful that we end up committing to things and then not being able to deliver on time, or even sometimes at all. And then we conspire with each other in a community to forgive each other for this, so that we can *all* be comfortable. You see, if I let you off the hook, you have to do the same for me.

If ever there was a time to go back to basics. Why not set yourself the simple challenge of adopting a new code of conduct in every meeting you attend:

1. Listen and ask questions (learn and create) rather than talk (defend and justify)

2. Be honest and direct – tell it how it is for you, and offer the meeting your honest views

3. Commit only when you truly intend to meet it, and honour every commitment you make

Why don't fish bump into each other? Because they are so much cleverer than us.

Summary

So here we are at the end of the section on teams. It's tough being a leader – always on show. It's tough being a high-performance team – always on show. We must subordinate ourselves to the purpose – the vision is the boss – and in return we are given money, status, the opportunity to create and achieve, and personal development. It can be a bitter pill to swallow when we discover that the price for liberation from autocracy is not freedom but the discomfort and exposure of having to take personal responsibility. If we've been brought up to believe that the reward for promotion is the bigger car, the office, the PA, the money, the lights, the glory and then when we get there it's all humility and self-sacrifice, well... bummer. But the rewards are extraordinary, the privileges immense. To be part of a winning team is a life-affirming and even life-changing experience, definitely to be recalled at the end, whenever that comes and whatever that looks like, as one of the most rewarding experiences of life.

The high-performing team simply have a 'knowing' that success is assured. This is not to say that they are arrogant or over-confident, or that they believe that every-thing will go smoothly, or even that they know precisely how they will do everything that is needed, but just that their trust and confidence in each other is so high that they feel nothing can stop them.

Section 4
Change

Chapter 12
Cultural change

Cultural change – just another form of control?

Everything I've witnessed and learned has taught me that in the corporation, culture is everything. How does it go? *'Culture eats strategy for breakfast!'* Ugh. A company can survive, thrive even, in the short term with a fabulous product that hits the market zeitgeist, but without attending to its culture its decline will be terminal. But cultural change is often simply another act of exercising power and making people conform to 'new' behaviours. So how do we facilitate genuine cultural change and development?

> *cultural change is often simply another act of exercising power and making people conform to 'new' behaviours*

I outline in this chapter the three stages of intentions, structures and behaviours as the fundamental process, and while these concepts may be familiar, the real key lies first of all in the total alignment of all three, and second, in the differentiation of values as a structure and not an intention, and of coaching as a structure and not a behaviour. In Chapter 14, I outline the eight steps of genuine cultural change, accenting the dynamic whereby in order to truly change, people have fundamentally to be more afraid of the status quo than of the change before them.

Let's repeat – a company can survive, thrive even in the short term with a fabulous product that hits the market zeitgeist, but without attending to its culture its decline will be terminal. What's more, everyone in a corporation knows this to be true and everyone says publicly they believe it. In 2008 I worked with the top 150 leaders of a multinational drinks company as they started to integrate their recent acquisition of a competitor, including their Russian and Asian businesses. In their own words they were leading their company from being a dodgy Danish conglomerate to being the fastest growing global brewer. The integration needed was to rapidly deliver €1.5 billion of integration savings while paying €25 million per month interest on the debt. I met a scarily formidable corporate finance specialist who'd been invited to speak at the leaders' conference, and she made this statement in her speech:

> Culture plays perhaps the greatest part in successful M&As; I can't put a value on a company's soul on my spreadsheet, but without one there's no hope!

The three pillars of cultural change

So how do you change the culture of an organisation? It starts with clear and inspiring *intentions*. It is anchored on clear and disciplined *structures*. It lives and breathes through desired *behaviours*.

It starts with clear and inspiring intentions

What intentions do we have for our business and how do we express and communicate these to our stakeholders?

What is the organisation's purpose or mission? What was the original founding idea or world problem that it set out to be the solution to? This may have changed along the way, of course, but when we go back to that initial and original spark that created the business, we have a chance of honouring our heritage and the often enormous well of goodwill, emotion and value of our history. Often this is expressed in the brand values curated by our PR or advertising agency, who may have been finer guardians of the purpose than successive management teams.

What is our vision for the future? What is the finest and clearest emotional picture we can create of what our desired future looks like and feels like as we look towards the horizon?

What are our values? What are the written and unwritten rules and guidelines we will lay down and enforce for the way we want to behave in our journey in service of our purpose and in striving to make our vision a reality?

What are the 'iconic' goals we will set? What are the big, symbolic, indisputable milestones we will set to guide and inspire us and for us to be sure we're on track, and that we've arrived? And what are our ambitions for each group of our stakeholders – investors, senior executives, middle managers, employees, customers, suppliers, the community in which we operate? If one group is overly favoured, worse still if one group is demonstrably *dis*-favoured, then once again we can achieve some apparently 'great' things in the short term, but long term we are doomed. So we need an 'iconic' goal for each group.

I use the term 'intentions' as the heading for these aspects for one simple reason. We are absolutely guaranteed not to achieve any plan we set out.

I use the term 'intentions' as the heading for these aspects for one simple reason. We are absolutely guaranteed *not* to achieve any plan we set out. Things will *not* go according to plan – we simply cannot control the universe to the degree required. External events *will* occur to blow us off course. So if we are rigidly wedded to making the world look precisely as we have said it will be, we are going to be inevitably disappointed. We simply set ourselves up (to fail) as machines in control of nature, corporate Canutes who will waste massive amounts of energy and resources, enslaving everyone involved to the fatuous pursuit of the impossible.

But if we have 'intentions' we allow ourselves to be human, and thus we are free from the emotional weight of ludicrous expectation, and free to adjust the tiller and reset the course if events dictate. We want the clarity, inspiration and guidance of vision and goals, but we must retain flexibility to be realistic and relevant.

It is anchored on clear and disciplined structures

Once we've set the course, we need to organise ourselves for the best possible chance of success. We need an efficient and enabling organisation structure, a sound and well accepted operating model, efficient (maybe even 'lean') business processes, HR processes that genuinely enable people to perform to their very best, and clear boundaries and disciplines for recognising, rewarding and sanctioning behaviours and actions.

And while we will establish our values in the first step, along with our purpose, mission and goals, we then need to bring our values into working for us as non-negotiable structures. While our goals might change as the world unfolds before us, our values are the one likely constant. They are 'the way we do things around here' and as such must be enforced as processes more than desirables.

And the same goes for coaching. Coaching is not a behaviour, it is a structure. It is a non-negotiable process we will use for the achievement of our goals. As a skill, of course, we understand that people will not be perfect coaches – clumsy coaching is the way – but just as people need to be educated in the business processes and conform 100 per cent to them for maximum organisational efficiency and collaboration, so it is for managers with coaching.

It lives and breathes through desired behaviours

The finest plans are often found in documents gathering dust on shelves or in filing cabinets, while chaos and failure inhabit the organisation. A great plan is essential, and the first two stages above will give us a phenomenal plan, but it is in the execution that we live or die. This is where the rubber hits the road. It is how we actually behave, what we actually do that brings a plan to life. And this is the biggest aspect of potential disconnect in an organisation – that the actions and behaviours of all involved do not fit with what's in the plan.

So the important aspects of this start with the way the senior executives role model, then run through how the middle managers and team leaders coach their employees, culminating in the empowerment of employees to willingly and voluntarily do the best/right thing in pursuit of the plan. I cannot over-stress the importance of what leaders pay attention to in guiding employee behaviour. I might even be tempted to say that this is the single greatest factor in guiding how employees behave and what actions they take and do not take. And again we come back to the power of the hierarchy, and why leaders have to massively over-index on their role modelling. Having put the work in to create the plan, they obviously need to keep a check on progress, but this takes just a few moments each week. The vast majority of a senior executives' time should be spent ensuring the behaviours are those desired. They need to focus on how people are prioritising and making decisions, on the quality of communications and relationships, on how people are feeling.

> *I cannot over-stress the importance of what leaders pay attention to in guiding employee behaviour. I might even be tempted to say that this is the single greatest factor in guiding how employees behave and what actions they take and do not take.*

The bottom line is that the behaviours are merely the outcomes of the cocktail of ingredients that have gone to make up the environment. Leaders need to work proactively on the intentions and the structures, and then monitor the behaviours adjusting their inputs through leadership and coaching as they go. And since the intentions piece should only take a very short space of time to establish, the vast bulk of leadership and management time can be focused on the structures piece, ie, constantly refining the processes and constantly coaching.

What is culture? More importantly, what is a 'winning culture'?

Culture is often defined as 'the way we do things around here'. Culture can often be the written vision and values, but more usually it is the *unwritten* rules that truly govern; the unconscious communication between people of how things are done and what is never to be done. So the really important question is what is a 'winning culture'?

A winning culture is one where people are working to a set of desired values and behaviours in pursuit of an inspiring purpose, vision and goals; where this collective way of working leads *directly* to the achievement of exceptional results and where the community is so inspired by the shared experience that people come to believe in ever-more extraordinary possibilities and are moved to strive for ever higher ideals.

Why do we need to change?

Change is constant, inevitable and largely unpredictable. Companies should there-fore be geared up for constant change, but in order to be mentally healthy and open to giving their best efforts, human beings need some constancy. It is the job of the leaders, therefore, to manage the environment in such a way that change is navigated and executed in the most effective way.

Leaving aside the frequent and individually minor adjustments to everyday working that allow the company to survive a constantly changing external environment, there are three classic reasons why organisations embark on 'major' change programmes or initiatives.

1. New leadership
2. 'Crisis' event in marketplace
3. 'Crisis' event in company's finances

1. New leadership

We've all witnessed the arrival of the new CEO, and the all-too-familiar tactics that are then employed – not exactly the sucking of teeth and uttering of the word *Cowboys* as the new workman surveys what was done by the last incompetent, but the cor-porate equivalent: a strategic review, a clear out of executives, maybe a sacking of advisers, a re-negotiation of costly contracts and agreements, but most of all a piling of anything and everything possible into the next set of accounts to 'clear the decks' for the new regime. If the share price drops, the new CEO can legitimately claim that the old guard had actually been fooling the market, and this now is the correct new baseline, from which the new team can create shareholder value.

A new CEO knows that their honeymoon period will be short-lived, but nevertheless it can be used to great effect, dumping everything that was wrong and the fault of the last CEO. Next year's results will absolutely be laid at the door of the new incumbent, so they need to start by knowing that there are no more skeletons. If you think this sounds manipulative, I might agree with you – but remember the new CEO will have negotiated share options based on an increase in the share price from a base value, and they are likely to have negotiated that, since they cannot know in advance what the true base value is, and it is in their interest to force the base value as low as possible.

And notice that new CEOs bring with them the hangers-on who also smell money. Advisers who charge thousands, millions even, for their advice – mostly, of course, for their patronage of the new team. This is why a company with a value of £100 million can consider paying £10 million in fees to initial public offering.

New CEOs always have their way of doing things, their trusted people and agents, their view of the industry and its future, their (objective) view of the company's state of health and their prognosis for the patient. By definition this will be very different from their predecessor, even where all parties agree that the predecessor was stunningly successful. And new CEOs are desperate to demonstrate the personal difference they can make, otherwise they look in the mirror with that most haunting of self-destructive questions, 'What is the point of me?'

So get ready for a new vision, values, goals and strategy. Get ready certainly for a new culture.

2. 'Crisis' event in marketplace

The great thing about a crisis is the completely galvanising effect that overcomes the fear of taking action. When things are calm it can feel like we've got too much to lose; it can feel like it's just too risky to change when things are actually going OK. But in a crisis... well, here we go. Tell an employee they need to take a 10 per cent pay cut in advance of a major competitor launching an initiative that could see our market share drop, and they'll stubbornly or even actively resist. Tell an employee they need to take a 10 per cent pay cut or else the company will fold on Friday, and you've got them. A crisis enables us, licences us, gives us permission as leaders to take severe actions that we probably should have taken before but were too scared to. This is actually the lifeblood of the market economy – that companies compete with each other for customers, and in doing so constantly strive to improve the quality and price for the customer, not necessarily because of the positive desire for excellence, but more likely because of the Darwinian desire to beat the competition, be the fittest and thus survive.

The leaders in this situation have a convenient ogre to set up to be the focal point of the change message and the hardships people will have to endure to beat the competition. Setting up the 'enemy without' means as leaders we can scare our people into accepting changes that are not strictly necessary, and that we would never dare to propose in 'normal' times, in the corporate version of Jo Moore's 'it's a good day to bury bad news'. Leaders position themselves as some form of messiah, to be trusted absolutely and without question, and bring out their very best Henry V rhetoric to seal the deal. In this phase we can do things to people without all that usual crap of having to communicate, discuss and debate. We can give the company a good dose of old-fashioned autocracy and we'll all be the better for it. Well, those of us still in employment will be the better for it, those of us still earning the same money, those of us not having to change our family arrangements to work different patterns, those of us whose prospects for promotion and greater pay in the future are still intact. OK, I'll rephrase – we can give the company a good dose of old-fashioned autocracy and as the new leadership team we'll be the better for it (because all others may not be).

And who wouldn't be inspired by Henry V? Who wouldn't be inspired by a new freedom to be aggressive towards the competition? And if the department that we rely on internally aren't up to it, then they're also the enemy and we have the same licence to be aggressive with them. After all this is a crisis. This is heady stuff and incredibly appealing, and even if we see thousands of our colleagues sacrificed along the way in the name of efficiency, this just serves to remind us of the scale of the crisis, and our self-survival instinct is just relieved that it's not us being discarded.

3. 'Crisis' event in company's finances

This is the same as a crisis event in the marketplace, but leaders have to construct a slightly different ogre to be the focus for aggression – past CEOs, CFOs, management teams or owners usually, although advisers and auditors can also come under fire. We will blame whoever is most culpable, obvious or convenient for creating the black hole in the finances, or for creating the legacy costs that are now crippling us.

If we cannot really blame the past governors, then we do have to focus on the external parties who acted (so calculatingly and personally) against us – maybe the government or a regulator or maybe a competitor who enjoys freedoms that we don't have the luxury of, but you get the gist. The strategy is actually pretty similar to the crisis event in the marketplace – create fear, create the ogre, do things in the name of the crisis, protect and grow ourselves in the process, for as long as we can get away with it.

> *Now I'm all for using fear. For using it, not creating it I hasten to add. This might sound as though I'm contradicting myself. But fear (of change) is inevitable, so we need to ensure that it works for us, not against us.*

Now I'm all for using fear. For *using* it, not creating it I hasten to add. This might sound as though I'm contradicting myself. But fear (of change) is inevitable, so we need to ensure that it works *for* us, not against us. The trick is to channel people's fear into the status quo, not into the change. People have to be *more* fearful of staying as we are than they are fearful of changing. We can make the actual change process exciting (the other side of the coin from fear) but first we have to get people to accept that there is no choice but to change. And, of course, a crisis is a wonderfully convenient route to achieving this, but what if there's no actual crisis? How do we create a John Kotter 'Burning Platform'? (More on that in Chapter 13.)

The four dilemmas

1. People development v business results
2. Short-term v long-term results
3. The place for targets in maximising performance
4. When to add headcount

Dilemma 1: People development v business results

Intellectually we may understand, even agree, that if we focus on developing our people, the best possible business results will flow from that. If we focus every day on developing the finest performances and the greatest personal growth of our people, then we truly open ourselves to the potential and opportunity of astonishing and extraordinary results – results we would never have dared to commit to a plan or a forecast.

If you are a professional golf caddie, it is the same dilemma you face as your pro approaches the 18th green, with the leader in the clubhouse by one shot and no one behind you. If your pro chips in from 60 yards, they will win $1 million (your share is a tempting $100,000). If they don't it's a play-off for second place, and they're spent. This is it. One shot. So here's the dilemma – do you get them to focus on hitting the ball in the hole, or do you get them to focus on playing the best shot they are capable of? Of course the answer in this example is obvious. Not only would screaming at them to 'hit the f***ing ball in the f***ing hole' be of no help, it would probably cause them to play a poorer shot through fear. So calming them down, encouraging them to access all that solid and heavily practised technique, whispering to them to 'let the club do the work' or 'play the best shot you can and what will be will be' is by far the best thing we can do. The pro can only play the best possible shot and let the universe do the rest. The result will be what the result will be.

If this example is blindingly obvious for golf, why is it not so obvious in business? Because I have to tell you that my experience is not good with this dilemma. Leaders are habitually guilty of seeing these as mutually exclusive, rather than truly believing that focusing on people gives the best results. They are frequently guilty of putting the achievement of a result (making a sale, for example), ahead of developing a person (holding a one-to-one, for example). How many times have you approached the performance reviews of your people with a feeling of dread, of them being a chore that will get in the way, rather than a feeling of excitement, of them being a fabulous unlock for fantastic results to come? How many times has a boss cancelled a weekly one-to-one with you, or arrived late and stressed, or cut one short because they've got so much on their plate? When executives get busy and stressed you can bet your life they'll sacrifice the people stuff first. Because *actually* what they believe is that people development cannot help them today, might not even be able to impact things next week or next month. Therefore in moments of stress, let's postpone the people stuff until it's quietened down. What a missed opportunity, since our greatest opportunity to develop people is the very precise moment of stress and pressure.

If we do all our training and development when things are calm, we set up the most artificial of dynamics.

The major airlines don't train their pilots to fly in calm, clear and balmy conditions. The autopilot does that. No, they are trained to fly with one engine on fire, with failed hydraulics, into an airport suffering a typhoon.

The major airlines don't train their pilots to fly in calm, clear and balmy conditions. The autopilot does that. No, they are trained to fly with one engine on fire, with failed hydraulics, into an airport suffering a typhoon. Now *that's* when we need them to perform at their best. So if you simply have to attend a client meeting at the same time you were supposed to do a one-to-one, how about taking them with you? *Use* the moment to develop them rather than postponing and sending a message that a) their development is not critical, and b) you are more important than they are.

Dilemma 2: Short-term v long-term results

This dilemma is hugely understandable, but the way it is spoken about and the advice given internally to handle it often make the dilemma worse. The mirror of this is the 'intellect v pressure' piece, whereby our rational and intellectual thinking believes that focusing on people development gives the strongest and most extraordinary results, but our habits under pressure play to the *just get it done* dynamic. It is fundamentally about control. If I hit a short-term objective, I am demonstrating I can control events. If I miss one (however arbitrary the target) I appear not to be able to control things, and if I can't do that, what is my value as a manager? Since there is so much *self-generated* pressure within many organisations, leaders need to constantly reinforce their assurances around 'OK to fail' and then they have to reward the behaviours when people do fail, rather than punishing them for making mistakes. In very exceptional circumstances, a leader might decide that hitting the short-term target really does supersede every other consideration. If we are facing not making the payroll at the end of the month, with the bank then closing us down, we certainly need to do some extraordinarily short-term things, but are there really such crises in profitable organisations?

Dilemma 3: The place for targets in maximising performance

It has to be a good thing to create a model of what it looks like when a business is running perfectly, and to see, therefore, what the absolute optimum outcome is. Inevitably the bottom right-hand cell of this spreadsheet will be exponentially bigger than current results. The dilemma comes in how to share this information, and on what basis to set the targets. If we simply go on a 'last period +' model, we'll get good incremental growth but we won't access the quantum leap stuff. If, however, we set the targets at or close to the 'theoretical optimum' we risk demoralising people who come to realise they can never achieve the goal. Most companies get round this dilemma through a balancing of a growth factor with a stretch factor, and/ or separating financial rewards and incentives from the target in some manner. The added factor in many modern corporates is that the word *exceptional* has changed meaning. *Exceptional* in the outside world means unlikely to be repeated or maybe not appropriate to even *try* and repeat. With corporatism *exceptional* simply becomes benchmark. If I have a quarter where I beat quota by 30 per cent, that becomes my new objective. This is relentless and exhausting.

Dilemma 4: When to add headcount

This is a much bigger dilemma than ever before, since in the past adding head-count has been in itself a growth driver. Now, under severe competition, and with the potential for machine learning and AI to replace human jobs, we are really head-count restrained. This means that people feel they now have a legitimate excuse for underperformance – '*I didn't have enough resource, so I had to leave sales on the table. I would have made the number with more resource.*' The counterargument is 'use your current resources better' and there is much to be said for this, since as we know when managers are, for example, better coaches, the productivity of their teams rises. But we also have a management community at near breaking point, with the vast majority of managers putting ten-plus hours a day into meetings, and then getting through their emails during the evenings and at weekends.

Execute successful growth strategies *through* transforming the culture of an organ-isation – where the very act of changing the culture leads directly to the most fabu-lous business results.

The three classic mistakes and the two philosophical foundation stones

People have been through change programmes so often that they've stopped believing in them. That's largely because leaders make one of three common mistakes:

1. Communicating that improved customer service is the reason for change, instead of being honest about profit, security and growth

2. Starting the change process with a restructuring, instead of the need for change and the vision

3. Having management, instead of the employees, design the change processes

So how can we avoid a change programme becoming another 'management fad'? Well we need to embrace two foundation stones:

1. Given the same knowledge and understanding of all the facts, the vast majority of managers and employees would reach exactly the same conclusions as us and would make precisely the same decisions about what is needed *(So why do we keep key information to ourselves and then expend so much energy forcing 'our' changes upon seemingly unwilling followers?)*

2. Once 'followers' are forced to engage in thinking about what is needed and deciding on required actions, they automatically start taking responsibility *(So why do we try and do so much of the thinking for them? Why do we effectively rescue them from having to make key decisions?)*

Chapter 13

The cycle of ownership

Five-stage 'cycle of ownership'

As a CEO and then as a consultant and chairman, I've implemented hugely practical and successful change programmes, refining their effectiveness over many iterations. Watching people go through change, I learned early on that actually you are leading people through an adapted cycle of grief – all change involves at first loss, and then an acceptance of changed reality, before finding the joy in the new situation. Dame Elisabeth Kübler-Ross gave the world the cycle of grief. It has five stages:

1. Denial

2. Anger

3. Bargaining

4. Depression

5. Acceptance

I realised that people in organisations go through a similar cycle when faced with a change that is outside their control. They react, they defend themselves, they resist, until they feel they have some control back. This is why emotional ownership is essential. So I developed a five-stage 'cycle of ownership':

1. Uncertainty

2. Resistance

3. Engagement

4. Reflection

5. Action

Stage 1: Uncertainty

Most of us live our lives according to some plan, even if it's not particularly conscious. Happiness for us is achieving something we've planned for – we love it when a plan comes together. And so receiving news of a change to be imposed upon us immediately brings up uncertainty for us, and we become 100 per cent focused on ourselves and on how this change will affect us.

A thousand unanswered questions rattle off in our heads – *'Will I still be able to book that holiday I've been planning? Does this mean I will have a new boss and if so, what will they be like? What new jobs will I have to take on, and how will I know what to do? Where will I sit? Is this change it, or is there stuff they're not telling us yet?'* We moan silently to ourselves, *'I've only just got used to my job, only just started to feel competent and comfortable in it, and now it's changing. When I came into work this morning I knew what was expected of me, and now it's all changing.'*

Uncertainty immediately brings up insecurity or, in other words, fear. We fear the unknown and we may even panic when it is clear that other people are now in control of our lives. If you want to know just how close people at work are to insecurity, try this simple test (actually, please don't as it's abusive!) – walk up to one of your employees, tap them on the shoulder and utter the chilling words 'Can I just have a minute...?' Watch the blood drain from their face and notice how they instantly think something bad is about to happen to them or that they've done something wrong.

> *Uncertainty immediately brings up insecurity or, in other words, fear.*

This is why communications about change need to be crystal clear and actually quite brutally simple and direct. Remember that once you have announced the change, people pretty much stop listening to you as their own brain chatter of insecurity takes over. So in the change message, there must be no room for ambiguity and the change message has to be non-negotiable. The reality is that since fear is going to be an issue anyway, whether we like it or not, we need people to be more fearful of the status quo than they are of the change we are making. It's called the 'Burning Platform'. Exciting visions and symbolic goals are crucial to any change plan, but unless the Burning Platform is established, getting people to accept the inevitable discomfort involved in change is going to be almost impossible.

However, once the change message has been communicated, it is vital for leaders to acknowledge the inevitable feelings of insecurity by enabling people to talk openly about their worries or their personal concerns about the change, and by then accepting these emotional reactions, without shirking from the change or retracting any part of it. And it is vital to start the process of painting an exciting future.

Getting the change message right is equally important as getting the change decision itself right.

⊛ Tell them what happens if we don't change

⊛ Tell them there's no choice

⊛ Ask them how they feel

⊛ Ask about their concerns

Stage 2: Resistance

Fear induces one of two different reactions in human beings – fight or flight. For people in employment, neither choice is actually possible. We cannot fight, since we would be sacked, and then how will we pay the mortgage? We cannot run away, since if we quit then how will we pay the mortgage? We are trapped, and so our only course of action is to hide.

Once we have absorbed the news of the change and our brain has started processing, we go naturally and predictably into resistance and denial. It's not the change that we are in denial of, it is the emotions that we want to deny. And it's not that we choose to be disruptive or

> *It's not the change that we are in denial of, it is the emotions that we want to deny.*

resistant or difficult (we may even 'know' that the change will be good for us), it's simply an inevitable process, because we have not yet psychologically accepted the change. Easier to deny what is happening than to accept it – we're simply not ready.

So our rationality kicks in and we start seeing the pitfalls and flaws in the plan that our leaders have clearly not thought through properly. We think about past changes and realise that not everything we've been told in the past has actually happened. We start second-guessing our leaders' motivations and intent, and endow them with Machiavellian strategising. We decide to lie low, and wait and see what happens.

Which is disappointing for our leaders, of course – they, after all, are very excited about the change. They've been living with the change for some months probably, agonising over it, strategising, creating the vision, and now they've announced these very exciting plans to the employees, they can't understand why people aren't excited too.

But the bad news for the leaders has only just started, because what happens next is utterly baffling to them. It shouldn't be, of course, and if they understood human nature then they would be expecting it, but I'm afraid that human nature can be highly inconvenient to leaders. So much easier to assume that people are resources who will simply do what they are told.

What happens next is that people start talking to each other. People ask each other what they think about the change. And, of course, if I am feeling insecure and going into denial about the change, then so is the person I am about to talk to. So when I ask them what they think, even if they are a bit hesitant and non-committal, I see their insecurity and I am reassured. *'It's not just me. Everyone feels the same.'*

We start to conspire against the change – not necessarily because we want to become active in our resistance, but because we want to feel safe again. And what makes me feel safe is agreeing with people around me either that the change will not happen or that it won't be as bad as it sounds. And since I cannot actively fight or run away, I must hide, which means I will hold my conspiratorial conversations out of earshot of my leaders. To them I must, of course, appear to be OK with the change.

> *The denial phase is thus characterised in corporations by people sounding as though they are in agreement*

The denial phase is thus characterised in corporations by people sounding as though they are in agreement, using political language and 'management speak' and avoiding anything that sounds like a specific commitment.

Leaders often feel like they can't win, and so the blame game starts. *'Don't they know these changes are inevitable/have been forced upon us/will be good for them?'*

While it is still OK for people to be inactive and not openly committing in this phase, they need to be challenged by the leaders to expose the truth of their position, and to move them towards the next stage as quickly as possible. Whereas in the first phase leaders should ask people how they *feel*, and what concerns and even anxieties the change brings up for people, in this phase people should start to be asked what they *think*, and what obstacles and barriers people can see that might stop the change happening or that might cause the plan to fail.

- 🌐 Ask them what they think

- 🌐 Ask what obstacles they can see

- 🌐 Coach and facilitate

- 🌐 Don't start negotiating!

Stage 3: Engagement

Once people accept that change is going to happen whether they like it or not, they quickly move to negotiating, which is their way of wresting back some element of control over their life.

This is one reason why leaders should contemplate making the change not just inevitable from the outset, but *irreversible*. People can resist a planned change for a long time, but it's much harder to resist a change that is already executed. I know that we have all been taught that consensus is a good thing to aim for, and that involving people in future decisions is an effective way for them to truly own the plan, but this is the modern conundrum of leadership, and it's why probably the most critical aspect of any change is for the leaders to decide right up front what is non-negotiable for them.

> *the most critical aspect of any change is for the leaders to decide right up front what is non-negotiable for them*

Why? Because the negotiation phase is coming, and when we get there we need to be able to *genuinely* negotiate with our employees, not simply try and manipulate them into coming up with the right answer. So leaders need to be aware of this and to be clear over any non-negotiable elements of the planned change, and thus by definition be clear over elements of the plan that they are willing to allow people to design themselves. Otherwise this stage will be mishandled, and either too much ground or not enough will be given to those expected to follow. People know when they are being manipulated and behaviour is all too often geared towards *sounding* like compliance, so the leader needs to be crystal clear in handling this stage.

A simple place to start in the negotiating phase is to go back to the list of all possible obstacles or barriers created by the employees in the denial phase. And we *have* this list, since we asked them the right questions when we were there, knowing that the time was rapidly coming when the employees would be ready to start discussing the details of the change with us.

And since as leaders we were crystal clear at the outset what was genuinely up for negotiation, we can genuinely let go of trying to control the outcomes of this phase. There is no finer way to give control back to a workforce than to genuinely let them design the changes. Notice I have used the word 'genuinely' several times in this phase. Countless times I have seen leaders get this phase wrong – either granting too much latitude and therefore going back on some of the severity of the change as some kind of sympathetic reward to people who have been through so much in stages 1 and 2, or making it clear that although the employees are being asked to design the detail of the changes, their answers will only be accepted if they coincide with what the leaders decided in advance.

⊛ Ask how they feel they can contribute

⊛ Use their list of obstacles and coach for solutions

⊛ Reward positive ideas

⊛ Don't let them go back into denial

Stage 4: Reflection

Once human beings have exhausted their negotiations and have won as many 'concessions' as they believe possible, or better still when they have also become inspired by the excitement of the opportunities afforded by the change that was imposed all those phases ago, then we enter stage 4 – reflection. Before I can truly get on board with the change and take action towards helping it succeed, I must psychologically accept the change.

This is a private process, albeit that in modern-day life it will probably involve people close to me. I need to look in the mirror and decide that from this moment on, I accept the change and that I will embrace it and get behind making it successful. For it is now in my interests to do so. I may need to talk to my partner again, and have *them* accept the change too. I may need my friends to validate my decision to accept the change. But whether I do this privately or in conjunction with those closest to me and whose opinion of me I value the most, this is a process that does not involve me interacting with my leader.

This is why we often ask or advise people to sleep on it. Isn't it amazing how we feel differently about things when we've had a chance to sleep on it?

Of course back in our modern organisation, the compliance and even enthusiasm of employees during and at the end of the negotiation phase is often mistaken by the leader for total acceptance of the plan. This is a key mistake made many times, for the reality is that the reflection phase must be navigated.

The intellect was won over during the negotiating stage, in fact the intellect may well have been won over even earlier, as most changes are in fact agreed upon as being necessary and right by those affected. So the leader must allow, even facilitate, a short period of quiet calm reflection, even if this is as simple as telling people to take the weekend to think it over.

Have you ever noticed how smart leaders often refuse to accept a 'yes' decision straight away? They're smart because they know that it's better to take a risk that someone's enthusiasm for a change will be dulled or negated by taking some time, than it is to 'bank' a yes too early.

- ⊛ Give them space to reflect
- ⊛ Don't let them keep talking
- ⊛ Ask them to metaphorically 'sleep on it'
- ⊛ Don't negotiate any more

Stage 5: Action

There is no change without action. Ownership is all very well, but ownership is not an intellectual or passive state. Ownership has to mean commitment and commitment is evidenced by action. It's no good asking someone if they're committed; as leaders we need to observe the actions of our people in performance, and then we know just how committed they are.

> *Ownership is not an intellectual or passive state. Ownership has to mean commitment and commitment is evidenced by action.*

As human beings we truly feel back in control when we start living our life again according to some predetermined plan that we feel is ours and no one else's. So our actions might be small and they might even be mundane, but they are the everyday actions of employees who are working once more towards the common purpose and common goals.

And so finally we move through to ownership, defined as follows… that we believe in and evangelise the change as if it had been all our idea in the first place. This is the holy grail for most leaders – getting their people, their teams, their departments, their companies to 'buy into', to 'own' the change.

- ⊛ Coach for specific action
- ⊛ Show them they belong
- ⊛ Show them they are stars
- ⊛ Reward action over results

The job of the leader

People will go through the five stages outlined above on their own, 'naturally', but it will take a long time and there will be much cost, risk and stress along the way. The biggest risk of all is that we will need to launch the next 'generational' change before our employees have come to a place of acceptance of the last one! Sound familiar?

The job of the leader is to move (lead) people through these five stages as fast as possible – arguably the definition of leadership is to get people through these stages quicker than they would get there on their own. So how long does it take? For a big change with huge potential impact on the lives of individuals, some organisations never complete the cycle, indeed some never get out of denial! But with authentic leadership, a big change might only take a matter of weeks to gain total acceptance and maximum commitment.

Authentic leadership means creating an emotional journey towards an inspirational vision of the future – creating a compelling mission or purpose – and then communicating this in such a way as the people who want to believe get on the bus, and those who do not get off.

It means asking the right questions of people at each stage. It means holding people and listening to their answers without shirking from the discomfort of the resistance that will naturally come. It means being disciplined and boundaried and applying sanctions – not allowing people to go back a stage once we have all moved on. It means ensuring that all conversations are authentic not superficial. It means noticing and acknowledging the emotions that will, indeed *must*, be felt through the stages and celebrating them when they arrive on the scene – fear, uncertainty, guilt, sadness, grief, disappointment, denial, defensiveness, anger, frustration, jealousy, envy, betrayal, anxiety, depression, resignation, excitement, challenge, joy, happiness, calm, security, comfort, love, rejection, anticipation, elation, enthusiasm, energy, creativity, pride, honour, fulfilment.

Chapter 14

The eight steps of cultural change

Now knowing this immensely helpful psychological understanding, we can implement a change process that avoids the pitfalls and leads people through the cycle of ownership in hugely practical ways.

The most commonly used culture change process across the world was established by Professor John Kotter at Harvard Business School in 1995.

1. Establishing a sense of urgency
2. Forming a powerful guiding coalition
3. Creating a vision
4. Communicating the vision
5. Empowering others to act on the vision
6. Planning for and creating short-term wins
7. Consolidating improvements and producing still more change
8. Institutionalising new approaches

Over the years I have developed my own eight-step process. It has echoes of Kotter of course since it's hard to argue against proven and common sense strategies. However, in my experience of observing leaders implement the Kotter process, it can sometimes fail because of two factors – first, I believe it allows leaders to shy away from the starkness, the shock even, of the consequences of not changing. Some people will change when they see the light, but we're fundamentally wired to survive and not thrive, so most people will change *only* when they feel the heat. Secondly I believe Kotter's model is just too heavy on vision (three of eight steps) and therefore too light on pragmatism. People need to see the common sense and to feel the daily improvements very quickly in order to stick with programmes, which they are used to being overly theoretical and just too vague to be of relevance to their daily work.

1. Be honest about what happens if we *don't* change
2. Listen to customers and employees
3. Set clear intentions and symbolic goals
4. Slaughter some sacred cows
5. Police non-negotiable structures and processes
6. Turn the managers into coaches
7. Create champions and CI teams
8. Educate employees in the business model

Step 1: Be honest about what happens if we *don't* change

This really has to be a 'change or die' type message.

> *Everyone's job is at risk. It is vital to keep saying this over and over. In order to get everyone involved in change programs, we first have to persuade people that the company has no choice but to change.*
>
> James Champy

Now, in an organisation that is facing imminent collapse, it's not hard to get people on board. If we don't have the cash to make the payroll next month, employees will get the urgency and sign up to just about anything. When we've got nothing to lose, we can go with anything.

The hard part is introducing a change message when things are apparently going OK, when it feels as though change would be putting at risk what we already have. I've seen leaders use immense amounts of logic and irrefutable intellectual argument in such cases, and still they struggle to get people to change. The bottom line is that the fear of the status quo has to outweigh the fear of change. As an employee, I'm always going to fear change, so I'll resist it if I can. Intellectual arguments won't win the day. If I am going to venture out of my warm, safe, comfortable place to go out into the cold, dark unknown, I have to become more fearful of staying where I am.

the change message has to answer the question **What happens if we don't change?** *and this message has to be stark and unequivocal*

So the change message has to answer the question '*What happens if we* don't *change?*' and this message has to be stark and unequivocal, even if we cannot be specific on timescales. If we're making lots of money, but the customers are defecting in droves, then we have to change. If the profits are high but we have a toxic culture with harassment, abuse and high stress levels, then we have to change. If we don't change, then events will unfold and we will lose control of our destiny.

In this Step 1, we have to establish a mantra-like statement that we can repeat and repeat, because we're going to have to remind people constantly as they want to retreat back into the warm.

> *Change is always hard. My job as a leader in the organisation is to effect change on a massive scale, because it's required, and in a quick period of time because the industry is moving. To do that, you need to startle the organisation strongly enough so that change is possible. And yet you can't send the organisation into cardiac arrest. Getting that balance right – of enough surprise, enough seriousness, enough shock to the system so that the system starts to respond, but not so much that it goes into arrest – is vitally important.*
>
> Carly Fiorina, CEO Hewlett-Packard, 2001–2005

Step 2: Listen to customers and employees

Customers and employees always know what's needed. Customers can inform us as to what they want from us, and what they'd ideally like from us in the future. Employees can tell us everything that's wrong, given that they are on the front-line every day striving to do great work and having to cope with every poor process, every lack of adequate resource, every customer complaint, and indeed every complaint from suppliers and members of the community we co-exist in, and the agencies we have to interact with.

I recall a very satisfying exchange with a sceptical CFO who was adamant that if we asked the employees for their opinions, they would simply use the opportunity to ask for higher wages, and so it was too dangerous to set up a process that would ultimately serve to disappoint them. I asked him to trust me, and I even invited him to sit in and observe the employee listening groups. I knew that he would also believe that his presence would cause the employees to clam up and not want to be honest, and I wanted to demonstrate to him that his understandable fears were actually not real. Because the process was well managed, of course the employees were honest. His presence, under strict instructions not to speak or react, but merely observe and accept, did not contaminate the process one iota. After the very first session he came to me and said that he felt this was such an amazing process that he wanted to find a way to use it as part of due diligence before buying any more companies! He'd had his Damascene moment. Such moments pitch up every day as our employees walk through the factory gates and office entrances, if only we had the courage and belief to seek them out.

> People will fight for a community they have built themselves, no matter how flawed it may be; they will ultimately destroy one that is imposed upon them, no matter how good it is for them.
>
> Tom Peters

But we can also look for helpful external voices – analysts, market researchers, industry commentators and academic researchers. After all, sometimes customers don't know what they want because a product or market may not have been invented yet. We may be the innovators, the disruptors, who have to take our product to market and persuade customers that they need something they had no idea they needed.

Step 3: Set clear intentions and symbolic goals

Vision

While people rarely change unless they feel the heat, the moment they've jumped they want to be drawn towards the light. The moment as leaders we have the attention of our followers, we have to give them hope; we have to give them a reason to keep going and that reason has to be both emotional and logical. The vision we paint of the future has to be aspirational and it has to be common-sense.

The moment as leaders we have the attention of our followers, we have to give them hope; we have to give them a reason to keep going and that reason has to be both emotional and logical.

Where there is no vision, the people perish.

Proverbs 29:18

Without a vision, there is only work.

Michael Gerber

A vision without a plan is merely a dream; a plan without a vision is just a nightmare.
Anon

A vision without a task is but a dream. A task without a vision is drudgery. A vision with a task is the hope of the world.

Donald Zimmerman

The vision must directly link to the need for change, giving a common purpose through the adversity we may face in moving from current to desired state. This clear direction gives new security to employees and gives leaders the final part of the change mantra to continually come back to and repeat.

Managers, teams and employees then must be invited in to design their own parts, re-establishing a feeling of control through invention.

Perhaps the two most famous examples of visions in recent history are those of Martin Luther King and of John F Kennedy.

I have a dream that one day this nation will rise up and live out the true meaning of its creed: We hold these truths to be self-evident: that all men are created equal.
Martin Luther King, 28 August 1963

Notice the emotional draw; the idealism; the complete lack of 'how' – but that was not important, after all he told his audience '*I may not get there with you*', perhaps the most evocative line of the whole speech.

I believe that this nation should commit itself to achieving the goal, before this decade is out, of landing a man on the moon and returning him safely to the Earth.
John F Kennedy, 25 May 1961

Notice the audacity of the goal – a symbol that captured the mood and the imagination of the American people at a time when the biggest threat was nuclear war with the Soviet Union, who had also stolen a march on the Americans in the 'space race'. No one knew if what JFK had committed to was possible, indeed the legend is that when NASA scientists first got their hands on the plan, such as it was, at almost every step was inserted the words '*Technological discovery required here*'.

When setting goals, every stakeholder has to be satisfied. The all-consuming *maximise return to shareholders* cannot be dominant. It has to be balanced with desirable and aspirational outcomes for all stakeholders – leaders and managers, employees, suppliers, community partners.

Return on investment, of course, has to be in there, as does customer satisfaction and employee well-being. But do we also want to be a good citizen? What community, environmental and sustainability goals will we set for ourselves?

Values

I believe strongly that our values need to be set and communicated at this stage of the process – set as an intention and part of the future aspiration, the future vision. The purpose is the 'why', the vision and the goals are the 'what', and the values are the 'how' – and as such we will *use* them in the structures part of our strategy. So values have to move, and be seen to move, from an aspirational idealism, to a non-negotiable way of being, more important than any tangible result. There simply has to be a total integrity around this, not a manufactured one and not one that ultimately relies on the excuse of things being 'legal'. So integrity is not a value in itself, although I frequently hear it espoused as such. Integrity is *'an uncompromising adherence to a code of moral or artistic values'* (Oxford English Dictionary).

So integrity is acting in complete alignment with your values, and this is vital for mutual respect between people who may well believe different things. Our enterprise might involve collaboration between people from very different backgrounds and beliefs, and sometimes the only thing we can hold onto is that we respect them for their integrity. Given the range of personal values, all of which are likely to be fine and noble, just with differing manifestations, we have to have a common set of organisational values that we can coalesce around.

How important are our values? Well for me it's simple. When it comes to our values, you are either...

Living them,

Learning them,

or you are

Leaving!

(Or are they just 'laminated'?)

And of the three stages above, I love the 'learning' phase best, since that means people are honestly engaging with an openness and a vulnerability, being sceptical where appropriate and battling against ideas as they learn, all incredibly respectfully. For me this is the true meaning and value of 'diversity'. And as we've seen, values are an excellent source for coaching questions.

So are we changing a culture, or are we in fact developing a cult? A cult is a group bound together by a sacred ideology, venerating an ideal with rites and ceremonies and an utter intolerance of non-believers. While a strong culture will have elements of cultism, this is where our 'grip on reality' needs to kick in and save us from hubris and delusion. Our enterprise is important and may well change lives for the better, but it's not sacred and if it dies, it dies. People within it will go onto do great things in another enterprise.

> *While a strong culture will have elements of cultism, this is where our 'grip on reality' needs to kick in and save us from hubris and delusion.*

In my work as a consultant over the past 15 years I've come across some wonderful examples of corporate values and how they've been communicated.

Here are just a few of my favourites.

Hewlett-Packard Rules of the Garage

- Believe you can change the world
- Work quickly; keep the tools unlocked; work whenever
- Know when to work alone and when to work together
- Share tools, ideas; trust your colleagues
- No politics, no bureaucracy (these are ridiculous in a garage)
- The customer defines a job well done
- Radical ideas are not bad ideas
- Invent different ways of working
- Make a contribution every day – if it doesn't contribute, it doesn't leave the garage
- Believe that together we can do anything

When Carly Fiorina took over as Hewlett-Packard's CEO, she led a process that sought to take the company back to its roots, recreating the spirit and innovation of when Bill Hewlett and Dave Packard had founded their company in a garage in Palo Alto. So she went to the iconography and the symbolism of working in that garage, appealing to the engineering side of the business to once again lead the world in innovation.

Nestlé Principles

When Peter Brabeck-Letmathe became CEO of Nestlé, legend has it he wrote new values for the organisation on the plane to his first board meeting. The reason I love these values is the poetry and the humanity. They are taken from '*Basics of the Nestlé Culture*' – the main elements of the Nestlé culture to be respected everywhere:

- Nestlé people take a more pragmatic than dogmatic approach to business
- Nestlé people are realistic and base decisions on facts rather than dreams
- Nestlé people have a commitment to a strong work ethic, integrity, honesty and quality
- Nestlé people base relations on trust, expecting mutual integrity and rejecting intrigue
- Nestlé people take a personalised direct way of dealing with each other, reducing bureaucracy to a minimum

- Nestlé people do not show off but are conscious of their worth and take pride in the positive image of the company – they are modest but not without style and a sense of quality

- Nestlé people are open to dynamic and future-oriented trends in technology, changes in consumer habits, business ideas and opportunities, but they maintain respect for basic human values, attitudes and behaviour

The Lexus Covenant

In 2004, the year I first met Mike Morrison, founder of the University of Toyota, I spent a month in Los Angeles researching the phenomenon that was Lexus. Launched just 15 years earlier as a new sub-brand of Toyota, Lexus had already become the number one selling premium car in the US, outselling BMW and Mercedes and the luxury arms of the US manufacturers combined. Everywhere I went I asked people what was the key to Lexus' success, fully expecting them to reflect for a moment before telling me that the single biggest factor had to be product quality (which was, by the way, demonstrably ahead of their competition). Virtually every person I met surprised me by saying that while product quality was important, the single biggest factor in Lexus' success was the 'The Lexus Covenant' and in particular one line: *We will treat each customer as we would a guest in our own home.* This was revolutionary stuff in the motor trade, and a testament to the foresight of Cardiff University Professor John Kiff some years earlier.

The Toyota Way

With Lexus being part of Toyota, I became fascinated by the Toyota culture. My dealings with Tony Barnes 15 years earlier had given me a glimpse into the world of kaizen, lean manufacturing and total quality, and now here I was experiencing the 'Toyota Way' first-hand. The 'Toyota Way' is Toyota's values. It's a book, it's a training course, and it is a way of life. Forging a working relationship and then a friendship with Mike Morrison was one of the great gifts of my working life.

Toyota's Five Core Values

- Challenge: we form a long-term vision, meeting challenges with courage and creativity to realise our dreams.

- Kaizen: we improve our business operations continuously, always driving for innovation and evolution.

- Genchi Genbutsu: we practice Genchi Genbutsu... go to the source to find the facts to make correct decisions, build consensus and achieve goals at our best speed.

- Respect: we respect others, make every effort to understand each other, take responsibility and do our best to build mutual trust.

- Teamwork: we stimulate personal and professional growth, share the opportunities of development and maximize individual and team performance.

> *The most profound thing that studying the Toyota Way taught me, was how an adherence to a common set of working principles and practices did not restrict people – it liberated them.*

The most profound thing that studying the Toyota Way taught me, was how an adherence to a common set of working principles and practices did not restrict people – it liberated them. The absolute trust that Toyota employees have in their colleagues and how they are motivated and how they are operating, means that individual flair and talents can flourish within a safe and strong structure. The closest metaphor I found for this was when I met Dominic Alldis and his jazz group some years later. Dominic was a professor at the Royal Academy of Music and a hugely accomplished classical pianist and composer. But he had found a wonderful niche in leadership development in business, including running the highly acclaimed 'Maestro' programme for WPP.

The first time I met Dominic was at a meeting of the Academy for Chief Executives in a group of around 25 peers. Dominic was there with his jazz quartet and he started with a short presentation on what jazz was – that it was basically improvised playing around a common theme, a beat or rhythm or chord sequence or simple melody, with each individual musician improvising rather than following a score or any sort of pre-prescribed or learned music. And then they played, and in the middle of the day in a rather soulless conference room, four jazz musicians rocked the audience. They were brilliant.

With his audience in awe, Dominic repeated his description of the process they had followed – that he had introduced a basic beat and melody line, and that the next ten minutes was totally improvised. And then he delivered the killer fact – that he had only met the drummer and bass player for the first time that morning, and they had had no rehearsal time together whatsoever.

> *In companies with strong cultures based on common values, I see colleagues meet each other for the first time and immediately trust each other and start collaborating and creating and inventing.*

In companies with strong cultures based on common values, I see colleagues meet each other for the first time and immediately trust each other and start collaborating and creating and inventing. Pure jazz – but based on solid common fundamentals of rhythm, beat and basic melody line.

Documents with status

In creating the guiding purpose, vision, values, goals and plan, it's then important to create documents that articulate these, and to give those documents an iconic status within the business. Chairing board meetings, I symbolically place the key documents in front of me both for reference when needed (normally merely picking them up and waving them around!) and for the symbolism of their status within the business – the manifestation of 'the vision is the boss'. If every employee had a copy of the plan and carried it round with them, then we'd be far more likely to achieve the plan. So the trick is to design documents that are inspirational as well as informative; that can be used symbolically as well as serving as reference sources for information. I've often used quite 'cheesy' devices to give these documents status, including having leaders symbolically sign a flipchart sheet – the modern-day version of cutting our palms and exchanging our blood. If we are going to serve causes not people, if we are going to be inspired by principles and not personalities, then we need iconography and symbolism in our written plans.

Step 4: Slaughter some sacred cows

In all the listening, it's important to do an inventory of the key issues and start some form of prioritising. It's important in change processes to make commitments and then follow through, but equally as important is clearly stating what is *not* going to change, at least maybe for some time. Otherwise people can use these things as ongoing excuses.

Listening also allows the leaders to give an 'amnesty' on the truth – we value the truth more than we value being able to apportion blame or execute justice. We start from a compassionate belief that people are good, and that if they've done bad things, well they were probably conditioned into those behaviours or were only trying to survive or fight or right injustices from above.

The initial listening throws up some potential 'quick wins' – decisive actions that give people the start of the trust that leaders will listen and then follow through, and a clear reward and evidence that speaking up is worthwhile.

And this is where leaders need to look for some 'sacred cows' to slaughter. These are things that everyone knows are wrong, anachronistic, unfair or symbolic of the old way, the 'elephants in the room', and are therefore things that people have come to believe are untouchable. Basically, the things that despite the fine words of the new leaders will simply never be tackled. I look for outmoded status symbols, walls I can symbolically knock down, processes I can immediately scrap, policies I can tear up, and yes if appropriate, previously powerful people I can remove. These are the hugely public and visible signs that this time it's different, and that maybe, just maybe, we can trust this new leadership

Step 5: Police non-negotiable structures and processes

The leaders have to decide what is non-negotiable in terms of process. For example, if we decide that the way new managers are inducted is flawed and must change, then this will be established as a non-negotiable. Given its status, therefore, we need to establish the consequences of non-compliance. For example, you cannot take up your new management role unless you have completed and passed the new manager induction programme. Leaders have to be careful not to have too many non-negotiables, since that only serves to set people up to fail.

Wherever possible don't invent new processes; use existing ones where you can and insist upon compliance. Most processes are actually fine, the reason they're

> *Most processes are actually fine, the reason they're not working is no one is adhering to them properly*

not working is no one is adhering to them properly, or some are and some are not. Well, no wonder they're not working. Work the process, make the process work by using it. Then refine it if you have to, but only in agreement with all parties and then have all parties use the new process 100 per cent.

One of the 'harshest' things to do in this phase is banning people from finding 'work-arounds' – where well-meaning and nobly motivated people find a way round a process in order to get the job done. It's hard to criticise this at times, since people have also heard us talk about using their initiative, but we have to be insistent on 100 per cent compliance. One of the greatest culprits here is the spreadsheet. We may have a fully integrated ERP system, but it's all too easy for people to design a spreadsheet for themselves, especially if the system tools are a bit clunky or ugly. The issue, however, is that the spreadsheet starts to become an important part of the system, but one that no one else has access to or is even familiar with – and anyway they have their own spreadsheets! Banning these things is monumentally unpopular but absolutely essential.

Other examples of non-negotiable structures and processes are meetings – we should be prescriptive of the regime and rhythm of meetings that will be the structure of the way we manage the organisation. Team briefings, one-to-ones, team meetings, etc. There must be a formality to these to give safety and stability to employees and to give rock solid foundations for people to feel free to create, use initiative, flair, personality, potential, take risks, etc.

And our people processes will be firmly in this camp. Induction, performance appraisals, ono-to-ones, training and development, career planning, talent management, engagement surveys, manager and culture feedback surveys and exit interviews. Any process that is designed to assist people to develop, raise their performance or feel safe in their work must be non-negotiable. It cannot be acceptable for a manager not to do their employees' performance appraisals. It is, of course, acceptable for that manager to not be perfect at doing them, to be learning how to do them better and better.

Restructuring

Notice how everyone talks as if the organisation structure is a physical entity, whereas it does not physically exist. There are no solid walls that demarcate departments, although of course such physical projection is often backed up by people being located in buildings. But actually it's all symbolic – it's all in people's minds.

If you've worked for a company for a while, your experience is probably that you are only ever a few months from the last restructure or the next one, and while the answer to the question *'What's the best structure for us to have?'* is invariably *'The one we had five years ago that we abandoned for the current one'*, restructuring can often achieve a psychological shift that's simply not possible if you leave things as they are. Most people end up doing precisely the same work on the other side of a restructure, so you could ask 'What's the point?', and I'm certainly not one for changing just for the sake of it. Restructures are costly, time-consuming things and cause uncertainty and anxiety. But a restructure allows people the opportunity of an amnesty, of drawing a line and leaving behind the emotional baggage of things unattended to and unachieved, and gives them the fresh chance to launch themselves into their work with enthusiasm and confidence. I'm not convinced there is such a thing as the 'correct' structure for an organisation. I've been round the Boston Triangle countless times and it always seems to me that we want all three, and simply giving one aspect priority can oversimplify the complexity and ambiguity of the market and the whole supply chain.

In terms of desired structures, I always look for reduced management layers, with the flattest structure we can reasonably create. I am not a great fan of the 'span of control' ratio argument, especially where this is used to increase the numbers of managers. In an organisation with an open, fully engaged culture, one person can easily manage a team of 10+, 20+ direct reports, and more with some self-managed team processes in place.

In terms of desired structures, I always look for reduced management layers, with the flattest structure we can reasonably create.

In self-managed teams, as we saw in an earlier chapter, 'management' is performed by peers rather than a single individual with a concentration of power. And the impact of reducing management has a double-whammy effect of saving large amounts of money *and* enabling empowerment. The only reason managers resist these changes is an anxiety over their own self-worth.

> *Everything I had learned and done had convinced me that if I didn't do it myself it wouldn't get done right. It was my job to create the plan and then motivate 'them' to carry out. My major obstacle was my self-respect. I believed that my value as a leader came from my being a problem solver and decision maker.*
>
> James Champy

When we are the designers of change processes, instead of sticking to working solely on the vision and values, we carry round a mental template of how everyone should do their job. It then becomes inevitable that we judge people unfairly – we see them in action, and they are *just not doing it right*. We must liberate ourselves from the belief that we know what is best for others, that we help people best by taking decisions for them, and that we care for them best by exercising responsibility on their behalf – paternalism may have noble motivations, but it creates dependent children not empowered adults.

We need to ensure that change activities are serious first, fun second. Employees have a keen sense of the ridiculous and are not at all fooled by leaders who promote 'fun' as some sort of value.

We need to ensure that change activities are serious first, fun second. Employees have a keen sense of the ridiculous and are not at all fooled by leaders who promote 'fun' as some sort of value. They know that work is serious, both because the purpose is worthy and because the marketplace is competitive. I'm not convinced by the 'fun' argument. I believe in warmth over humour (humour is so frequently used as a distraction, and is so often inappropriate, with someone being the butt of the joke – just be warm) and I believe in enjoyment over fun – I absolutely want people to enjoy their work, to come to love it even, and if they have some fun along the way then that's great. But not manufactured, and not used as bait to get employees into change activities. That's manipulative.

In engaging employees we need structures and processes that get the employees *ahead* of management competence, so change still happens even when management get it wrong.

Everything should be geared towards establishing pride in the company and the cause it is championing and fighting for.

Create a small central team of trainers and evangelists to support local leaders. Educate everyone in the management accounts of the business – put scores on the doors but always with explanations, and this is where having employees in management meetings and accounts review meetings by rotation is such a powerful tool. Short team briefings must be held to allow interaction and questions around the performance monitoring, and while the managers should start these meetings to ensure they are held consistently, get the employees to run them as soon as possible.

In order to keep things clean and tidy and to reduce spending on cleaners, put up 'vision boards' (literally photographs of how the rooms, facilities, offices, workshops, etc, look at their best). Every time a meeting finishes, the delegates should take out their own trash.

If you are going to use 'league tables', and they can be highly motivating in sales or competitive situations, then make the 'campaign' goals clear and be clear on the rewards for success. In retail in particular, never underestimate the power of every single employee feeling the buzz from a sale being made – or from watching the daily numbers clock up somehow. And this is where we need to be careful of the comparators we use. I've seen so much demotivation where sales results have been shown against target, when everyone knows the target is unrealistic. So a comparison to the budget when the budget has genuinely been created and owned by employees is fine, but always the comparator to same period last year, since we always need to know if we are moving forwards or backwards. And don't forget league tables on costs and ratios as well, since these are the things that are actually within employees' control.

My final piece of advice here: Just read *Maverick* by Ricardo Semler.

Step 6: Turn the managers into coaches

The empowerment cycle

Empowering a workforce is not a passive act of mere rhetoric. It is not sufficient to tell people they are empowered and then leave them in a vacuum to get on with it. Empowerment is defined as '*the largest amount of voluntary and discretionary action in support of the company's goals'*. It is people proactively, and habitually, doing the right things at the right time; people working out what's needed and acting without instruction; people looking within the team for support, not looking upwards for answers.

It requires that we dismantle or at least 'devalue' hierarchies, replacing 'command and control' structures with devolved power and authority.

Empowerment cycle

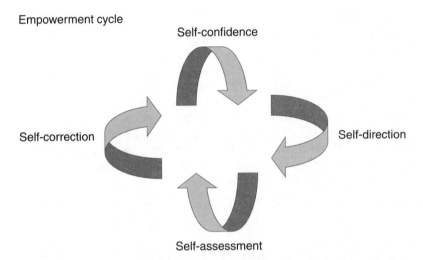

Notice that the journey of empowerment starts with people who have self-confidence, so the leaders' priority must be to build an environment that actively supports, encourages and develops self-confidence, creating cultures of 'inspired commitment' not 'dispirited compliance'. How many leaders do you know who spend most of their time and effort focusing solely on building a culture whereby people can be self-confident? How many do you know whose (albeit unconscious) use of fear and control knock the confidence of employees at every turn?

It is our willingness and our growing ability to coach that underpins empowerment. We have to change the historical and habitual conditioned behaviours and reactions in both managers and employees. Coaching must become the predominant leadership style, with a directive style then becoming more selective, and thus more effective when used.

Step 7: Create champions and CI teams

In order to accelerate change and ensure its maximum acceptance, leaders should ask for volunteers to champion the change; probably 5–10 per cent of the workforce who will be the eyes and ears, the role models and the true pioneers. Their role is predominantly to support the managers as they themselves develop into coaches. The champions will facilitate workshops and team briefings and set up the continuous improvement (CI) teams to energise and raise quality.

Leaders are responsible for initiating transformational change, since only they can. Kaizen or continuous improvement is not enough to transform – seeking to improve

> *Kaizen or continuous improvement is not enough to transform – seeking to improve something by 5 per cent does not inspire new thinking and does not break patterns or traditions.*

something by 5 per cent does not inspire new thinking and does not break patterns or traditions. Transforming things demands new ways of thinking and radical ideas, hence it's the leaders that must own that responsibility. Kaizen is then both appropriate and inspiring for employees, where change is best effected through gradual and incremental improvements.

Kaizen is from '*kai*' – to alter, renew, reform, or be corrected – and '*zen*' – good, positive. In everyday Japanese it simply translates as improvement. In industry, it is the relentless process of finding and eliminating '*muda*' (waste), '*mura*' (inconsistencies) and '*muri*' (physical strain). The other well-known Japanese 'lean' process is poka-yoke which means 'fail-safing' or 'mistake-proofing'. Poka-yoke was originally baka-yoke which means 'idiot-proofing'. Human beings make mistakes, so the question for the founding fathers of total quality was how organisations could design things so that understandable and predictable human errors could be eliminated.

When an organisation sets a goal to develop an already sound and successful culture into a truly 'winning culture', it begins a challenging journey.

A successful enterprise has a much greater challenge in changing attitudes and behaviours than one in trouble. When we are in trouble, we have no choice but to take some risks and do whatever it takes to turn things around. But when we are successful, somehow the risks are greater. After all there is no real *need* to change, and often the fear of losing what we already have gets in the way of changing anything at all.

Much falls on the shoulders of the leaders and managers; however, this is a dangerous dynamic. After all, they are but a minor percentage of the whole workforce, and while they, of course, seem to count for more than their collective number due to the authority of their management positions, the vast majority of the many hundreds of thousands of actions and events that occur every day as the enterprise moves forward, happen out of sight and sound of any manager. So critically a winning culture must get away from the typical dynamic in corporations whereby when things go wrong, the employees both blame the leaders *and* look to them for the answers as to how to get out of trouble.

A winning culture is self-sustaining, where the whole community holds itself to account to do the right thing. Thus the most critical aspect of creating and maintaining a winning culture, is the willingness of every single employee to carry the greatest positive intent into every single act they take each day, no matter how small, and no matter if there is no manager present to bear witness.

Governance panels

A powerful device to channel such behaviours is the creation of 'governance panels'. The best example of this I witnessed was working with a European cereals business in the late 1990s. The main factory producing porridge oats was in Scotland. As with many factory operations, the teams there were tasked with improving efficiency every year – year in, year out. This can become a very wearing, debilitating culture to live in. Kaizen certainly means continuous improvement, but it can so easily come to mean 'nothing's ever good enough', so leaders have to be acutely aware of the potential for fatigue and exhaustion to set in. The CEO's solution was brilliant. In tasking the factory management team to deliver yet another 3 per cent improvement in efficiency, he then asked them to form a 'governance panel' with teams from the other factories, to oversee the investment decisions for how to reinvest the savings from their efficiencies, with the business units pitching for those funds. The Scottish factory's contribution in the year in question was around £600,000 and one of the pitches was from the marketing team to support a BOGOF (buy-one-get-one-free) promotion on one of the company's most iconic brands, and the market-leading breakfast cereal. Its share had been in decline, and it had never had to rely on the 'usual' forms of promotional activity.

The amount requested was £600,000 to fund the promotion. The team from the Scottish factory listened to all the arguments and voted for the whole of their contribution to be used to support the brand BOGOF promotion, so that is what happened. It was a simply brilliant example of how trusting employees to make sensible decisions based on evidence and reality works beautifully. This was the factory producing porridge oats, working their socks off for 12 months to grind out efficiency savings and freely voting to give those savings to marketers of a completely different product – a solution that the leaders of the business could never have delivered.

Champions

Now, it is actually not that difficult to create an inspirational environment in which employees feel truly empowered and motivated to do their very best in everything they do. Stirring speeches, inspiring visions and ambitious goals can achieve much. The real problem is maintaining such an environment. This is a challenge because there are two 'maintenance pitfalls' that derail most cultural change initiatives.

First, human beings need a lot of positive feedback when they feel they are 'going the extra mile', particularly if they have taken risks in doing so, and since there are often no managers around to bear witness, who is going to give this to them? Employees will ask themselves, 'What is the point of secretly solving a problem that no one has yet noticed?' Second, the leaders and managers, being human beings too, will slip back into their old ways at times, thus giving an unspoken 'permission' to all employees around them to do the same.

human beings need a lot of positive feedback when they feel they are 'going the extra mile'

So a critical role at the heart of the organisation and at the heart of the cultural quest is the role of the champions – 'agents' dotted throughout the organisation who have been trained in cultural development and facilitation, and who are passionate advocates of the whole cultural journey, knowing both the form and the spirit of the vision and values, and knowing the form and the purpose of each of the cultural structures and processes.

Champions do not replace line managers, nor are they there to thwart the hierarchical authority structure (which must be sacrosanct). Rather they act as 'peer supporters' of both managers and employees, being constantly vigilant and aware of the 'maintenance pitfalls', stepping in when they see them arise, and generally being proactive promoters of the cultural journey. The champions are the accepted internal evangelists.

There should be one champion for every 30 or so employees. There should be a balance in representation between the divisions or functions within the organisation. Weight should be given to the relative numbers of employees in each area; however, this should not be the sole criteria or the biggest population will be too dominant. There should also be a balance in length of service. Champions should be selected and invited by the directors.

Selection should be on the following criteria:

⚙ Passion for the company's vision and purpose and values

⚙ Strength of feeling to see things improve

⚙ Development opportunity warranted

⚙ Willingness to be a role model

The skills that will be taught are:

⚙ Facilitation

⚙ Coaching (specifically for innovation, change, collaboration, challenge, etc)

⚙ Giving feedback

Once selected, there should be training and an induction workshop. The champions should meet regularly to share ideas and experiences, and to provide a written report to the board on progress, new ideas generated and recommendations. There should be a co-ordinator elected from within their own ranks, and this role should rotate regularly.

Champions do not replace any existing structures for representation, suggestions or complaints, for that is *not* their remit. The role of champion is the gift of the board, is a privilege, carries no monetary reward or additional benefits, and can be summarily removed. Champions should serve a maximum term and then stand down, being appropriately recognised and celebrated, so a rolling process of selecting and inducting new champions should be established. Finally there should be an annual champions' 'symposium' with the directors to maximise learning, develop the champions' process further, and set new and stretching goals for the future.

'Task teams' and the role they play

In 'normal' company cultures, it is the leaders who typically both identify and solve any problems. It's not that rest of the employees don't notice problems, for they are in fact usually the ones to catch the first whiff of smoke, and neither is it that they are incapable of coming up with and implementing solutions. No, it's usually simply that the leaders have established problem-solving as their domain – as in fact almost their whole reason for being.

This should not surprise us, since problem-solving and the subsequent martialling of people to implement solutions is *the* most rewarded leadership trait in most corporations. So no matter how we may exhort our leaders to become true perform-ance coaches, and to resist giving solutions to others, we are in fact asking them to break the habit of a management lifetime – to discard the very way of life that has served their success to date.

In a winning culture, however, where line managers are trained to become (at first clumsy and then progres-sively more skilled) performance coaches, focused heavily on the personal growth of their people, it must be the employees as a community that take on the almost entire responsibility of identifying and solving problems.

it must be the employees as a community that take on the almost entire responsibility of identifying and solving problems

I say 'almost entire'. Let's be clear then that there are problems that are the legitimate and exclusive territory of the leaders alone, and I would classify these as any unexpected event that is outside the current business plan, or one that puts the high-level goals or even the vision at risk. Typically there may be half a dozen such events in a financial year. Such events could be ones that *only* the leaders can see, given their helicopter view, or they could be ones that ignite from within the enterprise, but genuinely require a leadership call given the scale of risk required in exercising the desired solution.

So that's six major problems a year in the remit of the leaders. That leaves the other tens/hundreds/thousands (delete as appropriate) for the employees to solve. The smaller, everyday variety that crop up within functions can simply be solved by the employees affected, and the winning culture training facilitates this, as does, of course, the new performance coaching behaviours of the line managers.

But the problems we are concerned with here are those problems that arise that affect cross-functional working, and that could thus fuel inter-department tension and conflict. In a winning culture, there should be relatively few of these; maybe a dozen a year. One a month. This is where the task teams come in.

When such a cross-functional problem arises, a task team will be formed to solve it. The formation of a task team must be at the request of a director, although not always because they have identified the need personally. More normally the process will be that a concerned employee, catching the first whiff of smoke, identifies a problem and brings it to the attention of their line manager, or one of the champions. If that line manager or champion considers it worthy of a task team, then they should ask the employee to approach a director.

In forming a task team, the first step is to appoint a team leader. This will always be offered first to the employee who has identified the problem, in a sort of 'offer you can't refuse' style! However if the employee is simply too intimidated by the challenge, then the director will source an alternative leader. The employee will then be asked to join the team. If they refuse, the deal is that no task team will be formed and they will be asked to 'get back in their cage' and forget the problem. Tough stuff, but this is a winning culture we are talking about – one in which the *whole* community takes responsibility and accountability for things being the best they can be.

The task team leader then seeks team members. A task team always has six members and they must be as cross-functionally representative as possible.

A task team always has a life of one month and will meet three times for a maximum of 90 minutes per meeting. Meetings are as follows:

Meeting 1

⊕ Set up the remit of the team, define the problem and allocate tasks to each member for research, data collection, opinion canvassing, external benchmarking, etc.

Meeting 2

⊕ Review the findings, brainstorm solutions, draft the initial recommendations and allocate tasks to each member for any final further research and for the canvassing of opinions on the initial recommendations.

Meeting 3

⊕ Review findings, arrive at final recommendation(s) and decide who is to make the presentation at a board meeting.

At the subsequent board meeting, the commitment of the directors is to allocate 30 minutes to the topic – 15 minutes to receive the presentation, and 15 minutes to openly debate the recommendations and make a board decision, which could be to ratify all or part of the solution, or it could be to throw it out. If all or part of the solution is accepted, the board must give a timescale for implementation back to the task team. If the board decide not to proceed with the solution, they must give honest feedback as to their reasoning.

Whatever the board decision, the job of the task team is then done and it disbands, although the board must then hold itself to account for actioning the decision/solution, and must report back to the whole company on their commitment and their progress.

The final element of the cycle must be the review of outcomes – for learning about the whole process, but perhaps more importantly for recognition of those involved and the celebration of success.

The processes outlined above may seem overly prescriptive and inflexible; however, the rigidity of the boundaries and rules is a key part of the learning that the whole community needs to go through. Change is serious stuff and accountability cannot be avoided. Winning cultures are uncompromising places, and all constituents need to embrace this.

Step 8: Educate employees in the business model

Education is a key leadership responsibility – in fact when I think about how I predominantly spent my time as a CEO, it was as a teacher, an educator. The better

200

educated your workforce, the more meaningful their work and the more positive improvement they can generate. Leaders need to educate the whole workforce in the following:

- Vision and values
- New technical skills
- Industry and marketplace
- Business finance and KPIs

Everyone needs to understand the operating model so that they can put their part of the picture into the context of the whole, and make their daily kaizen adjustments directly contribute to the efficiency, productivity and profit.

When we give authority over budgeting and spending to highly paid CFOs, they simply round everything to the nearest £10,000 or even £100,000 and they are far more likely to set budgets on a last year + 0 per cent or 1 per cent basis. Give authority over budgeting and spending and cost management to employees raising three kids on £25,000 a year, and you get proper scrutiny of what's essential and what's profligate. It offends employees how highly paid executives spend money so wastefully, so we may as well harness that energy into the cause of tight cost control.

Sharing financial information

This is a key underpinning strategy for a winning culture. It has two elements:

1. Giving access to all employees to key financial information so that they can see for themselves how the company is performing, and can see how their own performance in their job contributes directly to the whole company's success

Everyone needs to understand the operating model so that they can put their part of the picture into the context of the whole, and make their daily kaizen adjustments directly contribute to the efficiency, productivity and profit.

2. Educating all employees into the business model, the way the finances work, budgets, management accounts and KPIs so that they can intelligently comment and have more criteria at their disposal to set priorities and do the 'right' things

The realisation comes that leaving cost control to the highest paid accountants can often result in budgets that are set by a method of 'last year plus a small percentage', whereas allowing the lowest paid employees to see the management accounts produces shock and horror at the amounts spent in absolute terms.

Giving access to and actively educating employees in the key financial information of the company ranks alongside the energy we put into giving employees the other tools they need such as the vision and the values, and all the other plethora of policies, procedures and processes around the business. Armed with all this guidance, why would *any* employee need to check with a manager before doing the right thing or going the extra mile?

However, there is a right way and a wrong way to do this stuff...

> *If you believe that putting numbers, charts or spreadsheets up on noticeboards is enough, think again. It's the same as believing that you could do the most technical job in your place just because there is a manual.*
>
> Tony Barnes, Sony main board director and member of the
> post-war Deming team in Japan

So it's not just about posting information on noticeboards, and trusting that people will read and understand it – it's about actively educating people. One way of doing this is for the members of the finance function to run internal 'Finance for Non-Financial Managers' courses and to regularly be out in the business promoting financial literacy.

Backing this up, however, and really making it come alive 'on the shop floor' should be an active education process with all employees, and one way of doing this is to involve, by rotation, employees in existing business review meetings, accounts reviews, budget setting meetings, etc. Having done this as a CEO myself, I view this activity as perhaps the single most valuable and effective process in changing the culture of a business.

It takes discipline and consistency, and it takes patience, since time has to be taken within the existing meetings, to stop and educate the employees attending. There has to be a contract of trust established with the attending employees at the start of the meeting so that they treat the information they receive with appropriate confidentiality, and that they respect the tone of the meeting, faithfully representing the meeting content and output to their colleagues when they come out of the meeting and 'report back'.

no money needs to be spent on this activity. Like all truly effective culture levers, it is an investment of intent and commitment, discipline and consistency on the part of the leaders

The investment in financial education is not inconsiderable, although interestingly no money needs to be spent on this activity. Like all truly effective culture levers, it is an investment of intent and commitment, discipline and consistency on the part of the leaders, and it further role models the crucial leadership focus on people growth as the fundamental driver of exceptional performance.

Once this new level of understanding starts to be part of the fabric of the whole organisation, additional levers can be designed in to internal processes to directly link employee actions and accountabilities to the financial goals. For example, any capital expenditure sanctions, as well as needing board sign-off, could come before an employee committee for comment, challenge and 'approval' first. Imagine the buy-in to such investments – where the *whole* organisation is behind the risks involved. This could even be extended to *any* strategic decision being passed through employees before being actioned. Of course, the leaders of the business must always retain the right and the authority to *lead*, but the power of creating a culture of co-ownership and accountability is too good to pass up.

Also the process of getting employee inputs (and therefore buy-in) to budgeting processes is made much more effective. This enables the leaders of the business to go to their company and say *'The target is £xxx...'*

Cultural change project planning – full steps example

1. Project planning

    * Board members sign up for the journey

        * What will the directors' personal commitments look like or be marked by symbolically?

    * Establish project governance

        * Who will be on the project governance body?

        * What will it be called?

        * Who will be its leader?

        * How often will it meet?

        * How will it communicate progress?

    * Establish the need for change

        * What is the 'mantra' statement?

        * How will this be communicated?

    * Establish the mission, vision, values and goals

        * Why does the company exist?

        * What is its rightful place in the industry/marketplace/supply chain?

        * What is the mission or purpose?

        * What is the vision?

        * What values do the leaders aspire to?

        * What are the symbolic or iconic goals the leaders will set?

    * WIIFM

        * What's in it for the employees?

        * How will this be established?

        * How will this be communicated?

    * Set KPIs and timescales

        * What are the project KPIs?

        * What are the milestones and timelines?

- ❊ Agree budget
    - ❊ What's the prize that comes from success?
    - ❊ How serious are the leaders about committing to the goals?
    - ❊ How much are the leaders prepared to invest to support the achievement of the goals?
    - ❊ What budgets are already allocated to activities such as marketing and training and therefore what existing budgets could be utilised?
    - ❊ What planned expenditure on development activities could now be cancelled?
    - ❊ Do we need a moratorium on any current development expenditure until we've decided what we are investing in and why?
- ❊ Select champions
    - ❊ Who will decide who to nominate?
    - ❊ How will the champions selected be communicated with?
    - ❊ What will be said to the other employees about who has been selected and why them not others?
- ❊ Plan the launch
    - ❊ How will the project be launched to the company?
    - ❊ What name/brand will the project be given?
    - ❊ Will there be a project logo?
    - ❊ What launch materials are needed?

2. Ask the employees
    - ❊ They feel included, valued and involved
    - ❊ They see themselves in what *you* say downstream
    - ❊ You can say, '*You told us...*'
    - ❊ Highlight the investment in people
    - ❊ Questions, stories and legends
        - ❊ What needs to change?
        - ❊ What must we keep?
        - ❊ How can we improve?
        - ❊ Just how good could it be?
        - ❊ How do we get there?
        - ❊ What do *you* want from the journey?

- This is based on the three fundamental animation questions:
    - What is your life like right now?
    - What do you need?
    - What can you do to help yourselves?
- How will the employee research be done?
- Who will conduct the research?
- Who will be asked – a sample or all employees?
- Will there be a paper based questionnaire or survey?
- Should there be focus groups?
- Who will co-ordinate and analyse the research results?
- What format will the results be produced in?
- What will happen to the results?
- How will the results be honoured in the project process?
- What feedback will be given to the employees?

3. Directors' leadership journey
    - Authentic leadership
    - Personal integrity
    - Executive team development
        - What training/development will the board do as a team?
    - One-to-one coaching
        - What coaching/development will be used to support each director in their own personal journey?
        - Who will give the one-to-one coaching needed for each director through the process?
    - Profiling
        - How could profiling be used as an aid to team development?
    - Discipline, consistency and role-modelling
        - How will the directors hold each other to account?
        - What key behaviours should the directors consciously exhibit?
        - What behaviours should the directors be on the lookout for to recognise and praise?
        - What behaviours should they look out for to sanction and eradicate?

4. Establish champions

- Select champions
    - Who will select the champions?
    - What criteria will be used to select them?
- Establish remit
    - How will the remit be concluded and agreed?
    - How will it be communicated?
    - How will the managers react and interact with the champions?
- Training in facilitation and feedback skills
    - Who will carry out the training of the champions?
    - Who will design the training?
- Monthly peer group review
    - How often will the champions meet with each other to check progress and share experiences?
    - Who will facilitate these sessions?
    - Who will coach the champions?
- Direct feedback to the board
    - How will the champions give feedback to the board?

5. Train the managers

- Core coaching skills – fundamental for culture change
- Break the 'managers solve all the problems' paradigm
- Using the values as a practical performance management tool
- Two-day programme, one month apart
- Groups of 10–12 managers
- Mid-point individual coaching
- Creates a culture of change being exciting, not frightening
    - Who should go on the training? Managers/supervisors?
    - How will the directors go through the experience to be role models?

6. Run employee workshops

- Three half-day sessions:
    1) 'It starts with me'; 2) 'In teams'; 3) 'To the future'.

- Teaches skills of:
  - Self-confidence
  - Creative thinking and problem-solving
  - Communications
  - Team-working
  - Using the values at work and in wider personal life
- What group sizes should we design?
- How far apart should the sessions be?
- Who will design them?
- Who will run them?
- How should the champions be involved?
- How will the directors go through the experience?
- Where should the sessions be held?
- How should delegates be chosen for each session, eg, cross-functional?

7. Set up CI teams
  - CI teams
    - What existing CI processes/teams are there?
    - Which of these should continue and which should disband and be replaced?
    - What needs to change about the current remit of any CI teams?
    - What projects need attention?
  - Task teams
    - How will the remit be designed and agreed?
    - How will the first task teams be initiated?
    - How do task teams fit with CI teams?
  - Buddying and mentoring
    - How should this be introduced?
    - What should the objectives be?
    - What process should people go through to prepare them for a role as a buddy or as a mentor?
    - How will the process be monitored and managed?

- Scoreboards and financial information
    - What KPIs will be chosen as the project focus?
    - How many will be chosen – what is the right number?
    - How will decisions be made as to what KPIs go up on the walls?
    - What process will be adopted for educating the employees in the finances of the business?
    - Who will take prime responsibility for this?
- Every action linked directly to improving KPIs
    - How will this aspect be linked into the existing HR processes for objective setting and appraisals?

8. Future growth responsibilities
- Culture roadshows
    - What might these look like?
    - When should they start?
    - Who will be responsible for organising them?
- Talent development
    - What enhancements need to be made to the existing talent development processes?
    - How should we enhance or redefine the qualities we are looking for from 'high potentials'?
    - What characteristics should we look for and recognise in non-management employees?
- Identify stars
    - Who will do this?
    - On what criteria?
    - For what ongoing purpose?
- Succession planning
    - What enhancements should be made to existing policies on internal promotions and succession planning versus recruiting from outside the company?
- Long-term strategic planning
    - How will the project be tied in to creating more ambitious strategic plans and goals for the future?

- ⊕ Knowledge transfer
  - ⊕ How will we categorise the key knowledge and experience within the business?
  - ⊕ How will we identify such knowledge and experience within individuals and teams?
  - ⊕ How will we actively process the transfer of knowledge?
- ⊕ When to call in external experts
  - ⊕ How will we know when we have exhausted the collective internal ability to improve things?
  - ⊕ How will we identify the best external experts to invite in to help us?

Section 5
Organisational strategies

Chapter 15

The business management bit

A plan that everyone owns

The plan is the unifying force within a business. The plan should be formed of a brief narrative that tells both the rational and emotional story of the year to come, plus a detailed budget for each area of the business.

Grand missions, ambitious goals and noble values are, of course, essential prerequisites, but many businesses have these. But how many businesses turn these noble ideals into reality? The plan is the engine that drives action and performance. As such it must be owned by every employee. Every employee must know that they're working to the plan and be emotionally invested in achieving it. And that process starts with their meaningful involvement in creating the plan.

> *The plan is the engine that drives action and performance. As such it must be owned by every employee.*

The classic dilemma of the annual budget is whether it should be 'top down' or 'bottom up'. The reality is that the best budgets are set through a rhythmic process of both top down and bottom up. It is for the leaders to look to the horizon, map the competitive landscape and come up with the parameters around market share, pricing, margins and products. To do that, the leaders need to add some parameters around investment, capital and resources.

At the same time, the employees should be auditing their own functions for what's possible with what they have. What efficiency improvements do they feel they can achieve with current resources? What could they achieve with some capital investment, and of what type? In my experience, only the employees can plan and achieve efficiency gains from current resources, and are also far better judges of the quality and return on investment in technology and equipment than leaders. This is not to say that the leaders should be absent from these 'bottom up' processes – this is where leaders can prove their worth as facilitators, asking the right questions, giving feedback and some gentle direction where required. For example, employees can get a bit carried away with their own enthusiasm sometimes, and can be guilty of arriving at an overly ambitious number. They may be eager to please, and to be praised for ambition. Leaders need to notice these things and be on hand to guide towards realism. Any plan needs to be a beautiful balance between what's possible if everything goes well, and what's realistic.

So now we have two sets of 'audits' – the external landscape and what's possible with what we already have. Now the two sides should present to each other to share all information, and the 'correct' plan is a synthesis of both. Having got feedback on their analysis of the competitive landscape (competing against other players in the market, but also competing for investment, space, brand profile, technology, innovation, etc) and having got the baseline efficiency gains from 'business as usual' (BAU), the leaders can now construct the ideal blend, matching the impact of what's going to be new – new investment, new products, new processes – on the baseline of BAU.

Setting a budget that is integral and genuinely valuable in maximising performance is an art form. Budgets must have that exquisite balance of realism and stretch, with 'bottom up' based on trust, education, facilitation and shared data, and 'top down' based on insightful analysis of the future marketplace.

Forecasting

show me the forecasting process in any business and I can immediately tell the level of fear in that culture

I've frequently said, show me the forecasting process in any business and I can immediately tell the level of fear in that culture. I've seen countless cultures whereby the forecast is nothing more than hope, and actually many where it's worse than that in that the forecast is a deliberate lie to stave off the pain of having to face up to reality. And that can go on for months, since many leaders are guilty of slipping into their Theory X dynamic, believing that the moment they accept a low forecast, they allow people to ease up. The strategy they are employing is that it is their resolute non-acceptance of a lowering of the forecast that will ensure all employees are doing whatever it takes to get there.

The plc CEO, of course, has the additional terrifying anxiety of having to make a call on profits warnings. Call too early and the CEO is guilty of spooking the market unnecessarily, with the untold damage that can do to a company's reputation, and to a CEO's credibility. Call too late and the CEO is clearly not in control of their business. But when is the right time? The only chance the plc CEO has of making a good call is to be absolutely assured that the forecasts they are being given are accurate.

I have a simple philosophy with forecasting. I err on the side of realism. Bear in mind that I have a plan that everyone owns and wants to achieve, and so I have a truly effective mechanism for analysing the factors causing us to miss plan, and I know about these in real time, not weeks or months after the event. Unforeseen external factors (ie, factors outside the control of employees) have to be accounted for and may well mean we must immediately lower the forecast; however, this might also mean that we change the plan – changing the timing or quantum of investments or product launches. And if we change the plan, then everyone is now working to the new plan, and so we'll be back on forecast.

If the reasons for shortfall are within our control – for example, we're not hitting the efficiency gains we planned for, or we're not achieving the level of sales planned – then we regroup, coach each other and determine what we need to do to get back on plan. Since everyone is emotionally invested in the plan, believe me *no one* likes being behind!

If we need to lower the forecast, then let's do it now, as I have great confidence that 'accepting' a lower forecast does not mean that people ease up. It actually means that I take some unhelpful pressure off people, allowing them to feel safe and thus to rejuvenate their creative energies to get back on plan.

Forecasting processes are frequently too opaque to adequately scrutinise, as the annual budget was not constructed properly in the first place, so there is no proper baseline against which to analyse what exactly has slipped and therefore what exactly is causing the forecast to be missed. So we're left with hard-pressed employees and managers presenting their new forecasts and being met with the fatuous and dangerous retort: '*That number's not good enough*.' How many times have you been met with that response when presenting your masters with what you genuinely believe is possible? Leaders really do need to eradicate this from their lexicon.

However, there comes a moment in the course of a journey towards a plan, whether a period end or a significant progress milestone, when the forecast simply has to change into a commitment – into the number we will deliver come hell or high water. When it's a forecast, teams can still be doing their utmost to balance short- and long-term tensions, acknowledging the urgency of what's possible in the moment, but cognisant of not doing anything that will ultimately do damage or cause unnecessary issues down the line. When it's a forecast, it can move and change with events and the passage of time. But when there is only a short time remaining before the final measurement, the event when we will be judged for periodic progress, then we have to deliver what we've committed to in our latest forecast. This is particularly true for quoted businesses in the public domain – the investor community demands that management are in control of their business, and while variances to and deviances from plans are understandable and tolerable, surprises are not acceptable.

I am reminded of a wonderful lesson I learned from an accountancy firm audit partner when I was a young plc subsidiary CFO. One month before the accounts had to be signed off, my group CEO came to me and asked whether I could produce another £1 million (representing an uplift of around 25 per cent) from the accounts as I prepared them for sign off. He said that results around the rest of the group were not going to be enough to hit the combined number given to the City. I said that in order to do that I would have to raid every provision, and do some further manipulation of accruals and prepayments, but that I could probably do it and maintain integrity. And so I got my team together, presented them with the challenge (which, by the way, included the not-inconsiderable task of managing the process with the Deloitte audit team who had already been given our draft 'final' pack). We set about our task, and three weeks later I sat down with the audit partner and his team and I took him through the rationale for the changes we had made since we had 'discovered' more profit, and why it was both ethical and prudent for us to do so. He looked at me and knew exactly what I was doing. And I looked at him and knew that he knew. And he knew that I knew that he knew. But there was enough real credibility in our case for him to agree to sign off the accounts at a profit figure £1 million higher.

Around a week later, just two days before the accounts needed to be signed off, my group CEO came to see me and told me it was OK, that one of the other group companies had actually hit its forecast, and therefore our additional £1 million was no longer needed and that I could go back to presenting the accounts at the original profit figure. I told him how I'd persuaded the audit partner to accept our higher figure already and that I could not now go back and say *oops*, or if I did that this would present me with a real personal difficulty for my professional integrity. Needless to say he wasn't that interested – that was my problem not his.

So I steeled myself for what would be a very awkward conversation with the audit partner, but I couldn't get hold of him until the following day – now one day before accounts sign-off. I went to see him at his office (always do the awkward stuff face-to-face) and told him that we had listened to his comments at the meeting a week earlier and on reflection we had accepted that our provisions needed to be increased, and therefore I was presenting accounts with a £1 million lower profit. He gave me that look again – that look that communicates '*I know and I know that you know that I know*'. I will never forget his response, and how he both reassured me and taught me a lesson. What he said was:

> *Mr Chick, you and I know exactly what has passed between us and you and I know exactly why we will respect each other's positions. But let me save you from any anxiety – because let me tell you my definition of materiality – materiality is turnover divided by the number of days before the accounts need signing off. One month ago, £1 million was absolutely material – which is why we were entirely comfortable with what you originally presented. One week ago, £1 million was borderline material and so we allowed your persuasive arguments to win the day. Today, with one day to go, £1 million is not at all material, so Mr Chick, you can basically do what you like.*

And he smiled a fatherly smile throughout (I was only 25 at the time).

There is of course more flexibility in private businesses; however, even here I believe there is something ultimately healthy about a culture that periodically demonstrates to its external stakeholders that it can deliver on commitments, and that it is healthy for managers and employees to operate in a working environment where delivery of commitments is built into the mix. The more our working environments mirror the realities of daily existence the better.

The operating model

As a young CEO, I always said that I needed two things to run a great business – employees who could make customers smile, and a spreadsheet that showed how the business worked at its best. I constructed my first Excel spreadsheet of a business in 1986. It was a model of the business, every bit as much as a Lego interpretation would have been constructed brick by brick, that I then used as the template for the budget. It had assumptions on all the critical operational ratios built in, so all I needed to do was input activity and trend information, and the model worked out the rest. It was a powerful 'what if' generator, and it forced me to know every aspect of my business, every tiny factor that could affect performance. It told me what was possible if everything worked perfectly. Of course I had to be wary of the potential tyranny of this. If the 'everything working perfectly' model spat out a

It was a powerful 'what if' generator, and it forced me to know every aspect of my business, every tiny factor that could affect performance. It told me what was possible if everything worked perfectly.

£3 million profit in the furthest bottom right-hand cell of the spreadsheet, I had to be careful not to have that as my target, with anything less being a disappointment. It's sometimes hard to accept anything less than perfection.

I learned (progressively) that the trick is to educate all employees in the 'what's possible if everything works perfectly' model, but then to demonstrate humanity and compassion in how long it could take for us all to get the machine working to that level of perfection. Truly the art of the budget is a rhythm of ambition and realism.

It's the new operating model that drives the required behaviours. If you wait for the behaviours to change before people are 'ready' to embrace the new model you'll have a long and frustrating wait. How do you get behaviour change?

⊕ You inspire change with the quality of the plan

⊕ You force change with the non-negotiability of the operating model

⊕ You reward change with inspirational leadership

⊕ You do these things reliably and predictably until the change is self-sustaining – until the culture has changed

The operating model should be based on a sound analysis of our deserved and legitimate place in the market and in the supply chain and the appropriate reward (margin) for our satisfying that deserved place.

Leaders of course need to look five to ten years ahead and predict what our market, our industry will look like and therefore the plans and investments we need to make now to stay ahead and manage our own destiny, but this innovative and transformational work can be done once the business has a sound foundation of a plan that the employees are working every day to achieve. Then the leaders can lift their heads to the future.

The philosophy of rigid disciplines

Forming a rigid structure of non-negotiable processes upon which to build a business is perhaps the most ancient of management skills. I was first introduced to this philosophy in 1982 by Anthony Househam who was deputy chairman of Gallaher Tobacco, and who chaired all 17 of their non-tobacco operating subsidiaries. At the time I was CFO of Ofrex, a leading national commercial stationery company, and we were bought by Gallaher as part of their strategy to diversify away from tobacco. We were in a basket of non-tobacco companies they'd purchased. The first item on the agenda of the first meeting I had with the new chairman was the Gallaher way of managing operating subsidiaries. Strategy, objectives and key tasks – that was the non-negotiable template that we had to plan and monitor our business by. Working closely with Tony Househam was my invaluable introduction to the crucial value of rigid disciplines. If our plan and our board pack did not align to the strategy, objectives and key tasks format, it wasn't even opened.

Ten years later and Tony Barnes was introducing me to Deming's 14 points for management, and to kaizen as a philosophy and practice of continuous improvement. Another ten years on and Mike Morrison was introducing me to the Toyota

Way. Through my exposure to these working practices and cultures, and through the mentoring and inspiration that Tony and Mike provided, I wholeheartedly embraced the philosophy of fundamental processes to which 100 per cent compliance was necessary. I learned that the trick was to first get 100 per cent compliance, achieved through there being consequences of non-compliance, and then to improve the quality and skill levels in using those processes. I learned that when the whole company ran on the same uniform values and processes, when everyone did the basics the same way, amazing things started to happen. Trust levels went through the roof. Commitments were not just words but got carried through. The transparency of what each person was responsible for, and how they were doing against their objectives, liberated colleagues from unnecessary anxiety and allowed them to focus 100 per cent on delivering their own commitments. The common language was bonding and reassuring and fostered collaboration rather than competition. Tasks or analysis that would have taken weeks before could be done in minutes, since all the data was really known; it was the decisiveness that had been lacking. Egos are put to one side as everyone submits themselves to the cause. And upon this solid united foundation, people became free to express their personality, to use their unique flair, to get truly creative and to uncover and then grow their amazing untapped potential. Truly the route into the 'unknown' box in the Johari window.

So first get 100 per cent compliance and do this in days not weeks. Start by explaining the philosophy and why it's vital, and then tell people what they're going to experience as it's implemented. Bright people who desire autonomy do not react well when given prescriptive and detailed direction, so this must be recognised and honoured. You are asking for a leap of faith; however, the alternative is resistance. Then explain the consequences for non-compliance. These consequences need to be in the form of exclusion, as people have to understand that these are the new rules of the game. Flout the rules and you will not be allowed to play. This might start with not being allowed to attend a meeting if the person has not adhered to the preparation process. Ultimately, serial non-compliance has to end with removal. There can be no exceptions. I know this sounds draconian and unbelievably autocratic, but if you want an efficient business that turns into a joyful place to work, these foundations simply have to be non-negotiable. What you'll notice is that the people who leave are the ones whose egos will not allow them to truly join a community. The people who are left can and will do great things together, and will personally blossom, thrive and have joy in their work. One hundred per cent compliance is the gateway to the good stuff. Pass through and you will be rewarded.

> **Bright people who desire autonomy do not react well when given prescriptive and detailed direction, so this must be recognised and honoured.**

Having talked about the 'consequences' phase, hopefully this does not last long, maybe only a week or at most a month. For once people show a willingness to dive in and conform, the positive reward phase can start, when the predominant leadership lever is reward and recognition for compliance, and for progressively learning and improving the quality and skill levels.

Key performance indicators

Trained accountant I may be, but even if I weren't I would love KPIs. Who doesn't? From the giant thermometer outside the church hall that shows the fundraising progress to the target, to our Fitbits, our scales, our speedometers, our fuel consumption computers and our calorie counters, we humans are programmed to seek to control what we can visibly measure. I know for certain that if all employees are given timely information on the KPIs, this in itself will cause performance to go up. We love to have a target and see our progress towards that target. It is motivating and causes us to focus on behaviours and actions that lead to progress. This is a fundamental cognitive ability humans have, to compare data and instantly devise strategies for improving. When leaders help employees to understand the KPIs and the relative impacts, human nature can do the rest.

It is relatively easy to see what the appropriate KPIs are in sales, production, design, marketing, IT and engineering operations. But what about the more supportive functions such as HR, communications and legal? The same question applies to coming up with objectives and key results (OKRs, see later) – but the very fact that it's harder to identify measurable activity and trend KPIs within these support functions should be enough to tell you to be wary of their power within any culture. All you need to do is to keep asking the question '*How will you know when you're being successful/adding value?*' And with any OKR process there needs to be an element of anecdote or subjective assessment, but still push for some measures. With HR there are factors such as attrition or absence rates, engagement survey scores, levels and spreads of professional and vocational qualifications, net promoter scores on internal training courses and numbers and lengths of vacancies – so it's entirely possible to set HR leaders and managers OKRs and KPIs, and this process forces these characters to be accountable for the business impact they bring.

But I really struggle when it comes to comms and legal, and this is why I'm in favour of outsourcing as much of the professional support as possible in these areas. I much prefer the clumsy and often inelegant communications of line managers (where they cannot rely on the wordsmithing of internal comms teams) since it is wholly authentic and is a skill that they can improve upon with training and practice. And it has to be a critical responsibility of line managers to communicate, and not be able to subcontract that to internal 'specialists'.

So if you have support functions in your company where you are really struggling to identify measurable and meaningful KPIs and/or OKRs, then you need to ask yourself why you need them, or at least if the professional expertise they offer cannot be bought when needed from contracted external agents.

One-to-ones

Once the disciplines of the plan, weekly and monthly reporting and management are going, we can put the cross-member in place to give the whole structure a strength, stability and safety. This is the format and rhythm of one-to-ones, team meetings and regular communications. Let's start with one-to-ones – this is a brief guide I prepared for a client company who were reintroducing one-to-ones to their working practices, having had failed attempts in the past. This company calls their vision and strategy 'The Way Forward':

1. Why are one-to-ones critical?

   a. We have the mission, the vision, the plan, KPIs and roles and responsibilities

   b. Now 'all' we need to do is establish a consistent, safe and disciplined performance management structure – one-to-ones and team meetings

   c. The one-to-one is the main formal point of contact between manager and team member

2. Introducing one-to-ones into the operating rhythm of the business

   a. Be 100 per cent disciplined in holding the one-to-ones

   b. Keep to one hour unless it would be unsafe for the team member to end the session

   c. It is the formality, the consistency and the discipline that make the team member feel safe

   d. Remember their one-to-one is there to give them permission to struggle and licence to be fabulous

3. The person, the role, the vision... and the problem

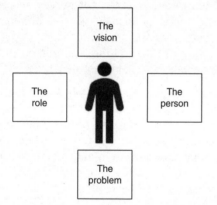

   a. The team member has everything they need to self-assess and self-correct. They have clear roles and accountabilities; they have KPIs that tell them how they are doing; they have the way forward to guide them in their decision-making, prioritisation and behaviour; they are clear on their own habits and traits, and clear on their agreed skill development areas

   b. Therefore when coaching team members in one-to-ones, the problems they present are merely the material to use to coach them to improve their own performance

c. The clearer the manager is on the roles and accountabilities, and the more the team member has what they need to self-assess and self-correct, the more the one-to-one becomes of intense value to both parties since it solely focuses on the deeper needs of the team member

4. Mapping your people and preparing for the first one-to-one

   a. Prepare well for the first one-to-one – this one will lay the foundation for the success of all future one-to-ones

   b. Be as clear as possible on the KPIs that will measure the team member's success in their role

   c. Establish a clear contract with the team member – what they can expect from you and what you can and will expect of them

   d. Establish the principles of the one-to-ones: that the team member must develop as strongly as possible in self-assessment and self-correction, and that the one-to-one is therefore their place to bring their concerns, anxieties and struggles, and to bring their hopes, dreams and ambitions

5. What is feedback? Part I

   a. This sets up the critical dynamic of team members having clear KPIs and access to regular accurate independently generated information that tells them how they are doing

6. What is feedback? Part II

   a. Johari window – feedback as observations on what is hidden to the team member; what everyone else can see but of which they lack self-awareness

   b. **Phrasing feedback to ensure it is not judgemental and therefore is not automatically defended or excused**

7. Handling 'difficult' conversations

   a. Two types:

      i. giving wholly unexpected news of a management decision that affects that person's everyday life

      ii. reaching a 'non-negotiable' moment after a build-up of observational feedback

   b. Transactional analysis – parent, adult and child and examples of what these 'voices' sound like in a business

   c. How to stay in adult mode as a coach

   d. How to prepare clear statements and clear questions

   e. Get the key statement across right up front!

8. Aspirations for the employee engagement survey of one-to-one quality

Many managers avoid one-to-ones, finding them uncomfortable and anxiety pro-voking. The typical defence contains comments such as *'but I talk to my people every day'*, *'if they need to raise something with me they do'*, *'there'll be nothing to talk about in a one-to-one'*, *'my people will feel nervous and they don't want me to do one-to-ones with them'*.

In my experience this is wholly about the manager's fear. Of course it can feel uncomfortable for employees to have regular one-to-ones, particularly if their man-ager is clumsy at them. But remember the mantra – get 100 per cent compliance and then work on raising the quality and the skill levels.

Observing many hundreds of one-to-ones over the years, I noticed that the most consistent feedback I was giving to the manager at the end of the one-to-one was that they'd missed an opportunity to do some work and make a step change in progress within the one-to-one itself. Typically when an employee is tasked with a project, they'll go away and think about it, but if it involves some courage in taking the first step, they'll frequently come to the next one-to-one and say they've been too busy to start. It's not that they are being deliberately dishonest, it's that they're scared and so they've procrastinated. And this is obvious, if the manager is paying attention. So many times I see the manager yield and give the employee more time. The trick is for managers to notice the fear that lies behind the procrastination, and to be of practical help right then and there. This could be by gently uncovering what the fear is, and pushing the employee to commit to the irrevocable step they've been putting off. Or it could be coaching the employee to complete the first draft of a project plan. Either way, a five-minute tangent and the employee can have made a breakthrough.

> **The trick is for managers to notice the fear that lies behind the procrastination, and to be of practical help right then and there.**

Team meetings and communications

We saw in the chapter on teams earlier the incredible value of the team in changing cultures, creating high performance and providing sanctuary and mental well-being for hard-pressed people. Suffice to say that the team meeting, whether weekly or monthly, is an essential structure and must be honoured consistently.

Finally, let's talk about communications, and here I am talking not just about written communications or access to information on an intranet, but mainly about face-to-face gatherings of people to receive briefings. A good rhythm and regime to establish is as follows:

⊛ Frequent short briefings within single discrete teams – maybe even every day to check in on daily changes to situations, promotions, customer activity, what happened yesterday, what's coming up today. These might be just 10 or 15 minutes, mostly of the team members sharing information and asking critical questions. They will be punchy, clear and take place *in situ* – at the end of a production line; in the sales office etc. I call these 'team briefings'.

- Regular gatherings of larger, maybe departmental or functional groups, of longer duration, maybe 30–45 minutes once a week (maybe with pizza, cake, fruit, juice or a new product to add to the ritual nature of this happening every week at the same time). Again this should be predominantly the team members presenting, but with the longer time allocation giving the opportunity for a more senior leader to attend to give a short presentation and answer questions.

- Periodic (but regular) 'all hands' meetings of sites or even all employees, led by a senior leader, probably of 60–90 minutes maybe once a quarter. The leader updates the employees on companywide performance, progress and initiatives. This should have a strong Q&A element and be a truly interactive communication forum.

Putting the discipline of team briefings into an organisation is one of my non-negotiable structures, and although I'm prepared to be a bit flexible as to when, where, how long and the precise format, I insist upon at least weekly team briefings. In my experience this is one of the hardest structures to install – managers often hate them at first, again resisting with the '*I talk to my people every day*', '*they don't want to be there*', '*no one ever has any questions*', etc. I've spent countless hours driving to sites for the 8am team briefing to be there to support the manager, in what I appreciate is a tough gig (at least at first). And I've spent countless hours being in such meetings to role model and facilitate – I'm a great facilitator and so I know how to get people to engage, ask questions and ultimately experience the value of the process. And I know that I will find employees in each area who are natural presenters and engagers, and the finest team briefings are the ones run by the employees themselves, with the site manager sitting on the side-lines supporting but not either rescuing or dominating.

Management by objectives or OKRs

Again these are not new. Arnold Weinstock was using them, so too Toyota, long before Intel 'discovered' them and made them sexy. Then Google reinvented them again with their objectives and key results (OKRs). So I'm going to use OKRs as the prime acronym in this section.

OKRs need a quality measure and an efficiency measure. KPIs (metrics in the US) are the key. Progress towards our goal is broken down into objectives for each area of the business, and then down into objectives for each manager and each team. Since only inputs can be controlled, and on the basis that no one can control outputs (outputs are the results or outcomes from all the inputs) we need KPIs for activity. For example, in a retail store, total revenue is an output. It cannot be controlled in itself. Some of the inputs that we can control are conversion rates (what percentage of customers who enter the store actually purchase something): the average number of items in a customer basket at the checkout and the average value of that basket. A store manager can do something about the activity and input KPIs, but the total revenue is merely a result, an outcome from all the activity.

And KPIs are able to be compared so we can see trends and progress. We can compare to prior periods, last week, last month, last year; we can compare to the plan we set so carefully, and we can compare to best in class. In the absence of a plan, as a manager I first of all want to beat last year, to demonstrate progress, and then I want to beat the best there is anywhere else out there. I want to be moving forwards, and then I want to be the best.

> *leaders' OKRs must contain transformational objectives, otherwise they are merely glorified middle managers who are probably interfering with their own teams and thus destroying value rather than creating it.*

OKRs need an element of ambition. This comes back to the fundamental role of leaders. When we have a plan that is owned by all employees, they run the day-to-day business using a continuous improvement culture to maximise efficiency from our current situation and set of assets. This means the leaders can focus on the future, predicting the market and creating transformational change and development for the business. So leaders' OKRs must contain transformational objectives, otherwise leaders are merely glorified middle managers who are probably interfering with their own teams and thus destroying value rather than creating it.

The OKRs set for operational teams and for middle managers need an element of ambition but cannot be out of reach. People can accept that they will not necessarily achieve all their OKRs, but this dynamic needs careful handling, as it can tip into becoming a mere manipulative device very quickly.

This dynamic is especially sensitive when elements of reward and recognition are geared to the achievement of OKRs. If your rating or bonus depends upon you achieving your OKRs, the risk is that you'll try and negotiate low objectives, and that your behaviours through the period could be skewed by your progress or otherwise towards them. Deming was always clear with us, in that he was against individual bonuses, promoting team awards as more efficient. We don't seem to have learned that lesson yet.

There must be total transparency in OKRs – everyone must know and understand everyone else's. This fosters trust, collaboration and mutual support. In team meetings I'm always on the lookout for whether individual managers are preoccupied with their own objectives and the degree to which they are looking out for their colleagues and expending energy and commitment to assist them to succeed.

So we come to how to set OKRs and I always start with one of the most haunting questions I am fond of asking managers – '*What would happen if you were not here?*' I am a great believer that it is better to run with a management vacancy than to put the wrong manager in place. Poor managers cause damage. They take things backwards not forwards. They create problems rather than solving them. And they create mirror behaviours in their teams that can take months if not years to turn around. If there is a vacancy you can get the team together, apologise for the fact they are going to have to manage themselves for a while, and then coach and facilitate even from a little distance. Self-managed teams work brilliantly.

So a manager has to be able to answer the question I pose them. And they have to be able to articulate the added value from them being in place. The starting point for that added value should be their salary cost as a bare minimum. But really we should look for their salary multiplied by a significant factor.

Then their objectives should reflect the critical activity KPIs in their area – move these and the big hairy outputs move automatically. Finally their objectives should reflect the comparatives and the trends. What progress over last year do their object-ives represent? To what extent are they managing their area to become world-class or at least better than the competition?

With OKRs a manager might have four or five objectives and then a handful of key results under each objective. It's not that every key result needs to be achieved in order for the manager to be judged successful; they're there to give substance and guidance to how the manager should achieve the high-level objectives.

And so to the thorny issue of performance ratings, management-level gradings and elements of compensation based on the achievement of OKRs. This is a really tricky area requiring care and sensitivity, for this is a key element in the dangerous power and control dynamic inherent in corporatism and so easily abused by those holding that power. I am not a fan of individual merit-based rewards. They are divisive and breed internal competition. If they are utterly transparent to all, then there is a chance they can work; however, decisions on OKR setting and on performance ratings can be seen as immensely subjective, with disgruntled parties seeing colleagues seem-ingly being rewarded for selfish or self-promoting actions and priorities.

These so-called meritocratic evaluation and reward systems can be the single force denying diversity in a business. The results-oriented, hard-driving managers do well because they know how to hit short-term targets and they know how to look good and to claim credit. And so there is a predominance of this personality type at senior levels in businesses across the world. Where does the more reflective, more creative, more collaborative, more thoughtful, possibly more cautious or more nat-urally hesitant personality type get their look-in? How is their contribution noticed, celebrated and valued? I believe it's the lack of diversity in personality type that is our biggest diversity issue, and I don't mean to downplay the immense struggles for those discriminated against because of gender, ethnicity, disability or sexual orientation.

So take care with how you create your reward and recognition systems. I know that human nature has become obsessed with comparing ourselves to others, but let's see if we can eradicate that from our working cultures.

Strategy one-pagers

One way of achieving a unified understanding and commitment to each individual team member's strategy is to have each team member produce a 'strategy one-pager' – literally a written one-page document that clearly sets out the agreed strategy for their area of responsibility. This can then be critiqued and challenged, with team members able and equipped now to comment on each other's perform-ance with intelligence and context. But also it can be used to counter any nega-tive intrigue that people may seek to use (consciously or unconsciously) to divert attention away from their own shortcomings.

Contents of a strategy one-pager

Function name and strategy owner:

1. State of the nation

2. The long-term strategy and objectives

3. The tangible business benefits of this strategy

4. The strategy for the next 12 months

5. Key objectives for the next 12 months

6. The KPIs

7. The potential risks

8. The budget and resources required

9. Reporting and scrutiny

Here's a fictional example:

Function name: IT

Strategy owner: CTO/CIO

1. State of the nation

   The IT systems are performing basic functions to an adequate level but nowhere near their potential. Different sites are still at different stages of adopting Navision and are still using many different processes and tools. The proprietary software's 'reputation' within the business is improving but many managers still see it as a blocker not an enabler. The x people in the IT team are skilled and committed and well-resourced, but are operating at a level way below their true competence. We are more of a helpdesk than a business enabler at this time. The business has invested £x million in hardware and software and has yet to see a proper return on this investment.

2. The long-term strategy and objectives

   To create industry-leading fully integrated business systems, achieving maximum automation, utter integrity in business controls and reporting, and to be a source of innovation to the functions. To be recognised by our customers as a source of IT innovation in such areas as online, handheld and smartphones. Ultimately for the business to include IT in the value proposition.

3. The tangible business benefits of this strategy

   - A direct impact on the bottom line of the business, through progressive reduction in absolute costs and in IT costs as a percentage of revenues

   - Account plans that are even more persuasive and compelling to customers because of the clear industry-leading IT innovations achieved

4. The strategy for the next 12 months

Move halfway towards the long-term strategy, with clear evidence of direct impact on the bottom line, and in making the lives of hard-pressed managers easier instead of more difficult.

5. Key objectives for the next 12 months

- To dramatically raise the reputation of proprietary software across the business
- To reduce headcount in areas X and Y through the successful implementation of A, B and C
- To be generating operating reports X, Y and Z from proprietary software
- Reduce IT costs as percentage of revenue from x per cent to y percent

6. The KPIs

- IT costs as percentage of revenue
- IT costs versus budget
- Accuracy of X, Y and Z reports
- System downtime

7. The potential risks

Our assessment is that the risks are low. We have good business continuity plans in place, so we are confident of supporting the business critical systems even in the event of a natural disaster or loss of third-party power or network connectivity. We have good protection from cyberattacks and hacking. We believe we are better placed now to stem the practice of some managers using workarounds to proprietary software.

8. The budget and resources required

- Total IT budget of £x versus actual spend last year of £x
- IT payroll budget of £x versus £x based on static headcount
- Third-party licence and support costs of £x versus £x
- Other costs of £x versus £x
- Capex requested £x in order to achieve Y. Would need to be spent in December 2011. This Capex is in line with previous forecasts for staged investments in Navision, and run rates for replacing failing equipment. We could get by without this investment, but the medium-term impact would be a postponement of a bottom line impact of £x

9. Reporting and scrutiny

- Monthly board report
- Monthly team review with FD
- Quarterly survey from users

Know your balance sheet

The balance sheet contains critical measures that can tell a story about what is actually happening within the business. It is an invaluable source of intelligence on the reality of things, not necessarily as they are being presented by over-zealous managers. So look at simple things in the balance sheet such as accruals and prepayments, provisions and intangible assets – all areas where creative or overly stressed accountants can 'hide' things for dealing with later. Taking over a new business, I always surprise the accountants by asking to see the latest bank reconciliation, and by asking them to take me through the trial balance.

Let me give you a great example of how valuable a knowledge and scrutiny of the balance sheet can be. When starting as chair of a housing association, I asked for the financial report to include a full analysis of accruals and prepayments. It took several requests for this to happen, but it was duly delivered. I went to prepayments first, since that is the place that costs can be hidden or delayed from hitting the profit and loss (P&L), and all appeared well – nothing alarming and no large items that looked out of kilter.

I then went to accruals and it immediately showed two things. First, there was a huge accrual for electricity charges. On asking for more detail I discovered that association had not received the main electric bill (hundreds of thousands of pounds per year in charges) for some months. Not one of the board was aware of this including the CFO! Since the utility charges in the P&L were roughly on budget, nothing jumped out from a P&L review. This could have turned into a very big problem, and I while I understood the accountants' noble desire to hold onto cash for as long as possible, therefore not to chase for a bill, I advised them that this was a decision that should have come to the board, and that we could have a problem when the bill finally arrived if it was way more than had been accrued for, leading to a large one-off adjustment in the accounts.

Second, there was a huge accrual (over £100,000) for repairs and maintenance. So again in the P&L, repairs and maintenance costs were on budget, but we'd clearly not received all the bills we were expecting. On further investigation we uncovered a very alarming state of affairs. The accrual was for charges for provision of the annual gas certification for some 500 homes. The plain fact was that this annual process had not been carried out, and that the association was in breach of the law. This breach could have had disastrous consequences. It had clearly increased the risk to tenants from potentially faulty boilers and pipes. We'd been lucky on that front. It also meant that the association was at risk of prosecution, which would have led to a substantial fine, possible legal action against officers, and the loss of reputation, seriously diminishing the association's ability to develop more homes. Although the expenditure had been budgeted for, and therefore accrued for to keep the P&L looking in line with budget, no one on the board had any idea that we were behind on the certification.

the expenditure had been budgeted for, and therefore accrued for to keep the P&L looking in line with budget, no one on the board had any idea that we were behind on the certification

Interestingly the operating report had a green light against all maintenance quality standards and checks, but how could that be if the certifications had not been carried out? Simple – the regime in maintenance operations when completing the board reports was to put green against everything! When we dug further into how the maintenance operation was being managed, we discovered that the measurement of fix times (the average length of time it took for a registered fault to be fixed – a measure that I'd already clocked as suspicious at around four days, since the complaints register and conversations with tenants betrayed the fact that it took way too long for faults to be attended to) was being deliberately falsified. If a registered fault slipped over five days on the system, the people in the maintenance department were simply changing the reported date on the system. We plugged that gap.

Documents with status (I carry these next to my heart)

In Chapter 14 I introduced the concept of 'documents with status'. Here are the ones I would recommend:

⊛ Mission statement/purpose statement/vision

⊛ Values/operating principles

⊛ Strategy one-pager

⊛ Plan/budget

⊛ Weekly KPI dashboard

⊛ Weekly flash forecast

⊛ Monthly reporting pack summary

The results

I'm just going to repeat here the diagram I showed in the section above on one-to-ones. The person, the role, the vision… and the problem.

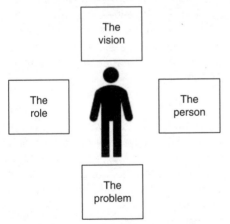

This is a great image for any manager to hold in their mind for any interaction they have with any employee. The philosophy is that the problem that the employee is facing is theirs and not the manager's. And the manager needs to keep it that way and not get drawn into the drama, however seductive it appears.

It's how as a coach we can be directive in our questioning, but directive towards existing and helpful processes that the employee can access on their own, not directing towards a specific solution.

By asking the employee some simple questions of context, the manager can guide the employee to solve the problem for themselves, without offering a breath of a potential solution themselves. It's how as a coach we can be directive in our questioning, but directive towards existing and helpful processes that the employee can access on their own, not directing towards a specific solution.

Questions can include *'What do the company values guide the employee to do about the problem?' 'What effect on the achievement of the plan is the problem having?' 'How critical is the problem to the achievement of the plan?' 'How big a priority is this problem in the context of your other objectives?'*

Also, because the manager knows the employee's personal development plan, the manager can also see the trait or habit that is getting in the employee's way and can give that feedback. The manager can also exhort the employee to use the problem as a learning example, a manifestation of the employee's progress on their personal development journey.

When managers hold this image in their minds, they can default to treating the problem as material for the employee's growth. Problems can therefore be celebrated rather than always causing reactions of frustration, impatience and irritation. This is a game-changing dynamic for managers and thus for entire working cultures. This is the cutting edge. If managers can learn to default to treating problems as learning opportunities, we will have fantastic businesses.

There is a beautiful thing that happens when people submit themselves to the cause. Things start to flow; organic processes emerge to take the business in the direction the universe is calling it to; people genuinely collaborate and support each other operationally but also emotionally; a healthy and sustainable organism starts to thrive as does every human being in it. I know this sounds spiritual, but that's because it is. And I know it's hard to trust that this is true, especially as there is inevitable discomfort to navigate to break into this nirvana.

But what is the alternative? Pressure, stress and anxiety.

And on a more prosaic level, the job of a manager and leader is made so much simpler when they can rely on the structures working. When approached by someone in the business, or when engaging with employees on a store or factory visit, and being presented with a question or an issue, how much easier it is to listen and ask some questions, and then to simply point that person at the correct process. So I frequently use phrases and questions such as these:

🉐 *That's a really important point for us to discuss – bring that to your next one-to-one.*

- How have you handled this so far with your manager? When is your next one-to-one? I suggest you bring it up there.

- That's interesting, what does the plan say you should do now?

- What's in the plan?

- How does that fit into the plan?

- I'd really like all your colleagues to hear this from you and to for us to be able to handle it as a team, so please make sure this is on your one-page update for the team meeting/please put this on the agenda for the next team meeting.

- It sounds as though all your colleagues need to be informed on this; add it to the Team Briefing for next week.

- That's an interesting dilemma for you. What would I see in your personal development plan that would guide you as to how you should be handling this situation?

These responses can, of course, be frustrating for people, including us as we have to deny ourselves a chance to show off, to solve a problem or to join in the drama. But we have to enforce the structures and processes that exist to solve issues in the right place and by the right people. And every time we do this, we make the system work that little bit better, we educate people to take personal responsibility and we relieve ourselves of an immense amount of counterproductive work.

Work the plan, work the system. Everyone benefits.

Chapter 16

Establishing a collaborative equity organisation

What is 'collaborative equity'?

I created the term 'collaborative equity' as the brand for my style of organisation. 'Collaborative' to stand for the encouragement of a truly collective learning, innovating, growing and thriving, and for the eradication of the aggression from competition. And 'equity' to stand for the inclusion and the equality of responsibility and rewards for every stakeholder. Collaborative equity is also conveniently shortened to the acronym CEQ, the same acronym I use to denote corporate emotional intelligence. So I'm really making it as easy as possible here – all you have to do is remember CEQ, and remember it stands for both the emotional and rational solutions to our problems.

> *all you have to do is remember CEQ, and remember it stands for both the emotional and rational solutions to our problems.*

A collaborative equity organisation is one where the people who gain from the success of the venture are the stakeholders who are *truly* invested – those seven stakeholder groups for whom the sustainability of the endeavour is paramount in their lives: the employees, the leaders, the suppliers, the long-term investors, the customers, the local community and the environment.

A collaborative equity organisation is one of shared ownership, shared responsibility and shared reward. Let's look at each of these in turn.

Shared ownership

This is an emotional state, not a financial or legal one. In a listed business, the owners are the shareholders and so it will remain. Of course we can tinker with share option schemes, LTIPs for the senior execs and share save type schemes for the employees, but these are just technical devices seeking to link the way managers and employees are motivated to some notion of medium-term rise in the share price. Many of these schemes are laudable but flawed. If the stock market was a sound medium-term arbiter of company performance then they might just work, but with such high degrees of speculative activity skewing values, they are notoriously unreliable. I have no issue with the separation of investment and employment, but I am heavily in favour of employees being generously rewarded for their daily efforts, with the 'bonus' of some capital reward for long-term contribution. In our materialistic society we have become obsessed with ownership of things as an emotional crutch, but in working for an organisation that we believe in, and in feeling attached to the purpose and the outcomes, we can transcend the material substitutes and feel the human rewards of connection.

> *in working for an organisation that we believe in, and in feeling attached to the purpose and the outcomes, we can transcend the material substitutes and feel the human rewards of connection*

Shared responsibility

This refers to that nirvana cultural state whereby every employee is working the plan to achieve the purpose and objectives, using all their potential, creativity and humanity. Yes there will be designated leaders and maybe even an inevitable hierarchy of authority to organise scarce resources, but fundamentally every single employee will gladly and freely take personal responsibility for achieving the plan. So leaders need to work hard to create a culture whereby every individual is willing, even desperate, to take personal responsibility for their area and for the collaboration across functions that will deliver outstanding results.

Shared reward

This means that every individual feels appropriately rewarded for their part. The market for talent will dictate that some earn more than others, but it is the secrecy around this dynamic that most upsets people. While a situation whereby a CEO might earn 200 times the rate of their average employee can be defended according to the 'market', it is surely both unethical and unsustainable. Unethical in the sense that one individual cannot be worth 200 times another, and if they are, then the organisation is overly reliant on one-off deals as opposed to having a compelling sustainable operating model earning a justifiable margin from its place in the supply chain. And unsustainable in the sense that this dramatically skewed dynamic automatically breeds hubris and damaging power, control and invulnerability in the leaders. If I earn 200 times what you earn, how can I legitimately come to you and ask you what you think?

Stakeholders are as follows, together with a simple statement of how each group is rewarded:

- Employees (rewarded by long-term job security, salary and a share of surplus)
- Leaders (rewarded by professional challenge, salary and a share of surplus)
- Suppliers (rewarded by long-term partnership security and growth)
- Customers (rewarded with the highest quality products and services)
- Investors (rewarded by a reasonable and stable return on their investment in the form of interest or dividends, and a share of surplus)
- Community (rewarded by regulated payments and taxes, and net positive impact)
- Environment (rewarded by total supply chain net positive)

But what about the alternatives?

Co-operatives and partnerships

The John Lewis Partnership was founded in 1929 by John Spedan Lewis to give all employees a say in the running of the business and a share in profits. This is a much-vaunted organisational model and constitution, which the company increasingly promoted to customers as an indicator of quality and more recently as an appeal to an ever-more discerning and ethically conscious clientele. 'John Lewis' became synonymous in the first part of the twenty-first century with an aspirational blend of quality and corporate ethics. John Lewis remains the darling of the middle classes, with its supermarket brand Waitrose and its internet delivery offshoot Ocado themselves entering the language as synonyms. It could be said that the reason John Lewis is able to distance itself from the vagaries of corporate short-termism is not because it's a partnership, but purely because it's privately owned. But that would be to ignore the palpable achievements on quality of products and service, and to diminish the genuine admiration its employees, past and present, hold for it.

My son Tom worked for John Lewis for ten hours a week as a 16 year-old, and experienced both fantastic training and the excitement of achieving sales milestones. There are many managers out there who've been through the John Lewis school of management as graduates or management trainees, and who have taken that sound schooling into other companies for mutual benefit. John Lewis is not, of course, immune to seismic market corrections, but it's significant that on the same day in 2018 that the partnership announced a 99 per cent decrease in profits (with the carnage going on in the UK retail sector) it also announced a rebrand as John Lewis and Partners. On a day when a public company CEO would have quit, been fired or at the very least had the humility to be utterly contrite for being so clearly inept, John Lewis proudly replanted their ethical flag.

> *On a day when a public company CEO would have quit, been fired or at the very least had the humility to be utterly contrite for being so clearly inept, John Lewis proudly replanted their ethical flag.*

Tomorrow's Company

Patrick Hosking in an article in the *Times*, 30 January 2017, entitled 'Building a Brave New World of Investment on Ghosts of the Past', wrote about the think tank *'Tomorrow's Company – a think tank having a stab at how we might get a little closer to this nirvana'*, which recommended the setting up of an investment trust for a total of £15 billion or 7 per cent of the UK stock market. The trust's shareholding was to be designated as a 'stewardship stake' for which, in return for promises not to sell the shares for at least two years, they would qualify for tax breaks and extra voting powers in areas such as executive pay. While I've heard the brand Tomorrow's Company banded about in recent years, I see no evidence of anything concrete.

Employee ownership

This is a growing phenomenon in the US and in the UK, whereby a significant proportion of the shares in a company are transferred to the employees, most usually in the form of a trust. This form of share transfer is typically chosen to facilitate the transition of ownership from a founder or founding family, to best ensure the sustainability of the company and its ethos. While owners know they could likely achieve a higher sales value from a trade sale to a third party, most likely a competitor, their motivation in seeing a continuation of their 'legacy' motivates them to accept less money.

The most surprising example of this type of transaction was in 2017 when KKR floated Gardner Denver on the New York Stock Exchange and awarded $100 million worth of shares to employees (over 10 per cent of the stake they were selling). Yes that's right, KKR, the private equity firm led by the legendary Henry Kravis, whose reputation was immortalised in the 1989 book by Bryan Burrough and John Helyar called *Barbarians at the Gate*, about the leveraged buyout of Nabisco. The *Washington Post* called Kravis the '*king of rough-and-tumble leveraged buyouts*' (in an article by Stephanie Baker and David Carey, 24 July 2014).

The epithet *Barbarian* also stuck. 'Letting Workers Have a Share', an article by Anders Melin and Melissa Mittleman in *Business Week*, 9 June 2017, reported on the KKR initiative and KKR's Pete Stavros, saying '*treating employees like owners and business partners – that's how you create value and make this more than just a feel-good story*'. The article postulates that

> employee ownership may be more appropriate in low growth, low margin industries where businesses must do a million things a little better to excel, and that front line workers know best how where operational inefficiencies exist and how to fix them. More than 25 million US workers are part of some form of employee ownership pro-gramme, and research shows that those who participate in ownership plans tend to outearn peers, accumulate bigger nest-eggs, and stay at their jobs longer.

Philip Aldrick, economics editor of *The Times*, writing in an article in 2017 entitled 'How the Barbarians Learnt to Share the Spoils – And Grow Rich' just after the KKR float, said:

> Study after study has shown that the gains of progress have been accruing to the owners of capital rather than labour, leaving just-about-managing wage slaves behind. The proportion of stock owned by individuals has dropped from 28% in 1981 to 12% in 2014. In 1998 individuals owned £250 billion of equity. In 2014 that had dropped to £200 billion. Only 2 million of Britain's 32 million workers are members of share save schemes. In France profit sharing is mandatory for companies with more than 50 employees. If the UK followed suit, 11 million more workers would have a stake in their company.

I can't resist pointing out that in 2018 when the Labour Party mooted plans to mandate for employee share ownership, *The Times* was one of the establishment newspapers that described the policy as 'robbery'.

WinCo Foods

WinCo Foods is a $6 billion US company that converted to being employee-owned more than 30 years ago, and has thrived ever since. It prides itself on comparison to Walmart, the behemoth with which it competes most, citing that while Walmart pays the US regulated living wage of $9 per hour, WinCo pays the same grade workers between $12 and $18 per hour, and that while Walmart provides those workers with no benefits and no pension, WinCo has employee pensions that rank in the upper quartile of funds deemed to provide 'living wage' pensions. And it claims lower prices than Walmart.

Information from WinCo's website states the following:

WinCo Foods is proud to be employee-owned...

We believe our employees should share in the success of our company in a tangible way. That's why we created an Employee Stock Ownership Plan ('ESOP') more than 30 years ago. Participating in the ESOP program means employees are part owners of the company and benefit financially from a job well done. In this way, there is direct incentive for employees to work hard and take pride in what they do; that is why our stores are cleaner, our prices lower and our smiles are bigger. Additionally, being employee-owned means WinCo Foods is owned by members of the local community. WinCo's ESOP never involves contributions from the employees; all contributions are entirely made by the company.

Our ESOP's Solid Financial Performance:

Unlike a publicly traded stock valued on the open market, the per share value of WinCo's stock is appraised annually by an independent valuation firm selected by the ESOP trustee. ESOP stock values have averaged increases of 18% compounded annually since 1986. That means an employee who received a company contribution of $5,000 worth of stock in 1986 now has stock worth almost $863,000 from that one year alone!

At WinCo Foods, being an employee owner means having a stable present while building your future. Our employees enjoy industry competitive wages and the long term investment that comes from company ownership.

While claim and counterclaim can no doubt be traded, defended and refuted, it seems clear that WinCo is a real-life example of a sizable company that provides great returns to all its stakeholders, not just to shareholders at the expense of employees.

According to the Employee Ownership Association (James Hurley, *The Times*, 25 June 2018, 'Why Do so Few Share Fruits of a Company's Ownership?'), in 2017 there were only about 300 employee-owned businesses in the UK, with a total workforce of 200,000. Hurley reports on the Association's June 2018 report called 'The Ownership Dividend', which *'found that employee-owned businesses consistently achieve greater levels of productivity than those with other ownership models... [they] also have stronger employee retention and appear to benefit from increased resilience when threats surface. They are more likely, too, to retain strong links with their local communities'.* Given the seemingly unarguable rationale for greater employee ownership, what is it that stops such models from gaining traction? Hurley is clear: *'More business owners would be willing to transfer ownership to staff if there wasn't such 'pressure' from self-interested financial advisers to follow a more conventional route.'*

Interestingly in our own personal case, with Rachel and I determined to transfer ownership of the Banbury Therapy Group to its members, the last thing we will be doing is seeking personal advice from accountants or lawyers, since I guarantee that their first reaction would be to try and dissuade us, probably politely pointing out that it is their duty to advise us that we could be selling for more, or saving tax by using some semi-questionable device.

No thank you.

The B Corps movement

Danone

A global food company present in more than 130 markets, and generating €24 billion of revenue in 2017, Danone has always had a purpose agenda, even in a time when it was an unusual idea. Danone committed to combine economic success and social progress in 1972, when the company's founder, Antoine Riboud, began Danone's 'dual project', saying 'there is only one Earth, we only live once.'

'One Planet, One Health' is Danone's Vision that the health of people and the planet are interconnected—a call to action for everyone who has a stake in food to join us in a movement aimed at nurturing the adoption of healthier, more sustainable eating and drinking habits, including fighting climate change, driving more sustainable ingredient sourcing, advancing packaging recyclability, reducing waste, conserving water, ensuring animal welfare, supporting food security and engaging our communities in these efforts.

The benefit corporation structure, created in 2010 and available in the majority of U.S. states, allows a company's directors to consider stakeholder interests alongside shareholder returns when making decisions. By creating the Danone North America division as a benefit corporation from day one, Danone was able to write Antoine Riboud's vision into its legal structure. Danone North America completed their B Corp Certification in April of 2018, making them Danone's eighth B Corp subsidiary and the largest Certified B Corp in the world.

Danone has a global ambition is to be one of the first multinational food companies to obtain a global, full-company B Corp Certification, which will help make sustainable business mainstream and create new business models of the future.

To help other multinational companies follow suit, B Lab has worked with Danone to create a case study, 'Danone and the B Economy: How Large and Multinational Companies Can Join the B Corp Movement.'

(12 April 2018, 'The World's Largest B Corp on the Future of Business')

Unilever

With a market capitalisation of $148 billion (November 2018), Unilever is Europe's seventh largest company by value. Most of Unilever's media coverage in recent years has been focused on CEO Paul Polman's long journey attempting to turn the company into a champion of ethical trading. He even held court at Davos in 2017. He famously scrapped quarterly reporting, publicly stated that he works for the customer not the shareholder, and banned the term 'corporate social responsibility', setting instead an ambitious goal to halve the Unilever environmental footprint while doubling sales. Under his stewardship sales have risen from €40 billion to over €55 billion and the share price has doubled. So far so good

In a somewhat patronising analysis ('The Fresh Scent of Success' by Thomas Buckley and Matthew Campbell, *Business Week*, 4 September 2017), Polman's strategy is characterised as '*trendy sentiment* with *syrupy pledges*'. At best they endow his strategy as being based on two fairly cynical arguments:

> First that ethically discerning shoppers in the developed world are willing to pay a premium for products that do less harm to the planet. And second that encouraging health and happiness in emerging markets will turn millions of the global poor into consumers for the first time.

While Buckley and Campbell acknowledge that '*his strategy seems to be working*', reporting on the success in bottom-line financials, and in examples such as '*reducing the volume of garbage sent to landfills at more than 600 factories and offices to zero*', they sit on the fence as to whether Polman's legacy will be as '*pioneer or outlier*'. They seem to conclude that the odds are stacked against him, that '*shareholder capitalism has other ideas*', with Polman '*fighting some fundamental laws of the financial system*'. And they may be right to have concerns, as Polman's rising star does appear to be waning with his investors, but if Polman fails it will be because he was unable to convince his power brokers, not because his vision, his strategy or even his operating models are flawed. Or maybe after ten years at the helm, he's run out of steam. Therefore the really interesting question is whether whoever succeeds him will enthusiastically take up the baton and run faster with it, or whether they will gently ditch it for more traditional methods. You see, we're clearly still too dependent upon 'white knight'-style leaders – we have yet to convince the system to fundamentally change.

the really interesting question is whether whoever succeeds him will enthusiastically take up the baton and run faster with it, or whether they will gently ditch it for more traditional methods

Etsy

Etsy was feted as the darling of the B Corps movement, and was, in fact, one of only two B Corps companies listed on the stock market, becoming a certified B Corporation in 2012.

In a 19 May 2017 *Business Week* article by Max Chafkin and Jong Cao entitled 'Leave My Etsy Alone', the Etsy story is examined, along with the many challenges the company faced from investors who became disillusioned by the company's performance.

First of all, the article describes B Corps as

> required to meet standards related to the environment, workers and suppliers. Some 2000 companies are B Corps, including Patagonia, but almost all are privately held.

There are just a handful of public B Corps, with Etsy being one of only two traded on a major US exchange...

Public market B Corps are rare because investors hate them... companies must reject the shareholder valuation model, and eventually reincorporate as a 'public benefit corporation' which are structured so that Boards and managers have a legal obligation to worry about more than just their fiduciary duty to shareholders.

Founder Chad Dickerson was eventually fired by the board, whose next act was to unceremoniously dump the internal 'values aligned business' group in charge of making sure that Etsy stayed true to its values. Surely the writing was on the wall right then and there, and lo in November 2017 Etsy gave up its B Corp status.

Chafkin and Cao's analysis leaves me with the conclusion that Etsy's challenges as a B Corp were not actually philosophical but purely strategic. Although the *New York Times* characterisation of Etsy as *'an extremely cosy private welfare state for its employees'* was probably harsh, the reality is that the business could not solve its problem of a lack of growth, thus the costs just got way out of line. Coupled with some serious practical issues around IP and the definition of 'hand-made' (scaling genuinely hand-made products into a global marketplace exchange was always going to be tricky) and Etsy actually just plain old struggles as a business, irrespective of its form of governance.

As far as I can see from some research there are still only two publicly traded B Corps – Alterrus Systems and Natura. Unilever's CEO Paul Polman has publicly flirted with getting Unilever certified, but despite his Herculean efforts on purpose and ethical trading, he has shied away from this 'ultimate' demonstration of commitment.

Why haven't we listened to the voices before now?

As a student of finance 40 years ago, one of the writers that most attracted me was Charles Handy. I loved the simplicity, the pragmatism and the social conscience of his business strategies. Even before I really knew anything about business, and certainly before I'd had direct experience of working in corporate environments, Handy's philosophy was immensely attractive to me, speaking to me as it did of the capacity for business to be a force for good for all stakeholders. In my research for this book, my good friend Professor David Grayson reminded me that Charles Handy had given a seminal lecture on the subject in 1990.

he instinctively operated in a manner that did right by the local community, but was against classic business school and economic theory

In it, Handy recalled his days as a young manager sourcing nuts in Borneo for mass-produced chocolate bars and how he instinctively operated in a manner that did right by the local community, but was against classic business school and economic theory.

Out there in the real world of business it is producing things for people on time, in good condition, and at a fair price which matters, without mucking up a decent town like Kapit, or upsetting the local government, or taking unreasonable advantage of a short-term profit opportunity. I was not there, I felt, to maximise the earnings of some anonymous shareholders. I had, I was sure, a much more serious social function. My business school in America was wrong, I am now convinced. The principal purpose of a company is not to make a profit – full stop. It is to make a profit in order to continue to do things or make things, and to do so even better and more abundantly. To say that profit is a means to other ends and is not an end in itself is not a semantic quibble, it is a serious moral point. In everyday life, those who make the means into ends in themselves are usually called neurotic or obsessive. In ethics, to mistake the means for the ends is to be turned in on oneself, one of the greatest of sins, said St Augustine. Let us be clear, profits – and good profits – are always essential, and not just in business. But the myth dies hard, the myth that profit is the purpose.

(1990 Michael Shanks Memorial Lecture at the RSA entitled
'What is a Company For?')

Handy concluded his lecture with his '7 Heretical Points':

1. *Profits are a necessary but not sufficient condition of success. The bottom line should be a starting post not a finishing post.*

2. *Owners with limited liability will never be owners, only punters, so don't expect too much from them. Turn them into mortgage men instead.*

3. *Stakeholder interests will not count unless they can be counted, seriously. Accountants to the rescue please.*

4. *Owning people is wrong. Companies are collections of people these days; they are communities not properties.*

5. *The law does not recognise this. It should.*

6. *Asking our managers to behave better than the rule book is unfair and unrealistic, so let us change the rule book.*

7. *If we don't, we shall endanger our children's future, and maybe even bring down our opponents with us.*

Charles Handy remains one of the most revered management thinkers and practitioners of the past 100 years, but where is the evidence that those people who laud him as having inspired them have actually changed their organisations ethically for the better?

Some years after stepping down from a 41-year career with BP including a very successful and publicly lauded spell as CEO, Lord John Browne in a *Sunday Times* article entitled 'Our Duty to Engage with the World' (6 September 2015), wrote about Connect – a manifesto to heal the rift between business and society. Coming just five years after the Deep Water Horizon catastrophe, Browne's manifesto was heartfelt, if somewhat idealistic. He wrote, '*despite its centrality to human progress and happiness, business has provoked suspicion and anger for more than two millennia.* Creating Connect, his goals were to *articulate the recurring rift between business and society and to offer a practical manifesto for reconciliation'*. He boldly – and in my view quite correctly – condemned corporate social responsibility (CSR) as being *'almost always detached from a company's core commercial activities; the time has come to declare both the theory and practice of CSR as dead'*. Three years on and I've not heard a whisper more about Connect. Maybe Browne was too tainted by BP's horrendous environmental legacy to be publicly acclaimed or cited as a role model. We corporate citizens are a fickle and promiscuous community.

The modern-day crusaders

Ian Cheshire's Net Positive

In an article for the RSA magazine entitled 'Life Beyond Capitalism' (Issue 2, 2014), Michael Townsend advocated for a migration to a more sustainable economic system, eschewing the excesses of growth and consumption.

This has echoes of my own personal experience working with Kingfisher plc between 2011 and 2013, supporting the top leadership group on their 'Creating the Leader' cultural change needed to deliver on Ian Cheshire's Net Positive vision. Not content with simply ensuring that Kingfisher's activities had a neutral environmental impact, he wanted the company to make a positive impact. I suspect he also knew the value of inspiring a whole professional community with a BHAG (Big Hairy Audacious Goal)! But Cheshire's skill was not simply in setting a grand and noble vision. He backed it with a comprehensive action plan, a wonderful mix of some centrally dictated non-negotiable controls with clear boundaries and consequences for non-compliance, and the investment in supporting his leaders to handle the significant change. Kingfisher was effectively one big UK company and one big French company, and prior to the launch of Net Positive, co-operation had ranged from patchy, through non-existent, to positively antagonistic. Cheshire's leadership was courageous and inspirational, but the most clever thing he did was to attend to the practicalities of how to get leaders to collaborate.

the most clever thing he did was to attend to the practicalities of how to get leaders to collaborate

Cheshire regularly postulated that retailers such as Kingfisher should not be selling things like power tools, but renting them; that the days of consumers buying things that they effectively did not need or never used, or used once and then put in a cupboard in the garage, had to be brought to an end. Brave indeed for the CEO of a company with existing sales of power tools running into the millions (at nice margins too!). You might think that a CEO who was open in his disagreement with absolute shareholder primacy, and who openly attacked one of his own major revenue streams, would not be long for this world, but Cheshire kept delivering growth. He delivered on his promise that he would do the right things for customers, employees and the environment, and that exceptional shareholder returns would be the bonus! And he was right.

In an open letter written by Cheshire to all Kingfisher employees and printed as a thought leadership piece in the *Guardian*, he said *'sustainability is a competitive business issue, it's not philanthropy'*. While some of his contemporaries were relying on eco-savvy customers paying more for ethically sourced products, Cheshire did not subscribe to this view, and insisted that his product innovation and sourcing people brought ethical products into the stores at the same price as their unsustainable counterparts.

Kering

Take a look at the article by Kim Bhasin in *Business Week* entitled 'Where Did You Get That Lovely Supply Chain?' (23 December 2016), which is about François-Henri Pinault and his extraordinary journey to turn his company Kering, a luxury fashion brands business, into a champion of supplier and environmental care. Based on his father's maxim that *'whatever the size, a company needs to pursue a cause that is beyond the profit target you usually have and be a part of the society where you want to do business'*, and having been inspired by Jochen Zeitz, CEO of Puma, acquired by Kering in 2013, Pinault set his company a series of ambitious environmental goals and then set about beating almost every one of them. Pinault recalls of Zeitz, *'Jochen is someone who was personally committed to the environment. He went very far with Puma and he gave me this new approach to sustainability. If you do it right, you can create... good for the planet, for your employees, for your shareholders, for stakeholders'*. Puma had developed an environmental profit and loss (EP&L) model, factoring in environmental costs using a *'methodology that is very complex. We did that with international partners, NGOs... allowing designers to calculate the impact of any product using a criteria of 5000 factors'*. Pinault also created a sustainability committee at board level and part of every executive's annual bonus was linked to sustainable goals. What really caught my eye from Bhasin's article was when Pinault spoke of the sourcing of python skins for Gucci. *'It's not an endangered species, but it will be if we don't change anything because there's no transparency in that trade. You can't just say we're compliant with the certificate needed, because we all know that most of the certificates are not really...'* The sentence is not completed, but we get the message. How many retailers are putting products out on their shelves and on their websites that are manufactured using child labour, or that are manufactured using processes that pollute or cause irreparable damage to natural environments, or that are causing endangered species to be taken further to the edge of extinction? And in all these cases the retailers will hide behind certificates that keep them legally protected. As the article concludes, *'what is striking is that the first learning from our EP&L analysis was that 93% of our footprint was outside our legal boundaries'*.

Why a collaborative equity approach might just catch on *now*

As I complete the writing of this book in late 2018, the world is a very different place from even just two years ago, with a number of hugely significant economic, technological, cultural, geopolitical and environmental factors colliding in tectonic fashion.

The digital revolution continues to disrupt everything at an ever-increasing rate, with technological advances in AI, medicine, travel, manufacturing, distribution and science transforming our world before our very eyes.

The 2018 IPCC report has shocked us (or has it?) into the realisation that climate change and global warming is already beyond a point where we'll be able to sustain the way we live for many more decades, with a bottom line that only unprecedented change on a globally collaborative basis will save us. The report basically says that avoiding an increase of 1.5 degrees in global average temperatures will require *'rapid, far-reaching and unprecedented changes in all aspects of society'*. With this scale of change seemingly beyond our capability for collaboration, and therefore inevitable, it lists the cataclysmic changes that will befall us in the next 30 years. The really frightening conclusion is that a projected increase of 2 degrees, itself increasingly unlikely to be avoided unless we act radically and soon, could bring extinction level threats to large areas of the planet (see www.ipcc.ch/report/sr15).

And talking of potential extinction, 2018 was the year when we finally seemed to take notice of what we're doing to our fellow living creatures on the planet. The website www.theworldcounts.com lists its 'Top 5 Facts About Species Gone Extinct':

1. *Species are disappearing – We don't know exactly how many species go extinct every year but it could be 100,000 – about 1 every 5 minutes.*

2. *And fast! – The current rate of extinction is up to 10,000 times higher than the average historical extinction rates. We, the humans, are almost wholly responsible for this increase.*

3. *It's getting worse – The worsening and loss of biodiversity are projected to continue, and even accelerate. Direct human activity and climate change is the cause of this – for example through the destruction of forests and coral reefs.*

4. *Possible mass extinction – There is a wide belief that a 'mass extinction' is underway. Some predict that half of all living species could be gone within 100 years.*

5. *Who are they? – Within the next 15 to 40 years it is likely that the following animals will become extinct: polar bear, chimpanzee, elephant, snow leopard, tiger, mountain gorilla, orangutan, giant panda, rhino, and the koala bear. Unfortunately, these are just a few of many...*

Then there's the new focus on plastic and what our appalling single use and crass disposal mentality is doing to our oceans. The website www.ecowatch.com/plastic-oceans-facts-images-2436857254.html lists the following facts:

❀ *At least 8 million tons of plastic enter the oceans each year*

❀ *More than 50 per cent of sea turtles have consumed plastic*

❀ *Cigarette butts, plastic bags, fishing gear, and food and beverage containers are the most common forms of plastic pollution found in the oceans*

And then there's the great garbage islands in the oceans. The website https://en.wikipedia.org/wiki/Great_Pacific_garbage_patch describes the infamous 'Great Pacific Garbage Patch', which we've all known about for years, but since we don't have to look at it or live by it every day, we can conveniently ignore. It covers 1.6 million square kilometres (an area roughly the same size as Spain, France and Germany combined) with an estimated 1.8 trillion individual pieces of garbage, weighing some 80,000 metric tons. By the way there is also a North Atlantic Garbage Patch, although not quite so big, so that's why you've never heard of it.

The UN Sustainable Development Goals became much more high-profile in 2018. These are a set of global aspirations aiming to address issues such as poverty, inequality, climate change, the environment, peace and justice by 2030. In what feels to me like a seminal article entitled 'Business Has the Tools to Answer Lagarde's Call for Sustainability' (20 September 2018), Sarah Gordon comments:

> The challenge for even well intentioned companies is how to translate these ambitious goals into business practice. The next is to convince investors that such measures should be rewarded. Companies still have a tendency to pat themselves on the back for saying the right thing...

This is an echo of the massive issue facing well-intentioned leaders, whereby they genuinely believe that if they say the right things then their companies will somehow magically deliver on principled behaviours and aspirational outcomes, and does, I believe, go to the heart of why business has failed to heal itself. However, I am not naïve in understanding the immense constraints that even the most enlightened, evangelical and fearless leaders face in standing up to the forces of global finance and investor pressure.

In her article, Gordon brings us some hope, reporting on the growing influence of devices such as positive incentive loans (PILs):

> where discounts or premiums are applied to the financing margin, depending on the issuer's compliance with a range of environmental, social and governance (ESG) goals. Put simply, behave well and your borrowing costs less; behave badly and it costs more. Danone issues one of the largest PILs to date in February 2018, at €2bn. Part of the syndicated credit facility's financing costs is indexed to Danone's ESG rating – measured annually by rating agencies which assess more than financial sustainability – and another part is tied to increasing the percentage of revenues generated by the bits of its business certified as B Corps. Danone has committed to achieving B Corps certification for its business as a whole.

As an aside, I smile when I hear Christine Lagarde's name in the media as I once coached a senior executive who reported directly to her. As with many senior executive clients I have coached, we spent a great deal of time discussing his relationship with his boss!

And finally, the workplace

The #MeToo and #TimesUp movements have put gender equality and workplace harassment centre stage, sending seismic shockwaves through organisations. The exposure of vile abuses and inhumanities has understandably put whole industries and institutions into a collective state of shock, and the eruption of shame, guilt and anger is taking and will continue to take a great deal of time to process and heal. But ultimately this is a healthy healing process, and the world will thankfully never be the same again. It's completely understandable that millions of us are struggling to know just how to react and many of us are left with a nervousness in how we use the power and control that we have over others. And that is great, because our nervousness will help us err on the side of caution.

In a prescient article entitled 'Is the Corporate Bully the Next Workplace Pariah?' in *Business Week* (14 May 2018), Matt Townsend and Esme E. Deprez use the story of Nike to illustrate the issue of workplace harassment. They describe an aspect of the Nike culture and how they tried to deal with bullying, quoting Gary Namie, co-founder of the Workplace Bullying Institute:

> *Bullying is inextricably linked with capitalism. It creates a zero-sum, competitive work environment where people feel they need to obliterate their competitors. Workplace bullying is often defined as behaviour – including verbal abuse, derogatory remarks, humiliation and undermining work performance – that results in physical or mental harm. About 1 in 5 Americans say they've been the target of it... and surveys show that such behaviour is four times more prevalent than legally actionable sexual harassment.*

So just as almost every woman has a story of some level of discrimination or harassment they've experienced in the past, so many employees have a story of how they've been bullied. But I believe those one in five stats bely a deeper secret: that many more employees have experienced a low level of bullying that they've come to normalise and thus deem acceptable corporate workplace behaviour. Watch out corporate world, for this area is the next to come under intense scrutiny, as employees across the world wake up from their collective hypnosis to realise they've been subject to corporapathic behaviours; that they have in fact been unconsciously and silently suffering the debilitating anxiety disorder that is CTSD – Corporate Traumatic Stress Disorder.

But I believe those one in five stats bely a deeper secret: that many more employees have experienced a low level of bullying that they've come to normalise and thus deem acceptable corporate workplace behaviour.

CTSD is a major contributor to what is now acknowledged as a global stress and burnout epidemic. In an article entitled 'Looking after Number 1 is Not Selfish', Andrew Hill, managing editor of the *Financial Times*, asked three entrepreneurs what they wished they had known before they'd started out. The answers he gleaned were mostly centred on how exhausting it all is, physically of course, but mainly emotionally and psychologically. One of his interviewees, Ariana Huffington, founder of the *Huffington Post*, now heads Thrive Global, which aims to end the '*stress and burnout epidemic*'. Hill also mentions Clayton Christensen's writings on the subject, including his '*shock on realising that the high aspirations of many of his Harvard and Oxford classmates had collapsed into personal dissatisfaction, family failures, professional struggles and even criminal behaviour*'.

Future leaders

Thank God our upcoming generations, the millennials and Gen Z, are different. They think differently and are driven by different principles. They are way less materialistic and way more health and environment conscious. They value friendship and experiences more than material wealth. They want to engage with companies, as both customers and employees, that demonstrably act ethically. Let's hope this generation can wrestle power away from the rest of us as quickly as possible.

In a 2014 White Paper, Doughty Centre for Corporate Responsibility Professor David Grayson differentiated between 'current' and 'future' leaders, with a marked contrast in values and beliefs between the two cohorts.

> While future leaders perceive social purpose and commercial purpose to be inextricably intertwined, many current business leaders do not equate social purpose automatically with corporate responsibility or sustainability...

> Future leaders believe that internal issues such as management attitude, lack of information and financial considerations are the biggest barriers (to fulfilling social responsibility), current leaders perceive external issues such as government, legislation and regulators to be the biggest barriers...

> Fewer future leaders than current leaders feel that focussing purely on economic value will have competitive advantage... future leaders cite engaged employees, increased innovation and increased trust in business as the major returns...

> Current leaders believe that profitability and shareholder value will continue to remain key, while future leaders believe that future indicators of success will include societal and environmental impact, innovation and the development of talent.

An appendix to the report referred to the 'Blueprint for Better Business' (www. blueprintforbusiness.org). This is a charitable initiative encouraging businesses to adopt 'Five Principles of a Purpose Driven Business', which are:

1. Honest and fair with customers and suppliers

2. A good citizen

3. A responsible and responsive employer

4. A guardian for future generations

5. Have a purpose which delivers long term sustainable performance

Why collaborative equity is the 'acceptable' solution

A collaborative equity organisation takes the development of strategy, client relationships, products and product lifecycles and brands, people and talent, and environmental concerns as the basis for business planning and guiding management focus and prioritisation. Leaders must do a ruthless inventory in each area and then set the plan and do the budget. All too many of our objectives currently are arbitrary, with no real relationship to reasonable market share, or sustainable relationships with all stakeholders. It's why executives can be delivering great absolute results, but if they're behind the arbitrary number they signed up to just a few months ago (or that was more likely imposed) they'll be stressed and therefore guilty of unconsciously managing through fear, control and manipulation. Once this takes hold, it feels like the only way through is even tighter control, even greater exertion of pressure.

Leaders should ensure the right operating model and resources. Employees should run the business day to day to best exploit that model and those resources. Leaders should keep their eyes to the horizon (on all sides) for competitive threat and market opportunity, and adjust or even disrupt the model if needed. Employees should watch the machine and continuously improve efficiency and productivity. Leaders should watch over the employees, encouraging, coaching, facilitating, teaching, nurturing, challenging, caring.

In conclusion, I put collaborative equity forward as a new approach to running an organisation, as opposed to a new form of legal entity. This is the essence of my evangelism around changing corporatism from within. However, the recognition of CTSD could scare corporate boards into looking to change themselves for fear of an endless and ultimately mortal tsunami of CTSD lawsuits. Corporatism then might be forced to open itself, for the very first time, to genuine changes in governance. And when it looks around, with an urgency for change, it will find in collaborative equity a state it can voluntarily adopt, integrate and promote. Corporatism will have time to heal itself before even the most concerted global movement could attempt to enforce change through legislation.

In conclusion, I put collaborative equity forward as a new approach to running an organisation, as opposed to a new form of legal entity.

And then the beautiful stage is reached when corporatism, which only changed through fear of death, and only adopted new behaviours in order to survive, suddenly finds that the world is actually better than it was before, not worse – that corporate life is more joyful and corporate performance is improved on all metrics. How collaborative equity, adopted earlier as the new medium for changing corporatism from within, could become the rallying banner for change for corporatism from without. The cycle of bio, psycho, socio and spirito plays out once more, this time for the glorious redemption of the corporation, and the ultimate survival of the human race.

No pressure, then.

The word of the moment is 'toxic'

And one last factor – the final 25 hours of writing of this book was done in hotel rooms in San Francisco and Los Angeles during a ten-day period while working with a major tech client in November 2018. Interspersed between my meetings in San Francisco's glossy corporate offices were the walks back to my hotel through the ever-more grungy streets, with thousands of homeless living on the streets, in ever-growing semi-permanent encampments reminiscent of the pavement dwellers of Mumbai. Current estimates are that 7,500 people live in San Francisco in this squalor. Once you get around half a mile from the swankiest areas of the city, the depravation and poverty and despair smack you in the face, as does the stench of urine, faeces and drugs. On every walk, irrespective of the route back to my hotel, I witnessed countless people shooting up, and one night I came across around 20 rats foraging, not in a back street, but in a wide open public area on the periphery of the United Nations Plaza. But the most harrowing aspect was the obvious and universal plague of mental illness within that community. Countless poor human souls in abject despair, and therefore either understandably self-medicating, or with their brains taking over and transporting their consciousness to another plain of delusion.

In one of the wealthiest cities in the world, the epicentre of the tech revolution of the past 40 years, for all the ingenuity of its more privileged inhabitants, human degradation and misery are getting worse.

Oh, and at the same time, 50 per cent of the people walking the streets (none of the homeless by the way) were wearing masks due to the poor air quality resulting from the worst wildfires in California's history just a few miles north of the city. Sixty people dead and still, as I write this, over 600 are unaccounted for.

WHAT THE F*** ARE WE DOING?

And in the same week the Oxford English Dictionary announced its 'word of the year'. Thankfully eschewing 'sunsetting' (a term that had been used by an American client of mine on a call just a week earlier – it means 'scrapping' in American-positive) the dictionary had selected 'toxic' as its winner. Defining the adjective as *poisonous*, Oxford said that the word was an '*intoxicating descriptor for the year's most talked about topics*'. The word of the year is meant to be a reflection of '*ethos, mood, or preoccupations of the passing year*', and according to Oxford's data, there was a 45 per cent increase in searches of 'toxic' on the dictionary's website. Oxford included a list of ten words used in collaboration with 'toxic', including 'environment', 'masculinity' and 'culture'.

So there you have it. The time is now. No excuses left. What will you do?

A beacon of hope

One week before my trip to San Francisco, a potentially seminal corporate event had taken place – the Google Walkout for Real Change, when 20,000 Googlers (that's around 25 per cent of the entire workforce) had come out onto the streets for an hour to protest at the company's handling of sexual harassment cases within the company. This was no strike, no attempt to destroy the company or even to remove a leadership with whom employees had become disillusioned. No, this was Google at its best, proving once more that it does culture better than any of the tech behemoths that have grown up alongside it. My perspective on Google at this juncture is that it has, and will take, an opportunity to reinvent itself, and in so doing will once again show the corporate world how it's done. With every large corporate striving to emulate the more caricatured elements of Google's workplace culture – the food, the office designs, the transparency, the autonomy and the making a difference to the world – Google can now kick on again and show the corporate world how to do a culture of diversity, equality, inclusion and well-being, and how to do social and environmental good. In my view, what it must do, however, is not simply expose and eradicate sexual and racial harassment and the worst excesses of bullying. These aberrant behaviours, while utterly unacceptable, will occur from time to time as they do in any family, town or community. What Google has to do is once and for all break the unconscious use of fear. It has to crack the conundrum of leaders saying fine and noble things, and then being perplexed when those things don't play out in reality; it has to crack the conundrum of managers under pressure believing that a culture without fear is a culture of lower performance.

If Google can't (or won't) then we're in for a rough ride. But if it can, then there is real hope.

And no, you're not mistaken – I have just made a direct correlation between fear in corporate workplaces, and our ability to save ourselves from environmental catastrophe. Deming was right 70 years ago when he said we must remove fear from the system. We have to change our default mode under pressure; we have to perform a 180-degree turnaround in how we automatically react under pressure, from frustration to love, from impatience to acceptance, from irritation to compassion, from 'Oh for God's sake' to 'Thank God'. So instead of reacting under pressure in a manner that puts the other person into fight or flight – or worse, 'freeze' – we have to react in a manner that celebrates their struggle and immediately rewards them for positive learning. At the very moment when we want the person in front of us to release all their fabulousness, we cannot react in a way that punishes them for taking that risk.

We have to change our default mode under pressure; we have to perform a 180-degree turnaround in how we automatically react under pressure, from frustration to love, from impatience to acceptance, from irritation to compassion, from Oh for God's sake *to* Thank God.

We have to develop our CEQ.

And now it's urgent.

Chapter 17

This is all very well, but does it make more money?

Unless we see a seismic change in the way capitalism is organised, and I just can't see that happening, there will always be a certain futility in the well-meaning attempts of decent people to bring corporate organisations to heel. When power and money hold sway, the system can tolerate some distractions and even some vaguely more long-term strategies, but it will not give up its addiction to the pursuit of short-term gains and something for nothing, and neither will it systematically care about saving the planet.

And while I believe that a recognition of CTSD as a condition caused by corporate cultures, and therefore as one that companies could be sued for, could cause turmoil in corporate boardrooms and lead to greater resources being invested in employee well-being, this is still picking a fight with vested interests who ultimately control local delegated executives, and those vested interests would not give up without a fight.

So surely the ultimate argument is to convince the hard-nosed capitalists and free-marketers that a collaborative equity approach makes more money. If they were convinced of that, they'd adopt these more 'enlightened' practices in a heartbeat.

So, does it make more money? Yes it does, and here's the proof.

> *So, does it make more money? Yes it does, and here's the proof.*

What follows are six real-life examples of how a collaborative equity approach creates greater value for *all* stakeholders. I can talk with authority on these examples since I lived them in a leadership capacity. The examples cover examples of my experiences as a CEO, chairman and consultant, in organisations from plcs to private companies, from public bodies to charities. Each one represents compelling and inspiring evidence. Taken together, they provide a body of evidence that is utterly irrefutable.

Example 1: Pendragon Plc (1998–2000)

My role: franchise group managing director

I waited eight months between jobs to join Pendragon, turning down offers from elsewhere despite not being guaranteed they could find me a role. I wanted to work for them because I admired their strategy; significant change in the retail motor trade was long overdue, and I thought that Pendragon's strategy of seeking to represent all manufacturers at national scale made complete sense. But that in itself was not what attracted me – what did it for me was their strategy for exploiting that scale, not through a typical command and control culture, but by a genuine culture of empowerment, with standardisation and centralisation of appropriate functions, and with local and franchise-specific considerations being handled by dedicated teams. I also wanted a crack at running a plc.

When I was recruited as franchise group managing director for Pendragon's Volvo division, I was confronted with the harsh reality that while the underpinnings of an empowered culture existed on paper, the reality was that command and control was still very much the order of the day from the plc board. Not only that, the business was in a complete mess – trading losses, huge and obsolescent inventories, lower quartile customer satisfaction scores and a manufacturer looking to dump us. The workforce was dispirited and angry. They had been seriously abused and thus come to hate the company, find customers irritating and mistrust the manufacturer they represented.

I inherited a management team of mixed competency and attitude, but thankfully a workforce of amazing untapped talent; a balance sheet of unreported and hidden losses, but thankfully a hugely viable market opportunity; decaying buildings and equipment, but thankfully great locations and lots of space; antiquated and ana-chronistic business and people processes, but thankfully a ready-made inventory of employee engagement tools. All my training and experience to that point had equipped me to handle what I found quickly, decisively and effectively. The next 18 months were the most exciting of my 40 years in corporate life. The antics of the plc board were hard to navigate, and I frequently felt bullied, but nothing stopped me from revolutionising the Volvo business. What we did in that 18 months was pioneering, exciting, inspirational and massively successful.

> *The next 18 months were the most exciting of my 40 years in corporate life.*

In Chapter 14 you'll find my eight steps of cultural change, and my Pendragon experi-ence closely followed that process. The need for change was blatantly obvious so I gave myself one month of research – one month to assess management competen-cies and attitude, to build as many relationships, listen to as many people and learn as many names as possible, to expose the absolute truth of what was lurking in the balance sheet, and to set the outline of a new vision and strategy.

Here's a flavour of what I found in those first 30 days, and the urgent diktats I made accordingly:

Balance sheet

The oldest car in stock was an unregistered 'new' car that had been in stock 583 days – close to two years! It had stood in one spot for so long it had a sapling growing out from under a front wheel arch. That car cost £4,500 to get roadworthy to sell as a new car. The total value of overage stock of new and used cars ran into many millions of pounds and the value of obsolete

> *It had stood in one spot for so long it had a sapling growing out from under a front wheel arch.*

parts wasn't far behind. And no provisions! I immediately issued a diktat that man-agers (and there were an army of them, all entitled to drive company cars) would be allocated the next oldest car in stock as opposed to choosing their next loaded-up demonstrator, until we'd cured the stock problem. This immediately started saving stocking costs, although the P&L had to absorb the massive costs of washing through the stock, since there were no provisions. It also sent a clear message to those whose egos were rampant.

Internal competition

Although we had Volvo dealerships all over the country, there was zero collaboration and zero exploitation of economies of scale. The previous management regime had encouraged internal competition as a way of driving and motivating performance, but it was in reality destroying value. For example, if sales staff in one dealership found out that a customer had been in to see a sister dealership in an adjacent territory, they would cut the price to the lowest level to win the deal. We were competing with ourselves, cutting margins on securing a deal that one of the family would have got anyway. I outlawed that practice immediately.

Decaying employee facilities

The employee toilets in many of the workshops looked like the Turkish prison scenes from *Midnight Express*. They were disgusting and inhuman. No money had been spent on anything other than customer-facing areas and facilities for many years. I immediately committed to a major programme of upgrades to employee facilities as an absolute priority, to be paid for by savings from stocking costs and the economies of scale.

Egotistical managers

Within the first 30 days I removed two of my senior team who did not want to be part of the change (every behaviour I had witnessed from them told me that). Coaching first-time CEOs now, my main advice is to trust their instinct and go harder and faster. It takes a few iterations as CEO to really learn this, and this was my fourth iteration, so while I understood the managers' shock when I told them they were leaving, I knew they were going to slow everything down. Don't worry, they were well looked-after financially.

After that first month of research and some early changes, I set about evangelising the change message. I found voices that I could quote to let people feel the heat, followed immediately by an inspiring message to allow them to see the light. My 'feel the heat' messages were these:

> The internet will rip the innards out of the automotive industry, just as cash dispensers rendered whole layers of bank management obsolete over recent years.
> Tom Peters

> The risk is that while Pendragon can be successful in an industry where poor management is widespread, the new era could see it competing against world class companies from other industries.
> Charterhouse (our brokers)

Here were my change messages to the employees. The first played into the revolutionary nature of what was coming at us whether we liked it or not. And the second hinted that while we were OK at the moment, we were just about to be overtaken as our competitors woke up and managed themselves better.

252

At the time, in the late 1990s, it was a common rumour that Richard Branson wanted to open car dealerships. So I jumped on that one with a third statement. My 'see the light' message was this:

If Richard Branson opened a car dealership tomorrow, do we honestly believe he would do it the way we do now? So let's get there first – let's be the pioneers.

I toured the dealerships with these three statements and then listened to customers and employees. Having been exposed to kaizen philosophies and practices through Tony Barnes in the early 1990s, I was always keen to involve employees as early and as completely as possible in change. Listening to people, coaching them in the process, is always an incredibly powerful process to inspire the best kaizen culture, and we'll return to this later on. It's therefore important to demonstrate that you've listened by acting on the common themes as quickly as possible.

I'd wanted to join Pendragon because of their culture (or at least the culture I believed they had looking in from the outside). But while I discovered a very different reality, at least they had a ready-made toolkit that I could immediately start applying – one that had the benefit of having already been communicated and having the authority of the plc board behind it. So I had the advantage of applying processes and practices that could not easily be dismissed as the whims or evangelical rantings of a naïve madman.

The tools were as follows:

1. Five core values representing quality standards for each group of stakeholders

2. 'The Way' – a complete documented guide as to the way things should be done within the company, particularly the processes that affected the way people were managed – induction, one-to-ones, team meetings, team briefings

3. CANI – constant and never-ending improvement – as a cultural mantra

4. Stakeholder bonuses – a bonus scheme for employees based not upon achievement of target or budget, but as a share of any growth over the same period prior year

5. Quads not quarters or monthly – the budget year was separated into three quads or periods of four months. This made a huge difference to the operating rhythm of the business, minimising time spent on analysis and post-mortem and minimising the fear from evaluation

6. One HR expert at the centre, with a philosophy of everything pertaining to employee well-being and performance being handled by local management

7. The leading industry ERP system, with cutting-edge technology to facilitate the best combination of central non-negotiable processes and local decisions

I can be critical of the board for their behaviours, but I have to applaud their commitment and courage in creating the tools. It was a massive advantage for me, and I set about making all the tools work for me with alacrity. I knew how to implement them.

> *The tale of the next 18 months is one of prodigious efforts, ruthless adherence to processes, openness and transparency in all dealings and a total embracing of employee engagement as being the driving force for change*

The final piece of the jigsaw was when I offered to pioneer lean distribution of parts within our dealerships. This was an initiative created by Volvo with the assistance of John Kiff, Professor of Lean Thinking at Cardiff University.

The tale of the next 18 months is one of prodigious efforts, ruthless adherence to processes, openness and transparency in all dealings and a total embracing of employee engagement as being the driving force for change, progress and exceptional achievement.

This memo (we hadn't started using email in 1998!) will give you a flavour of the strategy – notice that although it was written to the leaders within the business, a copy was put up on every employee noticeboard; I needed all employees to see the content:

ACTION REQUIRED

To Volvo Group Leaders & Noticeboards

From Gareth Chick

30th September 1998

GUIDANCE NOTES ON NEW STRUCTURE OR 'LIFE WITHOUT A DEALER

PRINCIPAL'

We are now one month into our new structure and it was to be expected that some questions would arise, and indeed some confusion would be generated. Bala, Nick, Tony and myself are trying to communicate the philosophy and strategy at every opportunity but it has been a fundamental change and some more guidance might help.

Let us remind ourselves first of all of why our businesses need to change. As one of our Stockbrokers' reports put it recently: 'The risk is that while Pendragon can be successful in an industry where poor management is widespread, the new era could see it competing against world class companies from other industries.'

Imagine if Mr Branson sat down with a clean piece of paper and designed a retail experience that replaced what we do now. Would he design car dealerships as we know them? I don't think so.

The scale of change we have to put through our businesses is nothing short of revolutionary. Our job is to make this process energising and exciting, and to avoid, as far as possible, the uncertainty that arises from change. It is the fear and uncertainty that damages people, not the change itself. We know that our strategy is based upon market areas and technology. We know that we need a retailing revolution to give true customer focus. So why was the change in leadership structure the first key to unlock the door? Simple – because our success will only come from harnessing the energy, creativity and power of all our team members, and therefore we need to let everyone join in the game.

Our businesses need empowered teams; confident leaders; every team member focused on helping customers and colleagues; teams working to the 'rules of the game' (the Way Manual, agreed processes and procedures); teams making decisions guided by the Way Manual and by our 5 Core Values; leaders held accountable by team members (not the other way around!). In short we need to place 'The Way' at the centre of our business culture, for 'The Way' is about changing attitudes, habits and behaviour. We can design slick processes, we can have the greatest strategy – all this only works if the hearts and minds of all our team members embrace the changes. As leaders we have to start and we have to set the example. We have to show visible signs of change in the business and in ourselves. Only then do we have the right to ask others to join up.

I would like to remind you of the changes that we have discussed recently:

1. 5 Minute Meetings should be at a set time and day and should involve everyone in the business.

2. You should hold a weekly leaders meeting to make operating decisions for the business. Make them a maximum of one hour. Involve at least two team members, and rotate so that everyone gets a chance to sit in. Produce hand written action notes – maximum one page, and copy them at the end of the meeting. Put a copy up on the noticeboard.

3. Problems that need researching before a decision is made should be dealt with by putting a small team together. Again rotate the team members. Guide them as to the problem, the facts they need to collect and the timescale. Get this team to recommend a solution. Find reasons to go with the solution, rather than reasons not to.

4. Ensure all elements of The Way training are in place by the end of October. Visions boards (photographs), management of meetings (agenda, roles etc), CANI meetings, reading lists and libraries and communication schedules. Remember that The Way training courses are on Personal Development, not the elements listed above. Don't wait!

5. CANI meetings – don't be surprised if the first few of these meetings are 'gripe sessions'. Past broken promises and injustices are keenly felt and do need to come out. Be tolerant of a bit of 'whinging' but keep a balance on moving forward. Please make one change to the CANI meeting guidelines put out by the training team. It says in the notes to ensure that the CANI minutes and suggestions be published on the noticeboard within one week of the meeting. Please change this to 'Produce hand written action notes, suggestions and supporting reasons and put these up on the noticeboard at the end of the meeting'. This puts pressure on the scribe but let's not build delay into the system.

6. Put the following information on the noticeboards – weekly profit forecasts, cash position (weekly) and summaries of management accounts.

7. Update the Stakeholder board with the profit forecast figures on the 1st of each month. Change to the confirmed figure as per the accounts the day the accounts are issued.

8. Decisions; if you are about to make a decision please develop a habit of stopping for a few seconds and asking yourself:

   a) Could I let the team decide on this rather than me?

   b) Whose opinion can I seek before making this decision?

   c) Have I used the Way Manual or the Core Values to help me in my decision?

9. Decisions – if you are about to defer making a decision (in the old days it would have been one for the Dealer Principal) ask yourself (honestly) why you don't feel able to make it. Is it:

   a) because you genuinely don't know what to do?

   b) because you are frightened of making a mistake?

   c) because you lack confidence?

   d) because you don't want to take the responsibility?

   In any of these cases don't first look for the DP (they're not there) or call me or Bala, Nick or Tony. First of all ask the team. Collect more information. Go to the Way Manual. Value check against the Core Values. Get a team together and ask them. Find ways to make a decision, not defer one.

10. Accounts reviews, quad meetings, etc are now to involve team members. Again rotate them but in 12 months' time let us have given every team member exposure to our financial information and business processes.

Finally, let me repeat – The Way is about changing our attitudes, habits and behaviour, starting with the leaders. We need a culture where our team members hold us accountable for our decisions, for the money we spend and for value that we add. We do not mend cars, we do not sell cars – so what do we do? As Larry Tranquillian of Templars said to me earlier this week – 'I fix cars for eight hours a day – I don't talk about it – I do it'. For those of us who talk but don't do anything, there is a real challenge and there are no hiding places.

Enjoy the challenge; have fun with it; take (sensible) risks with it. Life without a head buffalo can be very exciting, if a little scary.

Regards,

Gareth Chick

Franchise Group Head

I read this now, 20 years on, and I am struck by fundamentally how little my strategies have changed despite my being 20 years older and wiser and despite the world being a very different place.

I am immensely proud of what I achieved in my 18 months as franchise group managing director. The results were truly extraordinary.

We turned losses into profits, even though the P&L took a dramatic hit from washing through all the overage stocks. We exploited the benefits from scale, in both cost and quality. We nurtured a proud and highly motivated workforce. We achieved upper quartile customer satisfaction scores. We pioneered lean industry practices. We achieved a superb reputation with the manufacturer, leading to them supporting us in taking over other dealer groups and giving us a share of their distribution which endowed us with unprecedented power that we could have abused. And we achieved a reputation as 'honest corporate citizen' with other dealers in the network. I was even asked to chair the Dealer Council. In other words, every single stakeholder was rewarded to the very highest degree.

Conventional wisdom said that these achievements were impossible to achieve within an 18-month period, and further, that they were impossible to achieve simultaneously. Conventional wisdom is nonsense.

Conventional wisdom said that these achievements were impossible to achieve within an 18-month period, and further, that they were impossible to achieve simultaneously. Conventional wisdom is nonsense.

Example 2: Longwood Park (2003–2009)

My role: chair of trustees

Being chair of Longwood Park remains one of my most treasured business experiences. Under the management of Slough Borough Council, the estate had become the archetypal run-down environment, with poorly maintained and decaying housing stock, with graffiti, drugs and vandalism rife, and was being used effectively as a dumping ground for problem families. On my first visit one cold October evening, my guide pointed out the local prostitute operating out of the back of a transit van, and the various drug deals going down in darkened corners. For me, a privileged, white, middle-class male, it was quite a shock, although I have to say it reinforced the prejudices I brought with me. I learned my first lesson that very evening, being introduced to Marian Green, deputy chair of the residents' association. In my arrogance, I believed I was going to meet someone who would ideally be wanting to live my kind of life. Instead I met the most wonderful woman, proud of her home, loving her community and wanting nothing more than the hope of some regeneration, to give her own children and grandchildren, living on the estate, safety and comfort. Marian was both a humbling and an inspiring force – as all truly great leaders are.

Slough had made the decision to pass control of the estate to a housing association, but which one? Longwood already had a strong tenants' association, and the council, whether through enlightenment or laziness, called upon the tenants' association to drive the process of selecting the best partner (since the economics were pretty fixed). Out of this came a new governance model, with the tenants being given the right to manage themselves, supported by the professional staff of a designated housing association. The tenants chose Parkside Housing, and after passing an interview by the tenants, I was selected as the chair of a new board of trustees.

The Longwood Charter contains a key phrase – I can still repeat it word-for-word having read it out probably hundreds of times: *'Longwood Park is a groundbreaking initiative where the tenants are in day-to-day control of their own affairs'*. The tenants put in countless hours of work, late into the night for weeks, before selecting Parkside. Part of this process was having a massive input into the details of the £35 million redevelopment plan for demolishing two tower blocks, building new homes and refurbishing the remaining stock with new kitchens, balconies, bathrooms and heating. The £35 million was provided by a consortium of banks and building societies, and secured on the future income stream of the rents.

The tenants were brilliant managers of their own affairs. They set proper budgets, they monitored income and costs, and they dealt with uncomfortable issues as they arose. They were not always elegant and pretty as they did this. Board meetings could be raucous and difficult events. Passions ran high, arguments were not restrained. But it was wholly authentic and honest, and sufficient mutual respect was maintained for the working practices to be effective and not divisive.

The tenants were consistently diligent in a way that most managers simply don't have the stamina for.

The tenants were consistently diligent in a way that most managers simply don't have the stamina for. A good example of this was the signing ceremony to mark the passing of title from Slough Borough Council to Parkside Housing as the new parent company. The main ceremonial boardroom in Slough Town Hall had been set up with around 20 stuffed-full lever arch files of papers representing the documentation effecting the transfer. The room was full of local dignitaries, local politicians trying to claim credit, local press and an army of lawyers. In walked the 12-strong tenant board and the mayor asked them to pose for pictures and sign the transfer documents. They politely refused, and then they went about their work, checking every document prior to signing. Three-and-a-half hours later, having checked numerous things with the lawyers and had many errors corrected, and only when they had satisfied themselves that what they were signing was OK, and with most of the hangers-on having departed muttering under their breath, they signed. I could not have been prouder of them. This was the level of diligence they brought to everything – because these were their homes and it mattered. Nothing could be taken lightly.

Some of the housing professionals supporting Longwood Park actually resented the tenants. After all they'd trained in professional housing management, and knew what was best for the tenants, with no sense of how patronising that was. But to them the Charter was a distraction and many even tried to tell me that it was just a convenient set of words that didn't really mean what they said. The reason I started my practice of reading out those words from the Charter at the start of every board meeting, was because I needed to ritualise the status of the tenants, reminding the professionals in advance that the tenants were in charge. Countless times I had to ask one of the housing professionals *'and what do the tenants think about that?'* I was frequently reminded of the wisdom taught to me by a woman called Sheela, a self-professed middle-class activist I'd met in India some years earlier, who'd said to me *'I have to liberate myself every day from the belief that I know better than the poor what's best for them'*. As an aside, Sheela also provided one of my favourite quotes when she was talking about the resistance she'd met against her pressing for public toilets to be built in disadvantaged town, with local politicians claiming that the toilets would end up being overrun by people from outside the town using them. To which Sheela had exclaimed, *'Do you really think that people are just going to come to the town to shit?'*

The key to sustainability on low rents is low voids and low rent arrears. Typically, an operation managed by housing professionals tolerates long periods of voids, and relatively high rent arrears. Longwood Park had the lowest voids and rent arrears in the sector, recognised when they walked off with the prestigious Housing Association of the Year Award in 2006.

> *Longwood Park had the lowest voids and rent arrears in the sector, recognised when they walked off with the prestigious Housing Association of the Year Award in 2006.*

Voids were lowered and kept low because tenants would not tolerate a delay of more than 24 hours in contractors coming in to clean a flat between tenants. In 'normal' housing associations, the two critical measures of voids (number of empty flats and average length of time a flat is empty) were pretty high – often as high as 5 per cent of flats empty, and with an average void of up to three weeks. Work it out – those ratios yield a loss of income of over 10 per cent. Longwood got the percentage down below 2 per cent and the void down to under one week. Those ratios yield a loss of income of just 4 per cent. That's a difference of 6 per cent of revenue – more than the targeted 5 per cent surplus that social housing associations are supposed to generate, and way above what the majority of commercial organisations earn in profits. And that 6 per cent was a bonus over the normal operating margins.

Rent arrears were lowered and kept low because there was zero tolerance of people being behind on their rent for no good reason. Threats of eviction were issued way earlier than 'normal'. But because the community board knew everyone, they knew when someone was behind on their rent for a legitimate reason – a delay in benefit payments, a loss of employment, disability, loss of a breadwinner – and those people were given time and understanding, and they were given help with benefits. One tenant made themselves into an expert on benefits, and then held surgeries to help other tenants, achieving breakthroughs in time taken to process claims and frequently getting people access to payments that they had no idea they were entitled to. I suspect that Malcolm singlehandedly facilitated hundreds of thousands of pounds a year of additional income into the community.

So Longwood created surpluses above the norm, and the most joyous debates I witnessed were the community board debating and then deciding how to allocate the surplus funds. Of course they went through a public consultation and 'bidding' process – eventually deciding (because people with little spare cash or disposable income are naturally cautious) to save part of the surplus for a rainy day, and spend the rest on new equipment and fittings for the community centre, the children's playground and the IT centre.

The tenants were never ever going to legally own their homes. Yet their level of commitment was total. Emotionally, their homes were theirs. This is what I mean by shared ownership. It's the emotional ownership not the legal or financial ownership that matters. In reality, what did it matter that the tenants were not the legal owners?

What is ownership? Do I need to own something to be committed to its upkeep or to fully savour its beauty? As long as I can enjoy the benefits and it's not being irrevocably consumed... even better if I have a stake in its thriving, to feel the pride in working to build and sustain something important. That's ownership.

Example 3: B&Q (2013–2014)

My role: consultant, coach and trainer

Having known the newly appointed CEO Kevin O'Byrne for many years, and having had many conversations on employee engagement and open cultures with him over the years, I finally badgered him into giving me two stores to work with. I told him that I could transform the performance of the stores at minimal investment, and without ever visiting them myself. This was not arrogance but a profound knowing.

So he gave me Crewe and Shrewsbury and I met Alan Sneddon and Geoff Webb, two amazingly open and talented store managers. And Project Maverick (the name stolen from my favourite book) was born. All we did was this:

1. Held a launch meeting to introduce the philosophy, the strategy and the plan.

2. Mandated that Alan and Geoff hold launch sessions with all store employees to communicate Maverick, and to make two personal commitments to their store teams – first, to ask for help as they entered their own inevitable personal journey of vulnerability and, second, to pledge total transparency in store performance for all employees.

3. Created a 'control group' performance comparison across nine store KPIs so we could demonstrate the impact on these two stores over a 13-week period, ie, an immediately identified impact on profits.

4. Took the store management teams through our standard two-day Coaching Excellence programme.

5. Trained the local People Partners to support Maverick with local coaching, and trained them to run a follow up 'Day 3' training for the store management teams.

The nine KPIs monitored were:

1. Sales like for like (measured against same period last year)

2. Number of transactions like for like (measured against same period last year)

3. Average transaction value

4. Items per transaction

5. Conversion rate (percentage of customers entering store and making a purchase)

6. Profit contribution

7. Employee absenteeism

8. Employee engagement (as measured by Pulse and Q12)

9. Recommend to a friend (customer satisfaction)

The two stores took on Maverick with enthusiasm and Alan and Geoff were just magnificent. They led with passion, vulnerability and confidence. They 'got it' and savoured every moment of the discomfort and the joy that came with the experience. While I supported them at every turn, I never went to their stores (until way after my part was over). They did it themselves. The results were fantastic with one store beating the control group on eight out of the KPIs, and the other excelling on all nine. Extrapolating the results across the whole store estate, profits would increase by 5 per cent within the 13-week period, representing a 15-fold return on the investment in training inside the first 12 months.

> *Alan and Geoff were just magnificent. They led with passion, vulnerability and confidence. They 'got it' and savoured every moment of the discomfort and the joy that came with the experience.*

We extended the pilot (to prove the facts to some sceptical members of the management team) to a further 12 stores. While frustrating, we repeated the success, with eight out of nine KPIs beating the control group across these 12 stores all within the 13-week period.

And so to roll out across the whole estate – but then Kevin decided to go and run another company, and the new leadership decided they could do everything themselves. Ah well...

Example 4: SOFEA (2016 to date)

My role: coach to the CEO

SOFEA (South Oxfordshire Food and Education Academy) is a charity providing education and pastoral support for disadvantaged, emotionally disturbed and excluded teenagers, where mainstream education has failed them or simply been unable to cope with their hugely disruptive behaviour. The young people come to work in a warehouse setting, recycling surplus food from supermarkets, and distributing that food to food banks and other charities providing welfare assistance to disadvantaged people and communities. While the operation benefits from the food being given by the supermarkets for free (and delivered), this process actually saves the supermarkets money as they do not have to pay to have the food destroyed safely and in an environmentally friendly way. So SOFEA provides a service and receives the food as payment – a totally commercial transaction. And SOFEA has become so

> *And SOFEA has become so adept at the whole process of sorting and storing, and of marketing and distribution, that the business now makes a surplus (or 'profit' in the corporate world).*

adept at the whole process of sorting and storing, and of marketing and distribution, that the business now makes a surplus (or 'profit' in the corporate world). Adding this to the contract payments from the education authority for the training of the young people, SOFEA is utterly self-sufficient, and generating sufficient surpluses to invest and to expand. Initially donations were a significant proportion of income, as with many charities, and this meant that the founders had to invest a great deal of time and creative energy in fundraising. Donations are also a notoriously volatile source of income, meaning that the trustees of charities dependent upon donations cannot in all conscience invest too heavily in expansion or growth, since if the funds dry up, they may not be able to honour the commitments they have made. And that can be fraud!

So for SOFEA to achieve self-sufficiency is remarkable. Of course, if customers go elsewhere, or if suppliers fail or change their terms, or if contracts for services are given to other organisations at the end of the contract period, most likely through a tendering process, then SOFEA will potentially suffer an existential crisis. But in this they are no different to normal commercial companies. And since they are far and away the best at what they do both educationally and commercially, they likely have a very rosy future.

The most remarkable thing about SOFEA is that they do not turn anyone away. Normal commercial businesses have the 'luxury' of selecting the employees they want and sacking the ones who don't fit in. SOFEA take every young person who needs their support. The culture, the processes and the methods they have designed and refined (their 'technology') ensure, first of all, that disruptive and aberrant behaviours are soon exorcised, and then that the previously hidden and maybe even denied talents of the young people start to shine through. With so many varied jobs and tasks to perform to operate a thriving warehousing and distribution operation, there is work for everyone. With counselling and pastoral care as part of the curriculum, with daily experience of teamwork, problem-solving and communications, and with consistent feedback, recognition, validation and achievement, the young people thrive. All they needed was a facilitated opportunity. All they needed was love and care and respect. All they needed was boundaries. All they needed was self-esteem.

> *the methods they have designed and refined (their 'technology') ensure, first of all, that disruptive and aberrant behaviours are soon exorcised, and then that the previously hidden and maybe even denied talents of the young people start to shine through*

Since SOFEA is a commercial operation in how it receives, stores and distributes food, it is subject to the brutal realities of life. So the other critical factor in the young people's development is ruthless consequences when something goes wrong – no artificial protection. When an infestation of mice was discovered, the site was shut down by the environmental health officer for ten days. This meant a loss of pay for people, and a ten-day backlog to clear up in 24 hours when the site was reopened. The team pulled together, and while, of course, there was some moaning and groaning, no one left and no one abdicated their responsibility in pitching in to put things right. And those young people now have a very healthy and positive respect for hygiene and environmental standards. They police themselves.

When a delivery goes wrong, it is one of the young people that has to field the call from the irate customer, staying calm under attack and owning putting it right. When a supermarket delivers five times as much food as contracted, causing massive disruption to the operation, it is the young people who pull together and sort things out, happy that they have more food to distribute than they thought despite the chaos it has caused. And it is one of the young people who gets onto the supermarket to calmly give them feedback as to the issues they've created.

SOFEA reminds me very much of the Hummingbird Centre in Sao Paulo – an inspiring organisation I've had the privilege of visiting twice. The centre takes young people off the streets of Sao Paulo (at the last count around 100,000 children under the age of 16 are living alone and rough on the streets of the city) and gives them a home and an education. I was struck by three things at Hummingbird. First, many, maybe even the majority, of the children are crack 'addicts' (and dealers or runners) but the centre takes them in, with the philosophy that when children are safe, nourished, loved and receiving education, the reason for the crack goes away. Not addicts in fact, just surviving. Second, the children are asked what they want to study as a specialism, alongside of course the staples of reading and writing, basic maths and history. Whatever they answer, the centre does its very best to facilitate. Because this is Brazil, at the time I was visiting during the period 2005 to 2015, many of the kids wanted to be break-dancers, hip hop artists or capoeira (basically a mix of a non-contact martial art with samba dancing) artists. And so they were encouraged and trained in those things. I witnessed displays not just of great skill and technical competence, but of abundant joy and enthusiasm.

Teaching young people how to set goals for themselves, how to find talents in themselves, how to follow tuition and instruction, how to maintain the disciplines of practice and refining of skills, how to perform in public, and how to achieve greatness with grace and dignity and humility – surely these are the greatest gifts that education can bestow in a young person's life.

Finally, the centre operates a progressive mentoring and peer responsibility system. Every newcomer is assigned a buddy who has themselves only been at the centre for a few short months. Every young person is assigned responsibility, first of all for keeping themselves clean, and then for keeping their bed made, then their room clean, then joining the canteen rotas for cooking, washing up, serving. Next comes responsibility for leadership positions within the centre, taking responsibility for teaching, counselling, mentoring, disciplining. This is a self-sufficient community.

SOFEA has so many elements in common. Walk the warehouse floor and notice who is supervising the shift – it's one of the young people who has been there for long enough to learn the operation and demonstrate some leadership qualities. And of course this being the UK, an NVQ or some form of accredited certificate is not far behind.

Every business leader should visit SOFEA (and pay for the privilege of learning). In fact every manager should be made to spend a day there. Never again would they bemoan the 'fact' that they cannot get the right people!

A small postscript: in the same email to me in which Richard Kennell, CEO of SOFEA, approved what I had written above, he told me this:

> Today I spent the day at our new site in Milton Keynes. The team I took with me today included an 18 year old autistic boy whose family moved to Didcot so he could come to SOFEA. He has developed the project plan – and it's very detailed! And Nay, who you have met, she's my warehouse supervisor and at the age of 20, having been with us for 3 years, is going to oversee the launch of the new site.

Example 5: Produce World (2016)

My role: chairman

This 150-year-old, £250-million fresh produce business had got itself in a pickle. The family owner-directors had recruited an external CEO, CFO and HRD to help them get the business in good shape for a sale. After three years of steady progress under this new and well-balanced team, a powerfully competent blend of longstanding family and seasoned external execs, the family were persuaded to step back and recruit a further three execs from the outside to drive the business towards an exit, and these execs were accordingly generously incentivised.

Having found a potential suitor, and having promised a certain profit to justify the high asking price, this exec team then ruthlessly pursued what were clearly very unrealistic profit targets, and the whole business suffered dramatically as a result. Turnover was 'bought' by signing fixed price contracts, an incredibly risky strategy given such a volatile product. Investment was cut on anything that wouldn't give a 100 per cent payback within a few short months, causing a loss of efficiency and a drop in morale. The long-nurtured culture of employee engagement was replaced by command and control. Customer relationships were sacrificed to cost savings.

The long-nurtured culture of employee engagement was replaced by command and control.

The HRD, now seriously concerned by what these new execs were doing, asked me to help facilitate some employee workshops to get to the bottom of the dramatic changes in morale. It was patently obvious to me that the new execs were doing serious damage to the culture, that they were pursuing a sale that was never going to happen, and that the business losses that had started to come through largely because of the insanity of the fixed-price contracts, were accelerating to a potentially terminal level. In the very same month the company breached a financial covenant that it had not seen coming. There are differing levels of sins of mismanagement, but breaching a covenant *unexpectedly* is one of the worst. Truly the business was completely out of control.

The family owner-directors, with laudable courage, acted decisively and sacked all but the HRD and CFO, and I became chairman in order to support them in turning the business round. I committed to serving for six to nine months, since I felt that was all it would need – the business would either go under or be saved in that time. And I knew in my bones we could save it, mainly because the heart and soul of the business, its people, had not been completely demoralised – seriously, but not terminally.

The level of fear in the business was extremely high. Forecasts had been consistently missed for months, as the execs put extreme pressure on managers to forecast unrealistic numbers. *'That number's not good enough'* was the mantra of the day. And any dynamic of running the business to the current annual budget had long since proven ridiculous. With mounting losses and no end in sight given the horrendous contracts, the bank was threatening to pull the plug.

first we had to eradicate the fear that had gripped the business and that was petrifying people

I knew that if the business could be brought swiftly back to equilibrium, then it would make profits again very quickly. We just needed to get through the immediate losses and be able to absorb what were clearly going to be very high one-off costs of correcting things. So we needed a clear plan, but first we had to eradicate the fear that had gripped the business and that was petrifying people.

My first act was to buy £50,000 of shares, which seemed like a crazy thing to do with the bank threatening to put the company into liquidation. But I calculated that I had as much chance of doubling my money very quickly as I had of losing every penny, and while I am not a gambler, I thought the odds were worth it. My act of demonstrating my belief in the team was fundamental to achieving a rapid increase in confidence. I ended up getting my money back after my nine months in post, and I was very happy with that.

At the first board meeting I chaired I walked the team through what would happen if we went into liquidation. The fear of liquidation was absolutely terrifying for the family owner-directors and I needed them to get out of their paralysis. I told them that while they would undoubtedly suffer some humiliation, they would still have their houses and their families and friends would still love them. I told them that in many ways, liquidation might even turn out to be the best thing for them in the long run, freeing them to 'start again'.

The next thing was to create a bold turnaround plan, demonstrating to the bank that the team were prepared to take the bold decisions needed, and fundamentally to do whatever it took to save the business. Parts of the business were put up for sale, surplus land was put on the market at very realistic prices, and a pretty ruthless cost-cutting plan was devised, including closing offices and cutting some headcount. Cutting jobs is a horrible thing to have to do, but we were as transparent as possible in all our decisions, and the people who lost their jobs were incredibly dignified. The many years of care the family had shown had not been forgotten.

Because we had to act quickly, we made some mistakes – one of these was when we made a number of employees redundant at a site, only to find two weeks later that the site simply could not cope with an unexpected increase in customer demand.

We were suddenly presented with orders on which we could make much-needed unbudgeted profits, and we simply did not have the employee numbers to cope. Bugger. But the amazing thing was that most of the employees we'd made redundant came back to help us out. It was humbling.

I knew that an inevitable cost of having the bank's ongoing support would be ludicrous fees to professional advisers they would insist on appointing. We ended up spending close to £200,000 on these advisers, a wholly needless expense at the very moment when we could least afford it, but such is the lunacy of the world of corporate finance. That £200,000 gave the company absolutely no value whatsoever. It merely allowed the managers at the bank who were responsible for our account to be blameless should we end up going bust. I read the 90-page report, produced by the accountants to give comfort to the bank on their ongoing support, from cover to cover. It was a superb analysis of the company's situation. And it contained not one shred of advice as to how the company should solve its problems. It was bereft of any value to us in our efforts to save the business. It stank. But it was a price we had no choice but to pay.

The sales teams did their level best to persuade customers to tear up the loss-making contracts, with varying degrees of success. They also boldly went about asking for price increases, completely contrary, of course, to the relentless downward pressure on prices coming from the supermarkets.

We needed a realistic operating budget as quickly as possible; one that was owned by the whole company, managers and employees alike, to enable the team to get a grip on the business and to get back in control. I cannot tell you how many times in that process I had to use the phrase '*I don't care what the number is*'. The only important thing was the number that the local management teams and employees felt was achievable and was owned by them. With the new financial year just three months away, we determined that we would have the turnaround plan executed and making a dramatic

> *I cannot tell you how many times in that process I had to use the phrase I don't care what the number is*

impact, so that we could take all the exceptional costs into the current financial year, and we determined that we would have that new budget in place for the new financial year. Even though I was saying over and over '*I don't care what the number is*', I knew that the managers and employees would come to a sensible conclusion on what they could achieve, and that this would likely come out to pretty much the profit that the company had made in the prior years of steady progress. So while every professional adviser, including the bank, was telling us that no business ever performs the 'hockey-stick' turnaround of big losses, followed immediately by good profits, I knew it was entirely realistic. And so it proved – a loss of £10 million followed by a profit of £6 million.

Finally I told the team that I would only deal with *them* – that I would not be out and about in the business listening to and inspiring the managers and employees, and that I would not be attending any bank meetings. In my nine months as chairman I never once visited a site or met anyone below senior manager level, and I never met anyone from the bank. My ego wanted to, of course, to be seen as a saviour, an experienced operator and an inspirer of people. But what the business needed more than anything was for the team to lead the change and achieve things on their own. If the bank believed that I was the turnaround king, they may not have backed the business as they did. They had to see the team's competence and back *that*, and the same went for the managers and employees, who needed to believe once more in the family.

Now you may be thinking that this is in fact not an example of CEQ in action, or of the amazing value of employee engagement, but merely an example of hard-nosed management. But who said that employee engagement and hard-nosed management were mutually exclusive? The Produce World hockey-stick turnaround was fundamentally driven by and based upon CEQ and employee engagement. It was the voice of the employees that broke the catastrophic damage being done. It was the collaboration, talent, competence, passion and dedication of the employees that created a realistic plan, and that then delivered the achievement of that plan within a very short timeframe. Without the employees, and without CEQ guiding everything we did, Produce World would have gone bust.

Again a small postscript – the family on reflection had felt pressured to sell the business. They have now decided to keep it in the family and have started working on a plan for the next generation (the fifth). Sustainability in action.

Example 6: Banbury Therapy Group (2009 to date)

My role: co-founder and chairman

My wife Rachel and I set this company up in 2009, with the original intent of providing non-residential addiction rehabilitation. Rachel had successfully pioneered this approach in other environments, and she believed that helping addicts into recovery while living every day in the environment that was contributing to their addiction was potentially a more effective and certainly a cheaper way of tackling the problem.

So we went looking for a building to house our new enterprise, but we knew that it would take time to build up the volumes we would need to make the operation viable, and while we were committed to personally investing considerable start-up funds, we knew we needed some additional income streams to help get the venture off the ground.

Rachel's personal experience of her own training as a therapist, and her experience in operating as a practitioner out of her own home and out of rented rooms, had led her to believe that things should and could be done differently. And she had a vision not just for the addiction services, but of building a home, a community for therapists, where the environment would be an integral part of the therapeutic relationship with the client, where clients could be seen in high-quality surroundings, and where therapists could receive professional support on the two activities they typically found challenging – administration and marketing.

And so the Banbury Therapy Centre was born. Ten years on and that centre is now home to more than 20 private practitioners, and five national counselling organisations have based their local representation within the centre.

We carefully constructed the operating model to be completely self-supporting, although it obviously took some time for it to grow to this stage. We decided to charge a membership fee or rent, rather than try and control the income from clients. We wanted the practitioners to remain commercially independent, and so we do not take any 'cut' from their client fees. They simply pay a fixed monthly fee for their space and their regular hours. The operating model was designed around our being able to almost guarantee the members a certain number of client referrals, because of our ability to promote the centre as the place within the area where people could go for help and support. Although in the early days local GPs were incredibly suspicious, and rarely referred anyone to us, ten years on and we have earned their trust through the sheer consistent quality of our service.

We created a set of values to guide everything we did. The version you see below is probably the third iteration, but it has stayed the same now for at least seven years.

The Banbury Therapy Centre offers universal access to therapy, which we promote as a positive and life affirming part of general health and wellbeing. We take care to make the environment welcoming, safe and energising. We champion autonomy, choice and respect for all who come through our doors, and we are proud of our community of therapists, any of whom we would wholeheartedly recommend to a loved one.

Internally the values are known as 'the boss'. It is not Rachel that runs the business – it's the values.

Our values guide everything that we do, and every decision we make. Internally the values are known as 'the boss'. It is not Rachel that runs the business – it's the values.

From very early on we realised that we were generating an increasing level of enquiries and 'leads' for our members. Our process was to invite an enquirer to the centre for a free assessment, after which the client would be referred to the most appropriate member and our policy was that a client could be assessed within 24 hours of enquiring, and could be in therapy within just a few days. What a service! And at either market rate or low cost. We wanted to create a mechanism whereby the referrals to our members would really be valued by them as a critical benefit, but we did not want to go down the route of taking a percentage cut on transactions. We calculated that if we could give each member six referrals per year, at average hourly rates and with an average number of sessions per client, those referrals would pay the entire annual membership fee, while only consuming 12.5 per cent of the time the members were paying for. So whereas the membership fee made many prospective members nervous when seen in isolation as a fixed-cost commitment, the moment they could see the return we were committing to on their behalf, they got it. Since that time we have trebled the number of members, and we now regularly achieve averages of 12 referrals per member – double that original commitment. Once a business is stable, trusted and consistent in its quality, the demand will grow.

One of the smartest decisions we made was over our use of student counsellors – these are people in training to be professional qualified and accredited therapists, who are required to do 100+ hours of client counselling under the supervision of a registered counselling organisation. Frequently this is a frustrating experience for students, who struggle to get placements, and even then struggle to be given the clients, hours and supervision needed to get them over this hurdle. At the centre we turned this willing (and free) resource into a positive in order to better satisfy the demand we were getting for low-cost counselling.

Because we mean every word of our values, 'universal access' means access to disadvantaged members of the community, who would otherwise go unserved, and this means providing counselling at low or even zero cost. We initially served this need by creating a bursary fund and then reimbursing our members to their full rate for taking on a low- or zero-cost client. This proved unsatisfactory since we were always having to put effort into fundraising, and this was quickly shown to be unsustainable.

And then we hit on the idea of turning the increasing demand from students for placements with us into a source of supply for the low-cost counselling. We do not insist upon any form of means testing to qualify, since our experience is that people genuinely pay what they can afford, and if that's full price, then they do not actually want a discount. The pricing dynamic is a key part of the therapeutic relationship in how they value themselves if they have the means, and how they access services if they don't, without having to feel patronised or feel like charity cases. So we introduced a flat nominal rate for low-cost counselling, with placement students providing the service to the clients. Of course students cannot be safely given complex cases and so our bursary fund still covers these cases, but actually they are few and far between. Most clients are simply in need of support through the normal stuff of everyday life such as grief, depression and anxiety. We now regularly have eight students on placement and we are delighted to have them, and they get a high-quality experience, with fantastic support and supervision.

Another part of the business that grew organically was the founding of the Banbury Counselling Academy. We'd already purchased a small therapeutic continuing professional development (CPD) training business that had been offered to us. It made great sense that, if we were growing and nurturing our own members, we offered them CPD training of high quality, and this business started to flourish. We wanted to bring it into the centre, but our existing building was not big enough. Also we'd started some basic listening skills courses in response to growing requests from our community, and these were also putting pressure upon the space at the centre. Then we heard that the local FE college was shutting down its counselling courses, and we saw an opportunity to fill the gap that was going to be left. Rachel was again driven by her own experiences in being trained – overly large group sizes, the inappropriate facilities of further education colleges, a lack of care and support, and no real robust challenge in the training – and she was determined that it could be done to a high quality without costing more. And so the Banbury Counselling

Academy was born, offering at first just level 2, then adding level 3, and finally adding level 4 diploma courses of two years' duration.

Rachel and the team worked hard to gain accreditation from a recognised national awarding body, and the moment we appeared on their website, the enquiries came in. Before we knew it, four years had gone past and we've just welcomed in excess of 100 students into the new academic year under our care. Group sizes are limited to 12 to maximise quality, and the business makes a strong contribution to the group's finances, in fact it has greatly accelerated the group's achievement of being a wholly self-supporting and thorough viable entity. Yet we only charge market rates for our training.

And then there's Beverley Charman, quite simply one of the most accomplished managers I've had the pleasure of working with. Bev came to us initially as a receptionist, after a good few years in retail. It was clear from day one that she had natural leadership qualities and after a bit of persuasion, and after we'd been through a couple of centre managers who were simply not right, Bev accepted the role as centre manager. And we've not looked back. Bev is passionate about the centre, making every decision as if she owns it, which of course emotionally she does along with the rest of the team.

> *Bev is passionate about the centre, making every decision as if she owns it, which of course emotionally she does along with the rest of the team.*

She never shirks the uncomfortable stuff – giving tough feedback, holding the team to account, having tough conversations with members who sometimes unwittingly and innocently step outside the boundaries, and with suppliers who simply don't expect to be treated as professionally as we do – of course, a double-edged sword for some. And she has grown and learned tremendously over the nine years she's been with us, almost from the start. She now does all the books and manages the whole business day to day including the team, and she is a passionate and active external ambassador, attending networking and community events and never missing an opportunity to promote the centre or leave leaflets. The centre runs smoothly because of Bev.

And then there's the team – Lynda, Jo and (the other) Rachel. They are an amazingly close unit, supporting each other and basically managing themselves, including covering each other for unforeseen or emergency absences. They have also grown tremendously as individuals – we continually throw stretches at them and they enthusiastically grapple with things, creating processes and then converting things to 'business as usual'. And they are the absolute living embodiment of the values, which they love and repeat to all who will listen, and many who won't! One of our early policies was to invest in the team ahead of what the business could really afford, as we believed that this was the best investment we could make in marketing. We do not spend very much at all on marketing, since our 'word of mouth' marketing is so effective.

And then there's Rachel, our leader. More than any other individual I've encountered, Rachel has taught me how to convert a vision into reality. Her vision, her creativity, her passion, her fundamental belief in human values and her prodigious work in making very detailed processes not just work but achieve accreditation by experts, are an inspiration to all. I'm just the lucky guy she chose as her partner.

The success of the Banbury Therapy Group is an inspiring example of what is possible when a community devises ways of exchanging its mutual resources to support itself. We just manage our costs well, and there is nothing 'fancy' in what we do. We do the basics brilliantly, reliably, predictably and utterly consistently. We are very boundaried and standardised, yet everything is done with love and flair. The Banbury Therapy Group is another wonderful example of why all this 'soft' stuff works. There is no charity at the heart of this therapeutic community, only respect. There is no single powerful leader, only an organic flow of energy around a transparent governance. And there is no fear or shame, only acceptance and encouragement.

> *The success of the Banbury Therapy Group is an inspiring example of what is possible when a community devises ways of exchanging its mutual resources to support itself.*

Rachel and I have just communicated our intention to transfer ownership of the business to its members in 2021. We have been clear about the transaction price – not a penny more or less, since the 'enterprise value' is not a multiple of earnings to be negotiated. The business is self-sustaining with massive opportunities to grow and develop further, but that will be for the next generation of passionate, enthusiastic and dedicated leaders to pursue.

Cynics, sceptics and evangelists

One of the lessons I've learned over the years is that the business world is made up of cynics, sceptics and evangelists. And I've learned that you can give cynics all the evidence, data and proof in the world, and it will not matter if they're fundamentally fixed in their fears. Sceptics I love – they're challenging and demanding and nervous, but are genuinely curious and open to being persuaded. They get that learning comes from honestly battling with and even against new ideas. Evangelists require no evidence or data whatsoever, they'll just jump in with alacrity. I love them too, but the sceptics are actually more involved and invested in the process, and so when the inevitable discomfort that comes with change shows up, they'll stick with it.

Faced with discomfort, the cynics claim validation and aggressively put a stop to the process. Evangelists simply jump to the next bright shiny thing.

So, it's sceptics I'm really appealing to. So be proudly sceptical about all this, but then take some action. Research, investigate, try some stuff out, take some risks, look always for the positives, rewarding people for every forward step and the slightest forward step, help people through discomfort without rescuing them from their own learning, and be prepared to welcome clumsiness (humanness) into your daily practice.

FURTHER NOTES

Chapter 1

Deming, W Edwards (2000) *14 Points for Management* in *Out of the Crisis*, MIT Press.

Chapter 2

Erica Jong is an American novelist and poet, known particularly for her novel *Fear of Flying* (1973), Holt, Reinhardt and Winston.

Peter Abelard, 1079–1142, was a French philosopher.

Chapter 3

Collins, Jim (2001) *Good to Great*, Random House Business.

Sutton, Robert (2007) The No Asshole Rule: Building a Civilized Workplace and Surviving One That Isn't, *Business Plus*.

Gladwell, Malcolm (2008) *The Outliers*, Little, Brown and Company.

Kipling, Rudyard (1900) *The Elephant's Tale* in *The Ladies Home Journal*, April.

Chapter 4

Waterman, Robert H and Peters, Tom (1982) *In Search of Excellence*, Harper and Row.

In 2001 I had the great pleasure of meeting Robert Dilts, one of the 'gurus' of NLP (Neuro-Linguistic Programming) in California. Further details are available at: www.logicallevels.co.uk/pages/robert-dilts.

Chapter 6

This oft-quoted poem by Marianne Williamson is from her book *Return to Love* (1992) Harper Collins.

Bellah, Robert (1985) *Habits of the Heart: Individualism and Commitment in American Life*, University of California Press, p 84.

Robinson, Ken (2010) *The Element: How Finding Your Passion Changes Everything,* Penguin.

Chapter 7

Frankel, Victor (1959) *Man's Search for Meaning,* Beacon Press.

Johann Wolfgang Von Goethe was a German writer and statesman. This poem was written by Goethe but is frequently ascribed to William Hutchison Murray, a Scottish mountaineer and leader of a famous early Himalayan expedition.

Jack Welch is an American businessman who was CEO of General Electric.

Alexander, Caroline (1999) *The Endurance: Shackleton's Legendary Antarctic Expedition*, Knopf.

Benedict of Nursia AD 480–547, *Rules of St Benedict*, in particular *The Qualities of the Abbot*.

Pyr Gyllenhamer was CEO of Volvo AB in 1992 when I attended an event at which he gave the keynote speech, and this is a direct quote I transcribed at the time.

Chapter 8

The Toyota Way – a set of principles and behaviors that underlie the Toyota Motor Corporation's managerial approach and production system. Toyota first summed up its philosophy, values and manufacturing ideals in 2001, calling it *The Toyota Way 2001*.

Chapter 9

Lencioni, Patrick (2002) *Five Dysfunctions of a Team: A Leadership Fable,* John Wiley.

Bruce Tuckman developed a four-stage team development process in 1965. Later a fith stage was added.

Chapter 10

Nestle values – not available in public print but from a copy I was given when working with Nestle in the Ukraine in 2003.

Chapter 11

One Million Heads, One Beautiful Mind was the sub title of part 2 of BBC's TV's programme *Superswarm* (1999).

Chapter 13

Kubler Ross, Elizabeth (1997) *On Death and Dying,* Schribner.

Chapter 14

Kotter, John (1995) *Leading Change* in *Harvard Business Review Press*.

Champy, James (1995) *Re-engineering Management: The Mandate for New Leadership*, HarperCollins.

Carly Fiorina was CEO Hewlett Packard between 2001 and 2005. The quote comes from a presentation she made to 3,000 HP managers at a conference not long after she'd assumed the role of CEO.

Waterman, Robert H and Peters, Tom (1982) *In Search of Excellence*, Harper and Row.

Proverbs 29:18.

Quote taken from a keynote speech Michael Gerber gave at a Dale Carnegie convention I attended in Charleston South Carolina in 1998.

Martin Luther King, 28 August 1963.

John F Kennedy, 25 May 1961.

Semler, Richardo (1993) *Maverick*, Warner Books.

Chapter 15

Hosking, Patrick (2017) Building a Brave New World of Investment on Ghosts of the Past, *The Times*, 30 January.

Burrough, Bryan and Helyar, John (1989) Barbarians at the Gate, Harper and Row.

Baker, Stephanie and Carey, David (2014) KKR Co-Founder Henry Kravis Works to Transform his Legendary Buyout Firm, *Washington Post*, 24 July.

Chapter 16

Melin, Anders and Mittleman, Melissa (2017) Letting Workers Have a Share, *Business Week*, 19 June.

Aldrick, Philips (2017) How the Barbarians Learnt to Share the Spoils – and Grow Rich, *The Times*, 19 September.

Hurley, James (2018) Why Do so Few Share Fruits of a Company's Ownership? *The Times*, 25 June.

The World's Largest B Corp on the Future of Business, 12 April 2018, available at: https://bthechange.com/the-worlds-largest-b-corp-on-the-future-of-business-673bccda1d54.

Buckley, Thomas and Campbell, Matthew (2017) The Fresh Scent of Success, *Business Week* 4 September.

Chafkin, Max and Cao, Jong (2017) Leave My Etsy Alone, *Business Week*, 19 May.

Handy, Charles (1990) Michael Shanks Memorial Lecture at the RSA entitled 'What Is a Company For?', available at: www.growthinternational.com/resources/Charles+Handy+1990.pdf.

Browne, Lord John (2015) Our Duty to Engage with the World, *Sunday Times*, 6 September.

Townsend, Michael (2014) Life Beyond Capitalism, *RSA Journal* (Issue 2).

Ian Cheshire in an open letter to all Kingfisher employees and printed as a thought leadership piece in *The Guardian*, 24 March 2011.

Bhasin, Kim (2016) Where Did You Get that Lovely Supply Chain?, *Business Week*, 23 December.

2018 IPCC report, available at: www.ipcc.ch/sr15.

Townsend, Matt and Deprez, Esme E (2018) Is the Corporate Bully the Next Workplace Pariah?, *Business Week*, 14 May.

Hill, Andrew (2018) Looking after Number One Is not Selfish, *Financial Times*, 9 May. Available at: www.ft.com/content/30f830c6-3c0f-11e8-bcc8-cebcb81f1f90.

Professor David Grayson, 2014 White Paper, Doughty Centre for Corporate Responsibility.

INDEX

'7 Heretical Points' (Handy), 240
14 Points for Management (Deming), 5

account management, in team, 133–4
ACRC concept, 119–23
action, in cycle of ownership, 181
advice, 21
Aldrick, Philip, 235
Alexander, Caroline, 155
ambition, comfort zones, 30–1
Arland, Gilbert, 29
arrogance, 87
authentic leader
    expression for, 76
    purpose and vision, 80
authentic leadership
    consists of, 75
    corporate cultures, 75
    overview of, 75–6
authenticity
    definitions of, 79
    demands leadership, 76–8
    description of, 78–80
    genuine, 75
    Golden Core, 80–1
    leadership, 102
    Shield of Pretence, 81–3
autocratic leadership, 83

B Corps movement
    Danone, 237
    Etsy, 238–9
    Unilever, 237–8
B&Q 2013–2014, 260–1
balance sheet, 228–9
Banbury Therapy Group, 267–71
Bateson, Gregory, 54
behaviour change
    open questions, 42–3
    overview of, 41–2
    practice, 42
behaviour, Dilts' logical level, 54, 56
being in rapport, 25
blaming, 12
BreakThrough Coaching
    closed questions, 67–8
    overview of, 66–7
budget planning, 213–14
building rapport, 25

business as usual, 213
business management bit
    balance sheet, 228–9
    budget planning, 213–14
    communications, 222–3
    documents with status concept, 229
    forecasting process, 214–16
    KPIs, 219
    management by objectives, 223–5
    one-to-ones, 219–22
    operating model, 216–17
    results, 229–31
    rigid structure of non-negotiable
        processes, 217–18
    strategy one-pagers, 225–7
    team meetings, 222–3

care, in team characteristics, 150
CEQ v EQ, 1–2
CEQ, four pillars of, 2–4
challenge, ACRC concept, 123
champions, 195–200
Cheshire, Ian, 241–2
closed questions, 35–6
    BreakThrough Coaching, 67–8
clumsy coaching, 9–10
coachee's plea, 71–2
coaching
    'soft and fluffy', 10
    boundaries, 40
    clumsy, 9–10
    definition of, 38
    directing versus, 9
    myth exploding, 72
    myths of, 10–11
    outcomes of, 39–40
    peer group, 129–30
    process of, 39
    purpose of, 39
    recalibration see triggers
    rewards, 70–1
    role play, 68
    teaching and knowledge transfer,
        69–70
    team see team coaching
coaching crafting
    closed into open questions, 46–7
    practical process, 45–6
    questions crafting, 44–5

coaching for ownership
  great questions, 48–9
  overview of, 47–8
  right-brain questions, 49–53
Cog's Ladder, 138
collaborative equity organisation
  acceptable solution, 246–7
  B Corps movement see B Corps movement
  co-operatives and partnerships, 233–4
  definition of, 232
  employee ownership, 234–7
  future leaders, 245–6
  hope and, 248–9
  listening to voices, 239–41
  modern day crusader, 241–2
  on the internet, 242–4
  shared ownership, 232
  shared responsibility, 233
  shared rewards, 233
  Tomorrow's Company, 234
  toxic, 247–8
  WinCo Foods, 235–7
  workplace, 244–5
collaborative, definition of, 232
Collins, Jim, 38
comfort zones
  ambition, 30–1
  coach and, 29
  cultural, 29
  examples of, 27–9
  leader and, 29
  personal, 29
  resources, 32
  targets, 29–30
commitment, 97
communications, 222–3
compromising, 117
conflict as creative force, 147–9
consensual leadership, 83, 84
constancy, 99
co-operatives, 233–4
core purpose, 92
core values, 91
  commitment, 97
  constancy, 99
  courage, 96
  leadership, 97–8
  optimism, 98
  respect, 98–9
  service, 100–1
corporate cultures, 75

corporate leaders, 75
corporate leadership characteristics, 102
corporatism, 247
courage, core values, 96
cultural change
  behaviours, 169–70
  common mistakes, 175
  crisis event in company's finances, 172
  crisis event in marketplace, 171–2
  definition of, 167
  foundation stones, 175
  intentions, 167–8
  leadership, 170–1
  reasons for, 170
  structures, 168–9
cultural change dilemmas
  adding headcount, 175
  people development versus business
    results, 173–4
  short- versus long-term results, 174
  target place for maximising performance,
    174–5
cultural change project planning, 203–9
cultural change steps
  creating champions and continuous
    improvement teams, 195–200
  educating employees in business model,
    200–3
  honesty, 184
  intentions and symbolic goals, 185–91
  listening customers and employees,
    185
  police non-negotiable structures and
    processes, 191–4
  slaughter, 191
  turning managers into coaches, 194–5
cultural comfort zones, 29
culture
  corporate finance specialist, 167
  definition of, 170
  in team characteristics, 150
  winning culture, 170
curiosity, 21–3
  in SuperListening, 62–4
current versus future leaders, 246
cycle of empowerment, 194–5
cycle of grief, 176
cycle of ownership
  action, 181
  engagement, 179–80
  reflection, 180–1

resistance, 177–9
uncertainty, 176–7

Danone, 237
Deming, Edwards, 5
Dilts, Robert, 54
directing
coaching versus, 9
definition of, 9
documents with status
business management bit, 229
in cultural change, 190

employee ownership, 234–7
empowerment
cycle of, 194–5
definition of, 194
engagement, 179–80
environment, Dilts' logical level, 54, 56
equity, definition of, 232
Etsy, 238–9
evangelism, 87

facilitation
challenge thinking, 129
definition of, 128
guiding process, 128
overview of, 127
planning session, 128
recognise individuals, 129
reinforcing vision and values, 128
fear, in team characteristics, 150
feedback
advice, 21
example for, 17
honesty in, 18
overview of, 17–18
pitfall of, 17
receiving, 18
SuperListening, 66
using values, 19–21
'Five Principles of a Purpose Driven
Business', 246
forecasting process, 214–16
forming, Tuckman's team development, 137
future leaders, 245–6

genuine authenticity, 75
Gladwell, Malcolm, 42
goals, definition of, 92
Golden Core, 80–1

Goldwyn, Sam, 22
Good to Great (Collins), 38
Grayson, David, 239, 246
group, definition of, 127

Handy, Charles, 239
Haworth, Martyn, 76
high-performance team characteristics
accepting individual idiosyncrasies and
personal circumstances, 146–7
commitment and personal subordination,
156–7
conflict as creative force, 147–9
honesty, 149–51
individuals' place of sanctuary and
solace, 153–4
leader as honest coach and facilitator,
155–6
overview of, 139
purpose, vision, values, goals, strategy,
139–40
rehearsal and celebration space, 151–3
respect for each other, 141–3
roles and responsibilities, 140–1
team dynamics, 143–5
holding person and not problem, 23–7
honesty
cultural change steps, 184
in feedback, 18
in high-performance team characteristics,
149–51
hope, in team characteristics, 150
Hosking, Patrick, 234
human emotional connection, 23
human potential, 11–14

identity, Dilts' logical level, 55, 57
integrity, 100

job of leader, 181–2
judgemental SuperListening, 61
Jung, Carl, 27

kaizen, 196
Kering, 242
knowledge transfer, 69–70
Kotter, John, 183
KPIs, 219, 227

leadership
ACRC concept, 119–23

leadership (*cont.*)
  authentic *see* authentic leadership
  authenticity, 102
  autocratic, 83
  consensual, 83, 84
  core values, 97–8
  corporate characteristics, 102
  hiring people, 102
  mistakes in, 113
  organising yourself, 119
  personal core values process, 91
  pointing at process, 113–14
  principles and beliefs, 101
  radical and drastic, 110–11
  setting goals, 108
  stewardship, 111
  styles of, 83
  theory, 9
  trust with truth, 106–8
  vision is boss, 111–13
Lencioni, Patrick, 136
Longwood Park 2003–2009, 257–60

management by objectives, 223–5
Maslow, Abraham, 53
Maslow's hierarchy of needs, 53–4
mentors, 91
meritocratic evaluation, 225
Millan, Cesar, 162

narcissism, 87
Net Positive (Cheshire), 241
norming, Tuckman's team development, 137

objectives and key results (OKRs), 223–5
one-to-ones, 219–22
open questions, 42–3
operating model, 216–17
optimism, 98
organising yourself, 119

parental synthesis, 91
partnerships, 233–4
paternalism, 39
peer group coaching, 129–30
Pendragon Plc 1998–2000
  balance sheet, 251
  egotistical managers, 252–7
  employee facilities, 252
  internal competition, 252
  role of, 250–1

performing, Tuckman's team development, 137
personal comfort zones, 29
personal core values process
  core purpose, 92
  core values, 91
  defining experience, 92
  leadership, 91
  mentors, 91
  overview of, 90
  parental synthesis, 91
  vision and goals, 92
pinnacle/purpose, Dilts' logical level, 55, 57
positive learning, 3
potential
  human, 11–14
  untapped, 12
problem-solving
  Dilts' logical levels, 54–8
  hidden depths, 59
  Maslow's hierarchy of needs, 53–4
Produce World, 264–7
psychometrics, 24, 146
purpose and values
  at work, 95
  finding, 95
  inspire, 94
  joy, 95
  leaders, 94
  leading, 94
  overview of, 93–4
  practical strategies, implementing, 94

quantum leap, 131
questions
  closed, 35–6, 67–8
  closed into open, 46–7
  crafting, 44–5
  open, 42–3
  right brain, 49–53
  statements versus, 37–8
  stewardship, 115
  superlative, 66

radical and drastic, 110–11
rapport
  being in, 25
  building, 25
recalibrated coaching skills
  attributes for, 33
  behaviour change *see* behaviour change
  closed questions, 35–6

difficulties of, 40
over talk, 36–7
prime examples, 34
statements versus questions, 37–8
statements, legitimate use of, 37
recalibration
coaching *see* triggers
overview of, 15–16
triggers *see* triggers
receiving feedback, 18
recognition, ACRC concept, 122
reflection, 180–1
resilience, 103
resistance, 177–9
resources, comfort zones, 32
respect, core values, 98–9
rewards
coaching, 70–1
collaborative equity organisation, 233
for mistakes, 14
right-brain questions, 49–53
right-brain thinking, 49–53
rigid disciplines, philosophy of, 217–18
rigid structure of non-negotiable processes,
217–18
Robinson, Ken, 80
role play, 68
roles
purpose of, 116–17
stewardship, 115
strategies and behaviours, 117–19

seeking adoration, 87
self-managed teams (SMTs)
challenges, 161–3
motivation, 160
overview of, 158
principles of, 158
skills developing, 160
structural processes, rules and
boundaries, 159
self-discovery, examples of, 88–90
self-reflection exercises, 88
Semler, Ricardo, 75
sensing SuperListening, 62
service, core values, 100–1
Shackleton, Ernest, 104
shared ownership, 232
shared responsibility, 233
shared rewards, 233
Shield of Pretence, 81–3

skills, Dilts' logical level, 55, 57
SOFEA *see* South Oxfordshire Food and
Education Academy
'soft and fluffy' coaching, 10
soliciting feedback, 18
South Oxfordshire Food and Education
Academy (SOFEA), 261–4
spontaneous role plays, 68
St Benedict, 104, 155
staged role plays, 68
statements
legitimate use of, 37
questions versus, 37–8
stewardship
as leader, 111
in roles, 115
questions, 115
storming, Tuckman's team development, 137
strategy one-pager
budget and resources, 227
definition of, 225
key objectives, 227
KPIs, 227
long-term strategy and objectives, 226
reporting and scrutiny, 227
risks, 227
state of nation, 226
strategy for next 12 months, 227
tangible business benefits, 226
superlative questions, 66
SuperListening
curiosity in, 62–4
examples for truth, 64–5
feedback, 66
judgemental, 61
overview of, 60–1
sensing, 62

targets, comfort zones, 29–30
task teams, 198–200
teaching, 69–70
team
account management, 133–4
adapting theoretical models, 138
coaching *see* team coaching
continuous improvement, 195–200
definition of, 127
dysfunctions of, 136
high-performance characteristics *see* high-
performance team characteristics
place for targets, 132–3

team (*cont.*)
  purpose of, 131–2
  three-dimensional matrix, 134–5
  Tuckman's five stages of development,
    136–8
  within business, 131–2
team coaching
  challenge thinking, 129
  guiding process, 128
  overview of, 127
  planning session, 128
  recognise individuals, 129
  reinforcing vision and values, 128
team meetings, 222–3
The Outliers (Gladwell), 42
three-dimensional matrix, 134–5
Tomorrow's Company, 234
transactional analysis, 39
transforming, Tuckman's team development,
  138
transparency, 3–4
triggers
  comfort zones *see* comfort zones
  curiosity, 21–3
  feedback *see* feedback
  holding person and not problem, 23–7
  problem-solving *see* problem-solving
  right-brain thinking, 49–53
  staying calm, 16
trust with truth, 106–8
truth for SuperListening, 64–5

Tuckman, Bruce, 136
Tuckman's five stages of team development,
  136–8

uncertainty, 176–7
unconscious controlling habits,
  15–16
Unilever, 237–8
unreasonableness, 87
untapped potential, 12

values and beliefs
  current versus future leaders, 246
  Dilts' logical level, 55, 57
values for feedback, 19–21
  proud, 19
  successful, 19, 20
  trust, 19
  valued, 19
values, in cultural change, 187–90
vision, 92
  in cultural change, 185–6
  in leadership, 111–13
vulnerability, 3–4

Weinstock, Arnold, 223
Welch, Jack, 85, 102
WinCo Foods, 235–7
Winning Culture, 196
workplace, collaborative equity
  organisation, 246

You may also be interested in Gareth's first book:

Corporate Emotional Intelligence: Being Human in a Corporate World

October 2018   276pp   ISBN 9781912508044

CORPORATE EMOTIONAL INTELLIGENCE

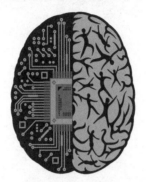

Being Human in a Corporate World

GARETH CHICK

Corporate Emotional Intelligence is a seminal work for business in the 21st century. It analyses how human behaviour is conditioned within corporate cultures, and how managers come to adopt unconscious controlling habits that are counter-productive and that create cultures of fear.

The book introduces us to the Corporapath and the Corporate Hostage and to the unique anxiety disorder CTSD – Corporate Traumatic Stress Disorder – yielding a profound new level of self-awareness for all corporate citizens. Success in business now requires a different kind of human intelligence: IQ + EQ is no longer sufficient. We now need CEQ – the ability to read, understand and manage the psychological states and behaviours that are unique to corporate cultures.

In the same way that Daniel Goleman's work on emotional intelligence (EQ) dramatically shifted our view on how non-cognitive skills matter as much as IQ, Gareth's CEQ will inspire a new wave of thinking.

Mike Morrison, University of Toyota